POPE JOHN PAUL II
AND THE APPARENTLY
'NON-ACTING' PERSON

POPE JOHN PAUL II AND THE APPARENTLY 'NON-ACTING' PERSON

PIA MATTHEWS

GRACEWING

First published in 2013 by
Gracewing
2 Southern Avenue
Leominster
Herefordshire HR6 0QF
United Kingdom
www.gracewing.co.uk

ISBN 978 085244 805 2

Nihil obstat: Reverend Monsignor Matthew Dickens, MA, DipLib, BTh, VG
Imprimatur: ✠ Most Reverend Peter Smith, LLB, JCD, KC*HS
                    Archbishop of Southwark
Date: 11 April 2013

The *Nihil obstat* and *Imprimatur* are declarations that a book or pamphlet is
free from doctrinal or moral error. No implication is contained therein that
those who have granted the *Nihil obstat* or *Imprimatur* agree with the contents,
opinions or statements expressed.

Typeset by Gracewing

Cover design by Bernardita Peña Hurtado

CONTENTS

INTRODUCTION

In his reflections at the end of the Great Jubilee Year 2000 and the beginning of the new millennium Pope John Paul II tells how he often stopped to look at the pilgrims queuing patiently to go through the Holy Door. He says that in each person he 'tried to imagine the story of a life, made up of joys, worries, sufferings; the story of someone whom Christ had met and who, in dialogue with him, was setting out again on a journey of hope'.[1] Profoundly disabled people, those who do not seem to be able to act out their lives in the same way as other people, were part of this flow of the pilgrim Church. Pope John Paul speaks of them, the 'differently abled', as passing through the Holy Door 'in the company of the crucified Lord'.[2] In his many encounters with the disabled Pope John Paul reflects on their stories and on the need to learn to recognise and meet them 'first and foremost as persons'.[3]

Pope John Paul's pontificate may perhaps be characterised by this notion of personal encounter: the encounter of Christ with every human person, and in carrying out Christ's mission, the encounter of the Church with God's people and the world where each encounter has consequences. Encounter necessarily entails the call to holiness and becoming a witness to the Gospel and this applies equally to the differently-abled and the otherwise-abled. Significantly, however, the Pope feels it necessary to draw attention to the fact that the profoundly disabled are persons. Of perhaps even more concern he has to remind people that the intellectually disabled in particular are 'fully human beings' with 'unique dignity and special value'.[4] He finds himself having to reaffirm the personal dignity of the profoundly disabled frequently because of certain pervasive attitudes towards the disabled where encounter is avoided, where the impaired human being is seen in terms of biological rather than biographical or personal existence, where the profoundly disabled are seen as useless, as redundant or as burdens to be eliminated. For apparently non-acting persons there is little room on the world stage and they are relegated to the margins.

In complete contrast, the many addresses and speeches that result from Pope John Paul's encounters demonstrate without doubt that the Pope is enlivened and encouraged by the witness of disabled people. This is because he sees that all the hopes and expectations that often lie hidden or unacknowledged in people who think that they live undiminished lives are brought to concrete reality in the lives of the disabled. Those who think that they live full and autonomous lives are short sighted: they tend to think that they do not need anything more but their own strength. With clearer insight Pope John Paul recognises that when living in faith the disabled in their bodies and in their lives 'express an intense hope of redemption'.[5] To be sure 'redemption' does not simply refer to a cure, a return to what is 'normal' or indeed full access to the community. Instead Pope John Paul sees that 'every person marked by a physical or mental difficulty lives a sort of existential "advent"', they are waiting in the 'living and active hope' for the redemption won by Christ in his Passion and Resurrection.[6] By bringing into question common apprehensions about the power of autonomy, appearances, function, speed and efficiency, by highlighting the way that 'inattentiveness sharpens suffering and loneliness'[7] the disabled can demonstrate that 'love is the last word'[8] and in this they are preparing the way for Christ.

Since love is everything, Pope John Paul sees the need to promote a 'spirituality of communion'. This involves 'the heart's contemplation of the mystery of the Trinity dwelling within us' and 'shining on the face of the brothers and sisters around us'. Encountering God in the self and in 'those who are part of me' in the Body of Christ 'makes us able to share their joys and sufferings, to sense their desires and attend to their needs, to offer them deep and genuine friendship'. This spirituality of communion means 'to know how to "make room" for our brothers and sisters, bearing each other's burdens' and seeing the positive in others not only as gifts for the person but also as 'gifts for me'.[9] Pope John Paul understands that learning to see the face of Christ in others, especially in the faces of those with whom Christ himself wished to be identified such as the hungry, the stranger, the sick, the disabled, is 'not a simple invitation to charity'. Instead it reflects an aspect of the mystery of Christ who is united in a sense with every human being[10] and who thereby guarantees human dignity.

Pope John Paul is especially concerned to bring attention to the vital contribution made by the disabled to solidarity and the universal call to holiness of all human beings. However he realises that this has become an urgent task given that in some contemporary thinking a 'conspiracy against life' has produced a 'culture of death' where 'a life that would require greater acceptance, love and care is considered useless, or held to be an intolerable burden and is therefore rejected'.[11] In his 1995 encyclical, *Evangelium vitae*, the *Gospel of Life*, Pope John Paul points out that not only are attacks on human life a 'war of the powerful against the weak'.[12] These assaults that diminish or indeed eliminate the disabled person also eclipse the full mystery of the human person whose dignity is founded in Christ. This culture of death has not only lost sense of the profound mystery of human dignity. It has also lost sight of God.[13]

As a prelude to his call in *Evangelium vitae* for an affirmation of a 'new culture of human life' Pope John Paul established the Pontifical Academy for Life in February 1994. He entitled the Motu proprio, his personal document setting up this institution, *Vitae mysterium*, the *Mystery of life*. In this document Pope John Paul observes that experts in science and technology are drawn towards research into the mystery of human life. However by mystery Pope John Paul does not refer to a puzzle that is especially difficult to unravel, an understanding perhaps held by many in the scientific world. Rather the term mystery indicates that the subject matter has such profundity that it calls for ever deepening reflection. Moreover this reflection is to be enlightened by the 'law of love'. For Pope John Paul human existence is indeed a mystery and this mystery embraces even if it cannot fully explain all aspects of the life of human beings: their strength and weaknesses, their freedom and action as well as their disability and apparent inaction, their frailty that can be moral, physical, intellectual. In his work as professor of ethics Karol Wojtyła sets about the task of deep reflection on human beings principally in their freedom and action. As Pope John Paul he continues this work about human beings not only in what human beings do but also in what they are, and in their apparent inaction and disability. Pope John Paul entrusts the Pontifical Academy for Life with the task of promoting and protecting life. He sees that the Church, as part of her evangelical mission and apostolic duty, is to enlighten the consciences of all people so that the dignity of every human person and his or her vocation is made clear. And he is in no doubt that this task is a particularly urgent one given that this culture of death 'threatens to take control'.[14]

Certainly some powerful and recurring themes emerge in Pope John Paul's work on disability and the frailty of the human condition. These themes are rooted deeply in the Christian tradition. In the same way that the earliest Christian writers respond to their own pastoral situations Pope John Paul is attentive to the 'signs of the times'. He explores the depths of these signs that more often than not refer to perennial questions concerning human existence and the place of human beings in the world. In keeping with the moral tradition he sees the significance of freedom and self-determination in the life of the acting person. However he is clear that it is a freedom linked to the truth of the human person. Even if this truth has been obscured in modern times so that human beings often assume a Promethean attitude to life, this truth has its reference in God and in the dignity of human beings made in the image of God. The image of God in human beings itself has reference to Christology and the emptying of the Second Person of the Trinity who humbled himself to become man. Christ becomes closest to what many consider to be the least of all, the poor, the marginalised, the sick and disabled through his own self-identification with them and through his total gift of self to the world. So it is the least among us that point to the dignity of all human beings and the truth that all are dependant on God. By forgetting, marginalising or dismissing the profoundly disabled, by exalting the strong, the autonomous and the powerful human beings distort not only humanity but also humanity's relation to God. Moreover as Pope John Paul points out everyone has a role to play in this 'mobilisation' for a new culture of life.[15] The disabled are profoundly effective witnesses to the work of God active in human beings whatever their condition or situation and so their lives are not only to be promoted and protected but also cherished.

Pope John Paul writes that the disabled person forces us all to question ourselves and the mystery of being a human being. He says that 'it is in the more difficult and disturbing situations that the dignity and grandeur of the human being emerges'.[16] It is in these situations that the modern outlook tends to be myopic. Just as the image of God in every human being is never lost so too do all human beings have personal dignity from the very beginning of life to its natural end. This dignity encompasses the whole human being as a unity in all his or her aspects: spirit and body, material and immaterial, interior and exterior reality. These themes are the starting point for profound reflection on the mystery of the human being who is at times strong, at times weak, at times acting and at times apparently non-acting.

This book seeks to explore Pope John Paul's thinking on human persons in such difficult situations in the light of his conviction that all human beings have the same dignity regardless of their abilities. We have this dignity because 'when God turns his gaze on man, the first thing he sees and loves in him is not the deeds he succeeds in doing, but his own image'.[17] As Pope John Paul explains, 'the disabled are not different from other people which is why, in recognising and promoting their dignity and rights, we recognise and promote our own dignity and rights and those of each one of us'.[18]

Not only do all human beings have the same dignity each also is entrusted with an exceptional task. According to Pope John Paul we all are 'workers in the vineyard' whatever our situation and so we are all called to build up the Kingdom.[19] However for Pope John Paul disabled people carry a particular calling: they are 'humanity's privileged witnesses' because 'they can teach everyone about the love that saves us; they can become heralds of a new world, no longer dominated by force, violence and aggression, but by love, solidarity and acceptance.'[20] Moreover every human being is another Christ and we are asked not only always to treat others as we would like them to treat us[21] but also to hold fast to a new commandment: to love one another just as Jesus has loved each one of us.[22] It is a love based on the truth about human beings and it is a biased love.

Pope John Paul's pastoral concern for the disabled extends over all of his writings, from his encyclicals to speeches and addresses directed at particular occasions, from his extensive reflections on the problem of suffering to his response to the 'signs of the times' and his interventions at the very specific level of patients in persistent vegetative state. The privileged space occupied by the disabled means that they have a prominent place when he speaks about the vocation of every human being, the idea that everyone is a gift for the other. It appears in his discussion on the significance of solidarity and participation of the marginalised as highlighted by liberation theologies. It is included in the concreteness of being a body in his theology of the body. However Pope John Paul's writings on disability appear to be somewhat neglected. This may be because they are wideranging and often dispersed among his other work or it may be because he is better known for his attention to ethics and moral theology, what some may regard as the realm of the acting person. Indeed the English title of his early and seminal work as professor of ethics, *The Acting Person,* seems to bear this out.

It is said that in purgatory all priests will be given a copy of Karol Wojtyła's *The Acting Person* to read. This saying can be taken in many ways: published in 1969 *The Acting Person* is after all one of the early works by arguably one of the greatest popes of modern times; it is philosophically significant as an example of Lublin Thomism, as a critique of phenomenology, the philosophy that looks to the descriptive meaning of things as they appear to us, and as an attempt to determine whether some aspects of phenomenology can be assimilated into Christian thinking. Also it is at times a dense, complicated and rigorously challenging work and priests may have plenty of penitential time, if indeed there is time in purgatory, to get to grips with the ideas it presents.

Whilst the *The Acting Person* is considered to be one of Pope John Paul's major philosophical works looking at it on the mundane level it may be that his book is more significant simply for what it says, or rather what it assumes about certain human beings even before it tackles ethics and action. This significance begins in the title of the book itself. Although much controversy has surrounded the book's English translation,[23] from the start it is interesting to note that its Polish title, *Osoba i Czyn,* actually translates as *Person and Act.* At first sight there does not seem to be an important difference between 'person and act' and 'the acting person'. However, this may be more of an issue if these titles are considered in the context of a common understanding of disability: according to the *Oxford English Dictionary* definitions of 'disabled' include 'rendered incapable of action' alongside 'want of ability' and 'incapacity'.

For many people it seems that a common though vague understanding of disabled people, particularly the intellectually disabled, is that they are not acting human beings. Such a view leaves the most profoundly disabled vulnerable to discrimination, indifference, loneliness or lack of respect, and sometimes even abuse as their lives are implicitly seen to be of less worth than other human beings. Moreover and arguably of more concern is the claim that human beings who cannot act in the sense of being able to make choices or hold desires or have a notion of themselves as existing over time are not only non-acting but also they are simply not persons.

Pope John Paul is especially concerned about the field of healthcare ethics since it is in this area that the culture of death perhaps most obviously confronts the culture of life. In contemporary healthcare ethics much of the focus is on patient autonomy and on empowering choice and action. Healthcare ethics seems to emphasise the value of the deliberate will of the acting person. This is no bad thing. Respect for autonomy in the field of healthcare is not merely ensuring that consent has been obtained. Rather, respect recognises that there is a level of partnership between patient and healthcare professional albeit at times an unequal partnership since it is the patient who comes with his or her need. Respect indicates the significance of self-determination that goes beyond simply the freedom to choose. It gives the patient responsibility and the opportunity to exercise good stewardship over his or her health and life. Autonomy and freedom, choice and action are central to personal activity and Karol Wojtyła clearly attests to this in *Person and Act* though in terms of general human activity not in the healthcare setting So certainly Karol Wojtyła's work on human action has made a distinctive contribution to ethics.

The down side of the current focus on autonomy is that there are many profoundly disabled people who cannot exercise the level of autonomy prized in contemporary healthcare ethics.

In some dominant and influential streams of bioethical thinking the profoundly disabled are placed on what the prominent
American philosopher Jeff McMahan calls in his book *The Ethics
of Killing* 'the margins of life.'[24] They are placed on 'the margins'
not because they are near to the beginning or the end of life but
because they are considered to be on the margins of personhood.
They are truly marginalised and this, according to some makes
them vulnerable to being killed often on the grounds that they
are seen as problematic, redundant or inconvenient. This is where
Karol Wojtyła's understanding of the human person is vital for
its corrective perspective. This is where Pope John Paul's more
widespread pastoral writings on disability and suffering, on the
apparently 'non-acting' person, can make a significant and practical contribution to a world that is beginning to forget or is
even deliberately ignoring the fact that all human beings are persons. Pope John Paul demonstrates that Church tradition has
profound insights, conveys practical wisdom and speaks for the
voiceless when the 'signs of the times' point to cultures of indifference and death.

Certainly Pope John Paul follows the established Christian
tradition that sees all human beings as persons even if not all
persons are human beings: God is three Persons; angels and
human beings are also persons although not in quite the same
sense. Moreover, in his juxtaposition of the culture of death and
the culture of life, and by his tireless championing of the marginalised and voiceless Pope John Paul clearly demonstrates that
all human beings are persons and their lives are of inestimable
and incomparable value. Among the voiceless are included those
apparently 'non-acting' human beings, the embryo, the anencephalic infant, the profoundly mentally disabled, the patient in
persistent vegetative state. Indeed they perhaps express being a
person more profoundly than many other more 'active' persons.

However in the light of apparent discrimination against some
disabled people and the devaluation of those who are dependant
on others for their care a rendition of *Osoba i Czyn* as *The Acting
Person* may take on more significance than *Person and Act*. Clearly Karol Wojtlya's book *Person and Act* does concern the human
being who acts. However it does not imply that it is only the acting
human being who is a person: *Person and Act* is about the person,

the human being who is always also a person, and about that person when he or she acts. Whilst this may appear to be merely a matter of semantics it also suggests that Pope John Paul II has something significant to say not only about the acting person but also about what some may perceive to be the 'non-acting' person.

At this juncture it seems necessary to point out that Pope John Paul II does not think that there is such a thing as a living human being who is a 'non-acting person'. All human beings are acting persons even if they are unable to express their personhood in terms of choice and conscious action. Those who are deemed by some to be non-acting and therefore not persons are, in Pope John Paul's view, simply radically dependent persons. Among other factors they are acting because in their very existence they make a gift of their humanity to others.[25] Nevertheless the point is that in a climate where defending and promoting life seems to have become heroic rather than the norm, where some human beings are not considered persons, or at least considered to be inferior persons either explicitly or implicitly, on the grounds that they lack certain capacities, capacities that imply at least the potential to reflect on and shape their own lives, then the contribution of an influential thinker like Pope John Paul II is invaluable. This is perhaps even more the case since some Christian writers have also embraced the view that certain categories of human beings are not persons and so are not entitled to the protections that go with personhood, most notably the protection from being killed.[26]

Furthermore some Christian writers argue that the Christian tradition, Catholicism in particular seems to dismiss the profoundly disabled person simply as a deficient human person.[27] They suggest that the tradition has a discriminatory attitude towards the disabled by viewing them as somehow inferior or lacking. What they do not seem to appreciate is that in the Christian tradition the 'non-acting person' does figure in his or her own right, though not as 'non-acting' or inferior but as a radically dependent person. As Karol Wojtyła's book *Person and Act* points out, albeit implicitly, it is not people who are physically or mentally disabled who are 'problems', are lacking or need mending. Rather it is all those human beings, whatever their capacities, who lack the will to offer love to others, who are crippled by pride, malice, negligent indifference. These are the ones that need help. Moreover in the Christian tradition as presented by Pope John Paul the human person who appears not to be capable of the kind of acts often attributed to human beings, acts that depend perhaps on a certain level of consciousness, intelligence or capacity to demonstrate some level of intentionality, is often closest to God.

Whilst Pope John Paul's early writings as Karol Wojtyła, professor of ethics, sit perhaps more easily in the world of academia his writings as Pope emerge more clearly out of encounters with people and so are also directed at practice. Pope John Paul offers a view of the apparently non-acting person that has resonance with those who call for the full participation of all the disabled in everyday living. He focuses on certain principles associated with Catholic Social Teaching: solidarity, subsidiarity, justice, an option for the marginalised and a theological understanding of participation that places the disabled person in the centre rather than on the margins of society. These principles are not simply lifted from Catholic Social Teaching. Instead they are seen as naturally underpinning the central concern of the Church as expressed in its documents of the Second Vatican Council and as taken forward by Pope John Paul II: concern for the human person regardless of the condition or situation in which he or she is found. Catholic Social Teaching does not single out the person with disabilities. Rather the disabled person stands alongside every human being as the subject of justice, solidarity and subsidiarity. Nevertheless the disabled person remains of greatest concern for the Church where he or she is being marginalised or where his or her dignity is being compromised.

Pope John Paul's thinking is also shown to have some resonance with current pedagogical research into intensive interaction therapies where these therapies are described as a form of personalised learning in its profoundest sense, that is, in the sense that they aim to help people communicate their personhood and where they support the full dignity of every human being. With Pope John Paul's insights the personalised learning that takes place in intensive interaction therapies discloses not only the personhood of the person with disabilities but also contributes in a profound way to the personhood of the other person: the teacher also becomes the learner. Still, Pope John Paul goes further in his reflection on the most disabled and vulnerable in society. For Pope John Paul, however disabled a person is, he or she does not remain passive. Rather Pope John Paul sees that God works particularly through those who are weakest and so every person has a particular vocation to fulfill no matter what their condition.

In order to bring together Pope John Paul's extensive writings on disability and to apply his thinking the trajectory of this book attempts to follow Pope John Paul's own methodology by looking first in Chapter 1 to the signs of the times in healthcare, bioethics and models of disability where there is much discussion of human beings with apparently diminished and non-active lives. The chapter explores the thinking of influential academic writers who place people with profound disabilities in the category of non-acting human beings and therefore human beings who are not persons. The assumption is that being an 'acting person' requires certain capabilities and characteristics often associated with the ability to exercise choice and express desires. Once personhood is no longer attributed to the profoundly disabled on the grounds that they do not possess these characteristics, they are 'non-acting'. Then they no longer have the protection and dignity associated with being a person. The strategy of these academic writers is to make a clear and explicit separation between the human being and the person and to establish a threshold for personhood. Discussion centres on which human beings and non-human animals are above the threshold and which human beings are below it and so on the 'margins of life' or personhood. However Chapter 1 also points out that whilst there is an explicit challenge to the personhood of the apparently non-acting person in academic circles this challenge is also raised in the more popular arena where there is not so much talk of human beings who are not persons. Instead certain human beings are considered to have lives that are not worth living not so much because of the amount of suffering they endure but because the value of their lives is seen as worthless. Implicitly rather than explicitly the profoundly disabled human being is seen as non-acting and therefore as a non-person with the result that his or her dignity is no longer fully respected.

This diminished view of the human being that reduces the person to expressions of wants, desires and choices seems to reflect a mind set based on philosophies of consciousness. So Chapter 2 responds to this contemporary scene of academic and popular views by returning to Karol Wojtyła's early philosophical writing *Person and Act* (the *Acting Person*) and more specifically to his series of lectures and articles published in 1950 as *Person and Community*. Karol Wojtyła's work focuses on the contrast between the philosophy of being and philosophies of consciousness and he presents a still timely and rigorous critique of philosophies of consciousness that claim to centre on human experience whilst forgetting that that subject of experiences is a concrete human being. Karol Wojtyła offers a new metaphysics that is built upon lived experience and that includes the real experience of what some may see as the 'non-acting' person, the human being who exists in radical dependence. Karol Wojtyła takes as his starting point the Latin tag *operari sequitur esse*, actions follow being, and he gives priority of being over activity. For Karol Wojtyła the significance of being a person is rooted in the Christian tradition though usually expressed in the incomplete thinking of Boethius. However philosophical traditions also contribute significantly to the profundity of being a person, particularly consideration of the 'I-Thou-We' relationship which involves seeing the other as another 'I', developing participation and being open to spirituality.

The Christian and Boethian tradition and the 'I-Thou-We' relationship find a place in the Second Vatican Council's Pastoral Constitution on the Church in the Modern World, *Gaudium et spes* and the reference to human beings as the only creatures on earth that God willed for their own sakes.[28] So Chapter 3 focuses on the theological aspects of Pope John Paul's thinking based on the long-established Church tradition that 'in whatever way the clay was pressed out, He was thinking of Christ, the Man who was one day to be: because the Word, too, was to be both clay and flesh'.[29] Pope John Paul's anthropology is built upon the fact that human beings are made in the image of God, redeemed through Christ and destined for a sharing in eternal life in friendship with God. This elevation of humanity by God is the grounds for the dignity of each human being. Pope John Paul considers each aspect, the image of God in human beings, redemption, and the destiny of human beings both as a call and as a vocation, most notably in his triad of encyclicals *Redemptor Hominis* 1979, *Dives in Misericordia* 1980 and *Dominum et Vivificantem* 1986.

Following in Church tradition from *Gaudium et spes* that itself is rooted in Scripture and clearly echoes the words of St Augustine that all are called to imitate the self-giving love of the Trinity[30] Chapter 4 looks at what is perhaps Pope John Paul's most well-known work, his *Theology of the Body*. This series of catechetical lectures is usually taken to refer to love in the context of marriage. However Pope John Paul himself says it is relevant to all whatever their state in life and his reflections particularly on solitude and *communio* seem to strike a cord with the experience of people with disabilities. The *Theology of the Body* has arguably come to be one of Pope John Paul's most relevant and popular texts for people living out their daily lives in relationships. As such it carries a message also for the profoundly disabled.

The experience of loneliness, sometimes seen as an aspect of solitude, is a reminder that the dignity of each human being is at times compromised by barriers that are physical and attidudinal, by discrimination and by the failure to see the other as an other. The consciousness of this experience has been raised by provocative ideas formulated by significant writers on disability notably Nancy Eiesland, Sharon Betcher, Hannah Lewis and Jennie Weiss Block. These four authors develop an understanding of disability that flows from the movement of liberation theologies. Undoubtedly the liberation of the disabled is a sign of the times that challenges some reductive thinking on human beings. Chapter 5 explores how these disability theologies emerge from the liberation theology that came out of the experience of thinkers from South America, how they appear to follow some of the principles of liberation theology closely and how they impact on the concept of the preferential option for the poor, indeed how they risk tending towards exclusivity in the disabled experience. The chapter indicates the extent to which liberation theologies of disability have significantly influenced disability studies.

Although Pope John Paul does recognise the contribution of liberation theologies in general, Chapter 6 reflects on Pope John Paul's understanding of a theology of liberation that differs in places from liberation theologies per se. Following in the footsteps of his predecessors and in scriptural tradition Pope John Paul extends the option for the poor beyond those who are materially poor to embrace the sick, the marginalised, and people with disabilities. By this extension he seems to be aligned with writers coming from the stream of liberation theologies of disability. However, he differs significantly from this stream when it comes to the often conflictual and arguably exclusive approach of liberation theologies of disabilities. For Pope John Paul the preferential option for the poor sits within the broader context of Catholic Social Teaching. Principles such as justice, solidarity, subsidiarity and participation apply equally to all human beings so the disabled need not be singled out. Moreover since Catholic Social Teaching is not simply about promoting good causes rather it seeks to serve the reign of God people with disabilities also have a role to play as 'workers in God's vineyard'.[31]

Whilst Pope John Paul travels alongside liberation theologies of disabilities when it comes to seeing people with disabilities as 'the main actors'[32], Pope John Paul's application of liberation theology to the disabled clearly allows a place also for those who have severe intellectual disabilities. This group of often forgotten people is more difficult to cater for in other liberation theologies that focus on empowerment and on the removal of attitudinal and discriminatory barriers. In Chapter 7 Pope John Paul's approach is discussed in the context of his addresses on the World Days of the Sick, annual occasions inaugurated by him in 1992. The chapter concludes with an exploration of Pope John Paul's apostolic letter on the Christian meaning of human suffering, *Salvifici Doloris* written in 1984, a meaning that embraces vocation and mission.

Pope John Paul's development of a theology of mission allows the focus of Chapter 8 to fall on the vocation of people with disabilities within Pope John Paul's perspective that 'we begin by imagining that we are giving to them; we end by realising that they have enriched us'.[33] In terms of what others do for the disabled, Karol Wojtyła's interest in *operari sequitur esse* is as a professor of ethics who sees that a person's acts reveal who they are as a person. However, this also demonstrates that every human being is a person and the apparently 'non-acting' person (in modern terms) is simply a person who is unable to express the person he or she is. It is in this area that participation and solidarity are both empowering and championing of the disabled person. Moreover, Karol Wojtyła's view that the person is waiting, as it were, to be discovered or to express himself or herself seems to be the premise behind some therapies of intensive interactive, a relatively new therapy designed with autistic children in mind but that has relevance for a whole range of disabled people of whatever age.

Intensive interaction is based in the early interactions of mother and child and this has correlation with Pope John Paul's own view that the early experiences within the family help to bring out and form the person of the child. This demonstrates that Pope John Paul's views can be appreciated in both a non-theological and a theological context, perhaps an important point since he is often criticised for his seemingly 'conservative' views on the family and on women in particular. However Pope John Paul's understanding of the significance of the family as 'domestic Church' goes deeper than merely being an influence on a child's personality or helping the child to express him or her self. The 'domestic Church' is a reminder that holiness is the path for ordinary life and part of that path is seeing and welcoming every human being, no matter what his or her condition, as a gift for others. Moreover Pope John Paul's own view of the 'genius' of women in his letter *Mulieris Dignitatem* deliberates on the importance of openness to the gift that is the human person. His reflection on the parable of the Good Samaritan in his letter *Salvifici Doloris* 1984 provides a striking counterpoint to intensive interaction therapy, a practice which is inevitably limited to the resourcefulness of its practitioners. In terms of the enrichment that people with disabilities provide, the call that every human being is given to be friends with God is one that focuses on the uniqueness of each person. This perhaps is in contrast to some modern views of disability that critique the Christian tradition for holding a view of the disabled person as somehow deficient and that sees the non-disabled person as the one who gives and the disabled person as the one who only passively receives. Pope John Paul's acknowledgment of the vocation of every sick, suffering and disabled person dispels this modern view and demonstrates that it is part of the rich Christian tradition that disabled people have a special part to play in building up the kingdom of God.

However some of the most radically disabled people seem to present a challenge for those who, like Pope John Paul, see that all have a part to play in God's work of salvation. Notably, the patient in persistent vegetative state is one such human being. Chapter 9 explores the situation of the patient in persistent vegetative state and other patients who are deemed, by some, to be better off dead. This chapter demonstrates that Pope John Paul is concerned not only about practicalities such as whether or not to continue to feed and hydrate such patients but also about assumptions underlying these practicalities that are both implicit and explicit, that appear to threaten human dignity and that seem to attack the bodily integrity of the patient. Pope John Paul has much to say about this patient and it is perhaps in this situation that what he means by the 'acting person' becomes definitive.

Nevertheless for some it is not only assumptions about consciousness or sentience that are taken as given. According to some writers like the Anglican theologian Nigel Biggar assumptions can be made about the spirituality of a human being so that once a human being can no longer respond to his or her vocation then he or she is no longer a person or, according to the Dominican bioethicist Kevin O'Rourke life is no longer of any benefit. Chapter 10 returns perhaps full circle to one of Karol Wojtyła's earliest works, his 1948 doctoral thesis on faith and the writings of St John of the Cross. Although this was not written with people with disabilities in mind, some of the aspects Karol Wojtyła explores from the range of natural and supernatural knowledge, the dark night of the soul who is not yet united with God, the primacy of the activity of God in the spiritual life of every human being, have resonance with the spirituality of people with profound disability. Moreover, the action of the Church as carrying on the mission of Christ demonstrates that whilst disability and the world of suffering appear to be isolating and a world within the world[34] it is also a world to which all belong.

Notes

1. Pope John Paul II, *Novo Millennio Ineunte*, 8.

2. Pope John Paul II, Angelus *Jubilee of the Disabled* (3 December 2000), 1p. 2.

3. *Ibid.*, 1.

4. Pope John Paul II, *On the Occasion of the International Symposium on the Dignity and Rights of the Mentally Disabled Person* (5 January 2004), 2.

5. Pope John Paul II, Homily *Jubilee of the Disabled* (3 December 2000), 2.

6. *Ibid.*, 2.

7. *Ibid.*, 5.

8. *Ibid.*, 7.

9. Pope John Paul II, *Novo Millennio Ineunte*, 43.

10. *Ibid.*, 49.

11. Pope John Paul II, *Evangelium vitae*, 12.

12. *Ibid.*

13. *Ibid.*, 21.

14. Pope John Paul II, *Vitae mysterium* (11 February 1994) quoting *Christifideles laici*, 38.

15. Pope John Paul II, *Evangelium vitae*, 98.

16. Pope John Paul II, *On the Occasion of the International Symposium on the Dignity and Rights of the Mentally Disabled Person* (5 January 2004), 2.

17. Pope John Paul II, 'Mentally Ill Are Also Made in God's Image' in *L'Osservatore Romano* (11 December 1996).

18. Pope John Paul II, *On the Occasion of the International Symposium on the Dignity and Rights of the Mentally Disabled Person*, 3.

19. Pope John Paul II, *Christifideles laici, 53*.

20. Pope John Paul II, *On the Occasion of the International Symposium on the Dignity and Rights of the Mentally Disabled Person*, 6.

21. *Mt* 7.12.

22. *Jn* 13.34.

23. R Buttiglione, *Karol Wojtyła: the Thought of the Man who Became Pope John Paul II* (Grand Rapids: Eerdmans, 1997), p. 117.

24. J. McMahan, *The Ethics of Killing: Problems at the margins of life* (Oxford: Oxford University Press, 2002).

25. K. Wojtyła, 'Parenthood as a Community of Persons' (1975) in *Catholic Thought from Lublin Vol.IV Person and Community* (New York: Peter Lang, 1993), p. 333.

26. See for instance N. Biggar, *Aiming to Kill* (Cleveland: The Pilgrim Press, 2004).

27. See for instance H. Reinders, *Receiving the Gift of Friendship* (Grand Rapids: Eerdmans, 2008), p. 124.

28. Vatican II, *Gaudium et spes*, 22, 24.

29. Vatican II, *Gaudium et spes*, 22 alludes to this quotation from Tertullian's *On the Resurrection of the Flesh*, 6.

30. St Augustine, *On the Trinity*, VI, 5.7.

31. Pope John Paul II, *Christifideles laici*, 53.

32. Pope John Paul II, *World Day of the Sick*, I, 5.

33. Pope John Paul II, *Address at Southwark Cathedral Anointing the Sick* (28 May 1982).

34. Pope John Paul II, *Salvifici Doloris*, 8.

1

HUMAN BEINGS AND HUMAN PERSONS:

IN THE 'SIGNS OF THE TIMES'

According to Karol Wojtyła philosophical anthropology and ethics present 'the great and fundamental controversy about the human being'[1] and this controversy is frequently being played out in conflicts of outlooks today. There is no getting away from the fact that someone's philosophical outlook contributes to how he or she sees the human being and a distorted philosophy inevitably distorts the truth about human beings. Yet a common misconception is that religion carries bias and that secular and philosophical perspectives are somehow neutral. A view further along the line is that only secular perspectives are reasonable; faith perspectives are tainted by superstition and the unproveable. The next step arrives at the point where a person with religious affiliation is viewed with suspicion: such a person cannot be relied upon to give an impartial, unbiased consideration of matters that affect society as a whole and any disagreement would make projects unworkable.

Certainly some atheistic approaches categorise all religious beliefs as superstition and therefore to be discounted. The same approaches view philosophy in whatever shape it takes as rational and therefore to be promoted. In their book *The Philosophy and Practice of Medicine and Bioethics: A Naturalistic-Humanistic Approach* the Austrian physician Barbara Maier and the American philosopher Warren Shibles present what they seem to think is an entirely sound and reasonable assessment of the 'battle' between religious 'supernaturalist' views and 'reasoned' scientific and philosophical views. The authors question whether a physician as 'a supernatural religious believer' has 'given up rationality and the scientific approach to medicine and should therefore be disqualified as a physican except for members of his or her own church'.

They quote the utilitarian philosopher and influential bioethicist Peter Singer who speaks of church 'doctrines about immortality, original sin, and damnation…doctrines so obnoxious…that if anyone did accept them, we should be inclined to discount any other moral view he/she held'. The authors make the rather unenlightened, reductive and dismissive claim that since there are no rational arguments for the existence of God religion is irrational therefore medicine and bioethics can jettison theology in favour of accepting 'rational, critical, naturalistic, consequentialistic scientific thinking in general'.[2] On a more practical level Suzi Leather, the then chairperson of the UK's Human Fertilization and Embryology Authority explained in response to a question about the desirability of having different views represented on so important an authority, to sit on the board a person must accept IVF and embryo research otherwise the board would not be able to make decisions; it is not pragmatic for members of the board to represent opposing views.[3]

In contrast to this kind of closed secular thinking Pope John Paul is keen to point out that philosophy can be 'the way to come to know fundamental truths about human life'. He adds 'at the same time the Church considers philosophy an indispensable help for a deeper understanding of faith and for communicating the truth of the Gospel to those who do not yet know it'.[4] However Pope John Paul is also well aware of 'forms of atheistic humanism' that see faith as 'alienating and damaging to the development of a full rationality'. Furthermore in the field of scientific research he notes a mentality that is in danger of putting 'something other than the human person and the entirety of the person's life' at the centre of concern.[5] Pope John Paul recognises that certain ways of thinking, particularly atheism, have serious repercussions for the dignity and freedom of the human person[6] and so rather than shutting off dialogue he is very clear that the Church both responds to the signs of the times and also has vital insights that it seeks to share with all human beings.

In this championing of dialogue Pope John Paul places himself squarely in the vision of the Second Vatican Council. Moreover, he sees that carrying out the vision of the Council is his main task.[7] He accepts that 'faith without dialogue' is certainly 'less exacting'.[8] Nevertheless he follows the Fathers of the

Second Vatican Council in acknowledging the importance of the problems raised by certain ways of thinking, notably those that threaten the dignity of the human person. Given this importance the Church Fathers call for 'an earnest and more thorough scrutiny' of the motives behind these ways of thinking.[9] Reflecting on this call Bishop Karol Wojtyła points out that such a dialogue both enriches faith and also makes 'grave demands' on Christians to give adequate expression and bear true witness to this faith.[10] As Pope, John Paul takes up this challenge of witness in his tireless defence of the truth of human dignity, especially where this is under attack in the situation of the profoundly disabled human person.

The dialogue envisaged by Pope John XXIII's project of *aggiornamento* and realised in the Second Vatican Council revolves around bringing the 'signs of the times' into the Church's orbit. Although *aggiornamento* is frequently translated as 'bringing things up to date' the concept is in fact much richer. It combines an understanding of *renovatio*, a conservation and appreciation of basic elements, with *accommodata*, accommodation to modern circumstances through timely changes and innovations in non-essentials. In the documents of the Council discernment of these signs begins with a thorough and profound study of the mystery of the Church and then this *aggiornamento* broadens out towards the whole of humanity.[11] The Council document *Gaudium et spes* recognises at the outset that human beings stand both in wonder and perplexity before the 'current trends in the world, about their place and their role in the universe, about the meaning of individual and collective endeavour, and finally about the destiny of nature and of man.'[12] The Council Fathers see it to be an 'expression of solidarity and respectful affection for the whole human family' to 'enter into dialogue' with all people about these difficult problems. It is then both urgent and necessary that the Church speaks up to affirm the dignity of the profoundly disabled and those who are often voiceless before a more vociferous world: a dialogue is after all a two way thing and those who cannot speak need someone to speak for them.

Engaged in this project of dialogue Pope John Paul's writings and his vision for human beings in all that they do from the Church and family, to the work place, to economics and to world wide issues are extensive. In his encyclicals Pope John Paul follows the practice found in papal writings on Catholic Social Teaching: he identifies and reflects on current issues from their contemporary relevance to their historical roots and to their future implications. He points out their promise as well as their mistakes and distortions. He offers powerful corrective insights that have a foundation in the sources of Catholic thinking, in Scripture, Tradition, reason and previous Church teaching. He does this in prayerful dialogue commending to God the task of the Church in enlightening the world. In order then to understand more fully what Pope John Paul is about when he speaks on disability and the acting person it is necessary to set the context from the signs of the times. Certainly some may suggest that at times Pope John Paul is too dogmatic in his responses and this seems to be an ongoing criticism of, for instance his stand on the issue of feeding and hydrating patients who are in persistent vegetative state. However when it is recognised that human life and human dignity are at stake, when his thought is put in the context of what is being said or implied both in the secular arena and in some strands of theology about the most profoundly disabled people then his voice becomes a powerful defence for the voiceless.

According to Pope John Paul in all areas 'the object' of the Church's care is the human being 'in his unique unrepeatable human reality, which keeps intact the image and likeness of God himself.'[13] However this is not simply a social mission for as Pope John Paul frequently says 'man is the way of the Church and Christ is the way of man'.[14] In its focus on the being and dignity of every human being the Church is following the way of Christ and the Father since all of God's saving activity is directed towards human beings. This is why philosophical and theological anthropology are key and also why perhaps Pope John Paul is especially noted for his views on bioethics and healthcare where the human being is often found at his or her most vulnerable moments.

Bioethics: a question of life

Bioethical issues concern every person at a most fundamental level, that of protection of the person and his or her health. The right to life involves not only healthcare but also the very dignity of the human person. When the discipline of Bioethics first emerged on the academic scene in the 1960s and 1970s it was arguably on the fringes of Catholic theology though the Church has always been involved in the ethics of healthcare. David Jones, the Director of the Anscombe Bioethics Centre, the UK's foremost Catholic biomedical centre, points out that when Pope John Paul wrote his encyclical on the Gospel of Life, *Evangelium vitae* in 1995 the Pope saw bioethics as 'a welcome development in the secular academy' and 'a sign of hope'. However David Jones describes how bioethics has gradually become the actual 'battleground' for a clash of cultures: the culture of death and the culture of life.[15] This is far from the battle presented by some as a conflict between superstitious faith and sensible reason. In setting up the Pontifical Council for Culture, a merger of Pope Paul VI's Pontifical Council for Dialogue with Non-Believers and the Council for Culture, Pope John Paul recognises the significance of culture for the full development of the human person.

Whilst this chapter is primarily directed at the signs of the times that demonstrate this battlefield Pope John Paul's concern with the culture of life requires clarification. Pope John Paul is not interested in human beings and the dignity of the human person in some humanistic sense as if they are supreme beings. Rather, he is concerned to foster the rediscovery in every human being of a 'deep sense of wonder' at himself or herself,[16] a wonder at the truth that he or she is the only creature on earth that God has wanted for his or her own sake[17] and that human beings are destined to become friends of God. This truth only comes to light in Christ because in His Incarnation human nature was assumed not absorbed and this means that human nature has been raised to a 'dignity beyond compare'.[18] Pope John Paul's understanding of the dignity of the human person and his conviction that the 'Gospel of Life is at the heart of Jesus's message' is not then limited to life in its earthly existence. Rather it extends to all aspects and stages of life, to eternal life and to the human person's calling to communion with God.[19]

Pope John Paul's traditional Christian perspective that human life includes the promised eternal life is not only theologically and philosophically crucial. It is also significant on a practical level for human life here and now. Not only does it challenge philosophies that have a materialistic view of the human person that may on the one hand forget or deny the transcendent aspect that all human beings possess, or on the other hand forget or deny that the person is a real living human being and not merely a conscious mind, it also provides a direction for bioethical decision-making. In contrast to materialistic philosophies that offer merely descriptive accounts of the human being that cannot be directive, the Christian perspective offers the possibility of the practical application of prudential wisdom and this is based on the fundamental dignity of each and every human being, no matter his or her situation or condition. Prudential wisdom is prepared to identify and challenge attacks or threats to the dignity of human beings and to speak up for the voiceless against injustices. Yet it also recognises that human beings are limited creatures and that fullness of life goes beyond earthly existence.

Since he sees that a key role is played by philosophy of the human being and by theological anthropology then inevitably Pope John Paul finds himself at odds with certain secular philosophies and understandings of the human person. As an ethics professor in the Catholic University of Lublin Karol Wojtyła is critical in particular of the a-historicism, excessive subjectivism and often unacknowledged limitations of phenomenology, existentialism and philosophies of consciousness. Phenomenology deals with how we experience things and the meaning things have in our experience. Finding both empiricism and rationalism to be inadequate when it comes to describing the phenomena of perception, phenomenology considers perception to be neither purely sensation nor purely interpretation. Rather we have a pre-reflective self-awareness such that experiences have a subjective feel to them: the fact that it is I who am having or living through this experience is not the same as what it is like to remember what it is like to have this experience. With a focus on how things appear to us rather than how things are questions of being are 'bracketed out'. In the same way that phenomenology concentrates on conscious experience existentialism and philosophies of consciousness concern themselves with a sequence of acts of consciousness and in the case of existentialism the radical experience of freedom of choice.

Phenomenology, existentialism and these philosophies of consciousness attempt to bypass metaphysics and traditional thinking and they discount any possible value these may have. The question is no longer 'is this description right or wrong' but what meaning does it offer. Whilst phenomenology does call attention to the subjective aspect of anthropology and so goes some way to addressing the focus in traditional anthropology of the objectifying of human beings phenomenology tends too much towards subjectivist reflection. Phenomenology and existentialism avoid analysis and explanation in their emphasis on what things mean for me and so any objective truth is lost. With phenomenology's focus on conscious experience and the absolutisation of consciousness it neglects semi-conscious and unconscious mental activity and bodily activity. It risks limiting anthropology to phenomena and in doing so it loses sight of the human being who does not appear to exhibit relevant acts of self-consciousness and freedom of choice: the non-acting person.

As Pope, John Paul comes up against what he perceives to be a more insidious threat: the development of a 'cultural climate' where some public opinion authorised by the State and aided by healthcare systems have distorted or even denied the full personal dignity of every human being.[20] Pope John Paul is moreover concerned by the tendency to categorise as rights certain attacks on the marginalised and voiceless so that a struggle of the powerful against the weak emerges whereby certain human beings are seen as inconvenient, burdensome, redundant and even as enemies.[21]

In keeping with Pope John Paul's methodology an exploration of the signs of the times points to some thinking that contributes to this cultural climate. Such an exploration seems vital in order to put Pope John Paul's thought and his frequently necessary and outspoken stand in context. These signs of the times indicate clearly that the very dignity of the human being at his or her most vulnerable state is at stake. On the one hand there is an explicit view, mainly found in academic circles that certain human beings are not persons and therefore are not entitled to the protection given to human beings who are persons. This may be because some writers hold that certain human beings fall below what they see as a threshold for personhood so are on 'the margins' of life, or because some writers wish to advance the rights of animals and so inevitably the status of some human beings appears to fall. However it is important to note that the argument is not in distant inaccessible academic journals. Rather it appears on book shop shelves, in textbooks on bioethics and it is discussed using real life case study scenarios. It is becoming an actual alternative and a possible way of thinking through and acting in difficult situations, made it seems more appealing where resources are tight or where apparent future benefits are held up as near achievements. On the other hand there appears to be a more subtle and pervasive implicit view that some people's lives are not worth as much as other people's lives and this is based more often than not on the fact that they are intellectually disabled. This view is arguably more insidious since it operates on the practical level of day-to-day dealings with the most profoundly disabled people and it seems to involve dismissive indifference to the situation and dignity of others notably by professionals and by those into whose care they are entrusted.

In academia, human beings and persons: biological and biographical life

In contemporary bioethics much has been made of the distinction between the biological life of the human organism and his or her biographical life as a human person. The notion that every patient has a biographical life, that is comes before the physician with his or her own life history and narrative and not simply as a body to be worked upon was brought to the attention of the medical profession by one of the founding fathers of bioethics, the American Protestant writer Paul Ramsey in a series of lectures, the Lyman Beecher lectures. These lectures inaugurated bioethics as a new academic discipline and led Paul Ramsey to produce one of its early written works in 1970 *The Patient As Person*. In his book Paul Ramsey seeks to draw attention to the personal life story of the patient; he does not intend to separate the patient completely from his bodily life. However, a different twist to the distinction between biographical and biological life emerges from the thought of the American moral philosopher Joseph Fletcher who also helped to plant the seeds for bioethics.[22] Joseph Fletcher develops this distinction so that it no longer functions as a way of considering two aspects of every human being. Instead Joseph Fletcher makes a clear separation between biological and biographical life such that in his eyes some human beings are no longer persons. It would seem that this separation best suits the new morality of situation ethics that Joseph Fletcher proposed in his wish to influence the American moral outlook.

Inspired by American pragmatism and the belief that the 'good' and the 'true' is 'whatever works'[23] Joseph Fletcher's book *Morals and Medicine* published in 1972 indicates from the topics covered that his chief concern is with patient autonomy and rights from the right to health and to know the truth to the right to control reproduction and the right to die. His ethical system of situation ethics further stresses autonomy in terms of the right to choose by its principle that maxims from the community and tradition are merely illuminators and the decision-maker can set aside such maxims '*in the situation* if love seems better served by doing so' (his italics).[24] For this new 'human centered' morality Joseph Fletcher formulates his celebrated indicators of 'humanhood', indicators for having a 'personal life': people who have them are 'subjects', truly human beings, deserving of great moral concern; those that do not are 'objects', subpersonal beings.[25] Personhood, he says, depends primarily on a minimum intelligence of an IQ above 20. This means that 'humans without some minimum intelligence or mental capacity are not persons, no matter how many of these organs are active, no matter how spontaneous their living processes are' and idiots are not human, they have no rights, rather they are 'outside the pale of human integrity'.[26] Unsurprisingly Joseph Fletcher's theological colleagues did not support his rather extreme views and Joseph Fletcher himself turned towards agnosticism and in terms of ethical outlook towards utilitarianism. However his radical turn to autonomy and rights remains influential.

Thus in early bioethical literature there emerges two competing visions of the human person: Paul Ramsey's 'embodied soul' who lives in his or her own particular narrative[27] and Joseph Fletcher's 'person' who exerts control and choice and is other than his or her body. These two visions have unfolded in the course of bioethics[28] and arguably Joseph Fletcher's vision with a focus on autonomy though without its more discriminatory aspects is in the ascendant. Joseph Fletcher's list of characteristics for personhood set in train a vigorous debate on what properties should and should not be included. Many influential bioethicists now seem to accept that a clear separation can be made between biological and biographical life[29] and many follow the line taken by list-creators like Daniel Dennett an American professor of philosophy who specialises in philosophies of consciousness[30]: they seem to take it as read that 'we' *all* recognise that most but not all humans are persons since 'we' recognise some conditions exempt humans from personhood and according to Daniel Dennett infants, the mentally defective, the insane are not persons; 'we' may not have yet discovered the formula for a definition of personhood, and he admits that there may be none to discover, yet 'we' would not abandon the concept of personhood since 'the idea that we might cease to view others and *ourselves* as persons….. is arguably self-contradictory' (his italics). It is perhaps notable that Daniel Dennett feels the need to use 'we' to give the impression that there is some kind of agreement and so gloss over obvious objections. It is simply not true that everyone accepts that certain human beings are not persons.

The division of human being from human person has taken root in two particular areas that have influenced bioethics: one is in life or death decision-making concerning human beings at what Jeff McMahan calls 'the margins of life', though from his 2002 book, *The Ethics of Killing: Problems at the Margins of Life* he clearly means at the margins of personhood; the other is in determining the threshold for personhood in the context of the animal rights movement whereby some animals, notably higher primates, are considered persons whilst some human beings inevitably fall below the threshold of personhood.

On the margins

The separation between a human being's biological life and his or her biographical life is more formally set out by another moral philosopher, James Rachels in the introduction to his influential book published in 1986 *The End of Life: Euthanasia and Morality*. Significantly as moral philosophers both Joseph Fletcher and James Rachels favour utilitarianism and both seem to realise that making inroads into bioethics paves the way for a change in ethics generally. In the introduction to his book James Rachels makes a distinction between having a life and merely being alive arguing that his 'moral' and 'reasoned' approach lessens the importance of some long-discussed distinctions between animals and humans, killing and letting die, innocence and non-innocence, ordinary and extraordinary means of treatment.

This in itself suggests that these long-discussed distinctions lack content and it overlooks the profound reflection and fine tuning made by theology to some particularly knotty problems. Of course it also fits in with the prevalent bioethical method of practical ethics, coincidentally though not accidentally the name of one of Peter Singer's books. Practical ethics, an offshoot of analytic philosophy, encourages an approach to ethical problems that focuses on ready answers. It is anxious to find consensus even where there is none in order to break through what appears to be interminable debate. Above all it claims that concepts such as the sanctity of life and human dignity are too abstract or contentious and they get in the way of decision-making. Practical ethics seeks to avoid foundational issues. It has been said that medicine has 'saved the life of ethics' by taking a practical rather than an abstract approach.[31] However in neglecting the deeper issues practical ethics fails to take complex concepts like that of the person seriously, it forgets that some things are worth struggling over, it does not seem to appreciate what is really at stake.

As an illustration of this practical ethical approach according to one of James Rachels's colleagues the motivation behind Rachels's book is to allow physicians and families to discontinue treatment of patients with permanent loss of consciousness.[32] To facilitate this James Rachels realises that he needs to challenge the prevalent principle of the sanctity of life, a principle implying that 'taking life is directly wrong'.[33] Perhaps recognising at least implicitly the significance and appeal of the principle he replaces it with a principle of 'sanctity of lives', 'lives' being the 'sum of all we hold dear: our projects, our activities, our loves and friendships and the rest'.[34] He says that killing is wrong simply because it is harming someone. However, in the absence of conscious life, where there is only biological life it is of no consequence to the subject of that life whether he lives or dies:[35] the more mentally complex the entity the more we have reasons for regretting its death and thus the more objectionable would be its killing; as lives become simpler protection weakens.[36] With 'subnormal lives' the value of life is diminished, indeed, if an entity lacks the mental and physical abilities to engage in simple human activities, according to James Rachels, it does not have human life.[37] The practical application of his approach is that where a patient has irretrievably lost consciousness his life is over and so he cannot be harmed by removing his vital organs or being killed.[38] Notably James Rachels speaks of 'our' regret at 'someone's' death by killing rather than, say, the injustice to that someone, and, like Daniel Dennett he presumes to carry his reader along with him. Moreover, James Rachels's rationale behind discontinuing treatment does not rely on the treatment being burdensome or futile for the patient or no longer clinically indicated. Rather, the focus is on the ease with which the patient can be deemed a nonperson from his or her apparent inactivity and on the worthwhileness of the life of the patient as if that can be easily and objectively judged.

James Rachels's separation of the life of the human being and his or her personal life fosters a social rather than a concrete view of the person. His influential view can be found in the more specific thought of many contemporary bioethical writers. For instance Jeff McMahan, an avowed specialist in practical ethics who explores end of life issues explains that there is a differentiation between two concepts of death, death of the organism and death of the person, or more precisely, mind or self. Death of a person often comes first so there is 'little reason to care about the exact timing of the death of the organism'.[39] Once again an apparently easy answer is offered to what is a most complex question, the human being in his or her living and dying.

Certainly the Christian tradition accepts talk of body and soul as aspects of the whole human person. However, body and soul do not correspond neatly to biological and biographical life: it is I, this concrete and real human being, who has a life story, a biography. This real human being with his or her life story is the person observed by Pope John Paul joining the flow of pilgrims in Rome at the turn of the millennium. Nevertheless writers like Daniel Dennett who argue for a clear separation of biological and biographical life ignore any theologically grounded philosophy and claim that this separation has a philosophical consensus. This claim stands despite the evidence that the criteria for making such a separation appears far from agreed and the apparent consensus itself is not subject to any rigorous critique. This lack of consensus is amply demonstrated by Joseph Fletcher who offers a list of characteristics for determining who is and who is not a person or has 'humanhood' and then invites others 'to add or subtract'[40] as if by refining the list 'we' might come to some agreement.

The lack of agreement is further demonstrated in the debate about defining death in terms of brain functioning, a debate that has serious practical implications. In 1968 the Harvard Medical School Committee looked at different definitions of death in order to respond to fears of overtreatment in the face of technological advances. At the same time the issue of organ transplantation was current. The outcome of the Committee's deliberations was the production of the *Harvard Report* in 1969 endorsing the whole brain death criterion. Robert Veatch, a prominent bioethicist and an early proponent of the higher brain death criterion, was involved in the Report and in the early debates on the redefinition of death to encompass brain activity. He explains that 'without really understanding what we were doing' we adopted 'a new and radically different meaning of the word dead' having little to do with biology, and 'we chose to classify them [humans with dead brains] as dead'. He adds, these humans may retain many bodily functions and are 'still living in the biological sense' however they are given a 'radically different moral status': 'the word dead has come to mean—for legal, ethical and public policy purposes—"having lost full moral standing as a member of the human community"' losing 'all the rights of living members such as the right not to be killed'. [41] Of particular concern here is that moral status seems to depend merely on the choices of others.

The ambiguity over brain definitions of death is perhaps illustrated by the fact that whilst some in the US argue for a definition of death based on the diagnosis of loss of functioning of the whole brain, in the UK it is based on the prognostic test of brain stem death. Furthermore others, like Robert Veatch, criticise the whole brain definition since some activity may still be present. So for instance Michael Green and Daniel Wikler, writers interested in brain death and personal identity, explain that the whole-brain redefinition of death does not show that the brain dead are dead rather it shows that they have a worthless existence and need not be cared for. The authors prefer to say the brain dead have 'no existence at all'.[42] Anencephalic infants, they say, have functioning brain stems so are not dead; they are just live human bodies rather than persons.[43] In the case of patients in persistent vegetative state, 'patients whose lives are stable but not worth living', a 'redefinition of death' might resolve problems. So just as organs can be removed from brain dead patients so too could an agent causing cardiac arrest be administered to patients in persistent vegetative state.[44] Michael Green and Daniel Wikler's apparently practical solution is that a person dies when his or her higher brain ceases to function even though his or her body may still live on.

The notion of this rather insubstantial self is perhaps best expressed in the philosopher Michael Lockwood's claim that 'the essential me is the mental me, which resides in the brain' with the rest of the body being 'merely a support system, toolbox, power pack and vehicle for getting about'.[45] Jeff McMahan takes a similar position. He says that human beings are 'essentially minds' and since an anencephalic infant 'is a fundamentally different sort of thing from us', since it is simply 'a permanently unoccupied human organism', there can be no real objections to taking its organs for transplantation whilst it is still living.[46] The same reasoning more or less applies, he thinks, to patients in persistent vegetative state. Notably the idea of an insubstantial self, a purely 'mental me' is not new. Theology considered and rejected this position as early as the fourth century though in the context of the Christological disputes. The heretic Apollinarius took the view that in human beings the mind supplied power to the flesh that was purely passive. Apollinarius was resoundly refuted by Gregory of Nazianzus and Gregory of Nyssa who rigorously explained that human beings are wholes, material and immaterial, and not separated into parts.[47]

Disagreement about what corresponds to biographical life continues in bioethical debates other than those defining death. Involved in these discussions are many prominent and influential bioethicists. Charateristics suggested by these bioethicists following Joseph Fletcher's lead are wide ranging and tend to favour higher cognitive capacities such as consciousness or self-consciousness, rationality, the ability to communicate, the ability to demonstrate self-motivated activity, the capacity to make choices, the possession of desires or interests. So for James Rachels some kind of mental and physical abilities to engage in activity is necessary; for the American bioethicist Baruch Brody there must be some higher brain activity;[48] for John Lizza, a bioethicist interested in philosophy of mind, some cognitive function;[49] for Jeff McMahan 'a mental life of a certain order of complexity and sophistication' is required.[50] Some speak from both secular philosophical and theological perspectives: the Anglican theologian Nigel Biggar links personhood to the capacity to respond to vocation and for that higher brain functioning is needed.[51] The evangelical theologian Robert Rakestraw thinks that the image of God in human beings requires a level of self-awareness and so 'the earthly life of a person' ends when self-awareness is lost even though the body is still alive.[52] The American neurologist and expert on unconsciousness Ronald Cranford also seems to think unconscious biological life is not what Christians understand by human existence since it cannot involve relationships, conscious choice, love, things that make existence meaningful and there is no special value in somatic life because this only has value insofar as it sustains consciousness. Consciousness, he suggests, allows humans to participate in God's creative and redemptive purposes so 'it is morally inappropriate to treat what no longer images God (in acts of intellect, emotion and will) as if it did'.[53] Significantly the claim that it is primarily human activity even if it is merely higher brain activity, that determines relationship with God or indeed the image of God in human beings is problematic in theology since it appears to limit the action of God in the lives of all human beings no matter what their condition or situation.

Not only do those who rely on some level of self-consciousness recognise that there is no satisfactory definition or understanding of consciousness,[54] some go even beyond consciousness. For instance John Harris, perhaps one of the UK's most well-known bioethicist, says of embryos that 'at no stage of its development through to the end of the third trimester of gestation and beyond' does the developing individual acquire the features relevant, as far as he is concerned, for personhood.[55] Persons 'properly so called', he explains are 'human individuals who have developed the capacity to value their own existence' and so he rules out from the category of person embryos, foetuses and neonates.[56] He argues that the question is not when does life begin and when does it end. Rather it is when does life begin to matter morally and when does life cease to matter morally. This he says is gauged by when life begins to have or ceases to have 'that special value we believe attaches to human life'.[57] According to John Harris what gives our lives 'special value' is autonomy in terms of the ability to make choices and to modify our lives through our preferences.[58] Once again the appeal to 'we' demonstrates a certain arbitrariness in his determination of 'special value' and this value seems to depend solely on the capriciousness of human choice.

The separation between biographical and biological life may be more formalised and explicit in academic bioethical discourse. However, it is also present in other forums. In the UK courts for instance in the case of Tony Bland, a patient in persistent vegetative state, it was clearly recognised that the patient was alive since the case concerned the legality of bringing about his death. Yet his existence in persistent vegetative state was described as a 'living death'[59] and his body called a 'mere shell'.[60] Less explicit perhaps are those who say they would not like to 'exist' in certain conditions or who see the lives of certain human beings as not worth living.[61] These views tend towards the notion that it is not so much the situation of the human being involved that is undignified. Rather it is the human being him or her self who is worthless. In contrast to a view that sees each and every human being as unique, irreplaceable and beyond valuation this almost hierarchical valuing of human beings is played out further in the fairly recent innovation of speciesism, a term coined by the British psychologist and philosopher Richard Ryder in 1973 to denote prejudice against non-human animals.

The non-human person and the human non-person

Championed in particular by Peter Singer, possibly the most influential utilitarian philosopher and bioethicist, speciesism has come to the fore in the context of animal liberation and rights and here the issue is not simply the separation of biographical life and biological life. As with those who separate out the person from the human being the only thing that matters is biographical life but for those who argue for the non-human person biological life, whether the entity is human or another kind of animal, is irrelevant. Peter Singer and his colleague Paola Cavalieri (mis)use Christian theology to prove the point.[62] They argue that when Trinitarian theology took over the term person and connected it to the 'person' of God this 'saved the life of the concept', it prevented it from being just another term for human being and so, they claim, person can 'overcome the species barrier'. They add that since the theological understanding of person is essentially relational then, given that the primary relationship is of the self to his or her consciousness, self-consciousness is the mark of personhood. Since self-consciousness and associated properties such as capacities to desire, choose and will do not depend on being a member of the human species then species membership is not morally relevant. What counts is having 'interests' and Peter Singer broadly defines interests as what a person desires.[63] According to Peter Singer the 'prerequisite' for having interests at all is the capacity for suffering or enjoyment.[64] So writers who follow the line taken by Peter Singer and who argue that species membership is not morally relevant accept the possibility of killing embryos, infants and the profoundly disabled indeed any human being without morally relevant properties.[65] David DeGrazia for one recognises this may be counterintuitive. Still he is prepared to accept the consequence that the presumption of equal consideration of the interests of all entities may deliver a 'moral blow': the suggestion that 'a lowered presumption against causing suffering to certain animals implies a lowered presumption for similarly situated, handicapped humans'.[66]

Peter Singer's own position is curious. On the one hand he uses Christian theology to support his claims for the personhood of some higher animals albeit he does not appear to be aware of the historical and theological journey of the concept of the person. Moreover he does not seem to appreciate that the relational aspect of Trinitarian theology simply cannot be translated into consciousness otherwise the three Persons of the Trinity would become three individual centres of consciousness and hence three gods. On the other hand he argues that the Christian tradition should be jettisoned in favour of a new ethic.[67] He believes that the Christian legacy in Western thinking with its emphasis on human beings as the crown of creation has drawn an arbitrary, speciesist line between humans and other animals. He claims with little evidence that the ethics of Judaism and Christianity is outdated and 'crumbling'[68] and on this basis he argues that what he sees as the overinflated status of human beings can now be reviewed though he states that his aim is 'to elevate the status of animals rather than to lower the status of any humans'.[69] Once, he says, we recognise that a boundary line between human beings and animals is speciesist and to be resisted then how we treat some disabled humans should be equally applied to non-human animals with similar levels of self-consciousness and capacities.[70] Again this is curious since his suggested treatment of the profoundly disabled includes killing them, albeit painlessly, for being redundant, inconvenient or unwanted. He explains that inevitably some lives of non-human animals 'by any standards' are more valuable than the lives of some humans. This being the case 'we must grant these animals a right to life as good as, or better than, such retarded or senile humans'.[71] However the standards to which he refers are the ones he has arbitrarily selected.

Peter Singer has been the target of much criticism by disabled groups for stating that the lives of some animals have a higher value than the lives of some human beings. However he does accept that as a group, disabled people are subjected to unjustifiable discrimination. So in keeping with his general ethical worldview Peter Singer advocates equal consideration of their interests: 'people with disabilities who want to live their lives to the full should be given every possible assistance in doing so'.[72] Whilst this appears a generous (and uncharacteristic) move, Peter Singer is talking here of already existing disabled people who can make their desires and interests known. His views on prenatal screening, the replaceablity of infants and what he sees as the 'reality' that the lives of disabled people are less worth living than the lives of people who are not disabled[73] belies his apparent generosity. Furthermore his preference utilitarian outlook still allows him to judge that 'people may be utterly mistaken in their expectations of happiness' such that 'a desire to go on living can be outweighed by other desires' and so from a classical utilitarian viewpoint he says it may be right to kill a person 'who does not choose to die' on the grounds that that person will lead 'a miserable life'.[74] The disabled cannot rely on Peter Singer. Certainly from this it is not at all clear that Peter Singer can take the concept of the person seriously even on his own terms. However his call for equal consideration of the interests of disabled people is not as equal as it appears: Peter Singer makes a clear distinction between disabled and intellectually disabled people. He claims that the severely intellectually disabled, like newborn infants, are not persons since they are not rational and not self-conscious.[75] By a pleasure-pain calculation the lives of such individuals may be shortened and they can be replaced by people who bring more pleasure into the world.[76] He also argues that it is better to legalise taking organs from living anencephalic infants and from those in persistent vegetative state (and so therefore killing them) rather than to declare them legally dead by changing the definition of death.[77] For Peter Singer these human beings appear to have worth only insofar as they provide a benefit to other more worthy human beings.

Human beings and worth: attitudes to disability

Whilst there may be an explicit separation between human beings and persons in some bioethical thinking it would seem that certain attitudes to people who are disabled, particularly the intellectually disabled, also attests to this separation though usually implicitly. Just as some bioethicists decide that some human beings are non-persons and so do not enjoy the protection owed to persons, so too do some deny certain human rights and dignities to people with disabilities whose lives they judge to be of less worth than 'normal' people. Both these explicit and implicit attitudes seem to have a foundation in philosophies of consciousness, the kind of philosophies critiqued by Karol Wojtyła, that see mental activity of a certain level as the criterion for being a full member of the human community.

Although a level of ambiguity seems to accompany attitudes towards disability, two UK commentators on disability studies, Tom Shakespeare and Nicholas Watson, suggest that Enlightenment dualism, with its focus on defining humans in terms of their rational capacities and its lack of recognition for the 'inherent frailty and vulnerability of our embodiment', has obscured the fact that illness, both mental and physical, is a part of the human condition.[78] Certainly research into the history of disability has shown that people with disabilities have been treated anywhere from rejection to being held in highest esteem depending on the prevailing culture and historical conditions; either they represent disharmony in the world or bring luck. Their disability, especially if it is physical, has often been regarded as a punishment and in legends it is frequently used as a warning to others to heed social conventions. However consistently it seems disability is linked to being 'other', different, hence perhaps the ambiguity.

Nevertheless every period in history developed its own strategies for making the disabled over into what was considered to be the norm of the day. As noted in Henri-Jacques Stiker's detailed book *A History of Disability*, the ancient Athenians provided funds to the disabled so that they could live like the able-bodied; in the fourteenth century almsgiving to the disabled became a way for the rich to achieve salvation and the inclusion of the 'fool' in royal courts allowed for comment on the pretentions of the ruling classes.[79] Perhaps what is more interesting is that in the Middle Ages friars in an almost opposite move lived alongside the disabled as outcasts so that they could share the lives of the poor and marginalised.

However there appears to be a significant shift in attitude in the seventeenth century with the belief that human beings had the capacity to intervene in what had previously been perceived as an immutable world order. Early Enlightenment thinking informed by the new science of atomistic theories took a mechanistic view of the world and in doing so lost something of the awe and mystery surrounding the world and humanity. This mechanistic view applied equally to human beings so for thinkers like Thomas Hobbes and Rene Descartes the human body is 'nothing other than a statue or earthen machine' whose physical components make it walk, eat and breathe.[80] The body as a machine, a church organ, a clock or automaton[81] with the heart as a spring, the nerves as strings and the joints as wheels[82] seems to lead inevitably to the view that human beings (and society) can be perfected.

For thinkers like Rene Descartes non-human animals have life and sensations but not thought or consciousness; behaviour is explained by mechanical and bodily processes, so it is not a crime to kill or eat them.[83] However, it became a short step to rationalise about certain problematic human beings. Sociological commentators Jan Branson and Don Miller record that where language was seen to separate human beings from animals, humans who did not match the required standard were dehumanised, called monsters, the 'mindless', considered less than human.[84] This redefinition of the problem so that it could be removed altogether seems to have been anticipated in the fifteenth century by Martin Luther who is reluctant to baptise some malformed children since he believes them to be the work of the devil. Moreover Luther seems to think it right to drown a misshapen child who he sees as being possessed rather than truly human or to suffocate a presumably disabled boy since he was simply a mass of flesh without a soul.[85] In the seventeenth century the philosopher John Locke also questions the 'precise and unmoveable' boundaries of species and he appears to think that 'monstruous productions' and changelings, something between a man and a beast, are the result of unnatural sexual practice.[86] Moreover, John Locke argues that if his contemporaries really believe that monsters have rational souls merely because they are the issue of rational parents then they would not destroy 'ill-formed and mis-shaped productions', a practice he suggests is common.[87] John Locke thinks that a very different outward shape or a lack of reason and speech is a sign of a different real constitution and species between a changeling and a reasonable man[88]: and if a defect in the body makes a monster and thus places the entity outside the human race then a defect in the mind does the same but more so.[89]

Whilst the rise of Enlightenment dualism perhaps began the separation of biological life from biographical life the rise of social Darwinism also seems to have contributed to the notion that certain people have less worth than others. Studies show that the nineteenth century conviction in the intrinsic goodness of science and progress saw disabled people as people who could be 'changed for the better' and part of this education was to prevent them from using sign language.[90] Moreover it was claimed that those who could only use sign language were less evolved than people who spoke, indeed they were considered to be more like apes.[91] With increasing interest in research and medical experiments there is evidence that disabled people were readily used as research subjects without their consent or the consent of their relatives.[92] Furthermore, with its notions based on the survival of the fittest some also saw progress in eugenics, forced sterilisation and legislation preventing marriage among the disabled community.[93] This view persists as medical conferences in the 1960s included speakers who endorsed eugenics[94] and contemporary writers like John Harris are keen to promote a eugenic mentality as illustrated by his book in 2007 *Enhancing Evolution: The Ethical Case for Making Better People*.

Despite the presence of some eugenic thinking, the rise in the twentieth century of human rights and equal opportunities encouraged a new view of disability so that it is no longer framed in terms of a lack to be addressed by medical technology. Marsha Saxton who writes extensively on disability points out that selective abortion after a prenatal diagnosis of disability may still be intended by some health professionals to eliminate categories of disabled people and so is seen by some as the 'new eugenics'. However, she says people with disabilities are now reframing the experience of disability: the stereotypical notions of 'tragedy' and 'suffering' and the negativity of a lack in ability result more from the isolation of the disabled in society; the disabled are 'afflicted with the social role assignment of a tragic, burdensome existence'. Certainly she agrees that disability brings difficulties and inconveniences. Nevertheless she argues what is 'most disabling about disability' is 'discriminatory attitudes and thought-less behaviours'. [95]

The minefield of language also has a part to play. Reference to the 'handicapped' has long been acknowledged to be demeaning since it has its roots in charitable handouts made to the less fortunate; 'impairment' and 'disability' indicate for some a lack, falling short of a norm or a difficulty in need of fixing. Indeed the very description of the disabled as 'disabled people' that places the disability before the person is arguably framing the person firstly in terms of his or her disability and only secondly as a person, hence the preference of some for the descriptor 'person with disability'. On the other hand 'people with disabilities' is critiqued on the grounds that we do not say 'people with black-ness' and reference to 'the disabled' or 'the blind' or 'the deaf' is entirely appropriate for those who consider themselves to be separate from 'the sighted' or those who hear. Of course some words offend some people and others are offended by their often euphemistic replacements; others seek to reclaim hurtful words in order to take away their power; others see that the problem lies in those who misinterpret terms. The kinds of attitudes to which Marsha Saxton refers and the dangers of the depersonalising language of disability are perhaps demonstrated in the debate surrounding what are generally called 'models of disability'.

Models of Disability

Models of disability provide a framework for thinking about how people experience disability whether it is from the point of view of the disabled or abled, of the professional or family, indeed of society in general. Models also indicate the kind of strategies that can be put in place to meet the needs of the disabled. Arguably, the different models are each incomplete and at times represent a narrowed perspective, indeed sometimes they conflict. However, they do provide a useful indication of the kind of thinking used by those who create and implement the model as well as the subject matter itself: disability. Models themselves change as society changes and in general there seems to have been a move away from models that are essentially paternalistic, that see disability in terms of 'cannot do', to models that focus on autonomy and 'can do' approaches. This appears to match the recognised progression of healthcare ethics away from medical ethics characterised by 'the doctor knows best' to the relatively new discipline of bioethics and 'ask the patient'. At the same time as bioethics began to emerge as a new academic field in the 1970s so too, it seems did challenges to the prevalent 'medical' model of disability emerge and the main contender is the 'social' model.

The medical model of disability has at its focus the impairment, restriction, lack of ability or disability that, in the words of the World Health Organisation in 1976, 'limits or prevents the fulfilment of a role that is normal for that individual'.[96] Given its emphasis on the individual's limitations the medical model is also known as the biological-inferiority or functional-limitation model. Since the medical model situates the 'problem' in the impaired individual it also locates solutions in the individual by aiming to help the individual overcome or cope with his or her impairment. The object seems to be to make the individual more 'normal'. However, this fails in the case of people with disabilities who cannot be 'cured' or 'improved' and so what remains is to accept the 'abnormality' whilst providing a level of support. Arguably the medical model has as its strength its goals of curing or alleviating the disabling condition of individuals. Still, from the perspective of the person with the disability its categorisation of 'normal' and 'abnormal' and its emphasis on dependence and care seems to fail the individual. Moreover, it seems to foster a culture where people with disabilities are cast in the role of 'the sick' and so are excused a role in society.

Whereas medical models of disability refer to an individual's physical condition such that the 'problem' tends to be in the individual, social models locate problems in social discriminatory structures.[97] The objection to the medical model is that it defines people solely on the basis of their impairment and those 'in charge' are clinicians who seek to cure or normalise no matter what the cost.[98] In contrast the social model of disability looks to the environment and society's attitudes towards the disabled. It focuses on the barriers that prevent people from participating in society. With its roots in civil rights movements especially movements in the USA it appeals to self-determination as a foundational principle so that people with disabilities are encouraged to take control of their lives. Within this model it is argued that disability has as its source the failure of society to see and act upon the needs of the disabled who are often therefore an oppressed minority in much the same way as, say, black people are oppressed by racist attitudes. Following this model, it is claimed that once physical barriers and barriers shaped by attitudes are removed then the lives of people with disabilities will be improved and the resultant equal opportunities to participate in society would virtually wipe out disability. Indeed, what Tom Shakespeare and Nicholas Watson call the 'strong' version of the social model claims 'the difference between disabled people and non-disabled people is not that we have bodies or minds which do not work, but that we are an oppressed minority within a disabling society'.[99]

However Tom Shakespeare and Nicholas Watson point out that the apparently ascendant social model loses sight of the fact that impairment is an aspect of the experience of disabled people so disability cannot be reduced to the outcome of social barriers alone.[100] Moreover the notion that empowerment of oppressed people or the removing of barriers is the answer seems to forget that for some people, notably the profoundly intellectually disabled, it is precisely their impairment that cannot be overcome. The authors offer their own model for consideration 'an alternative ontology of disability' that recognises that everyone is impaired and there is no dividing line between the 'normal' and the 'disabled'.[101] Nevertheless Tom Shakespeare and Nicholas Watson accept the priority is to analyse and campaign against social barriers[102] and discriminatory attitudes are included in this campaign.

Although approaches to disability are frequently considered in terms of the medical and social models as the two opposite poles, the 'cannot do' and the 'can do' there are also other models of disability. One such is the tragedy or charity model. Following this model people with disabilities are cast in the role of victims of circumstance, people to be pitied. In the charity sector they are often shown alongside victims of natural disasters, of famine and poverty. This negative image of disability tends towards a culture of handouts and dis-enabling, of lowering the self-esteem of people with disabilities whilst suggesting they take an attitude of gratitude to their benefactors. It seems to foster pity rather than respect.

It is noteworthy that the 1976 definition from the World Health Organisation benefited from the input of doctors. However, in response to the many challenges and discussions WHO is now revising and updating its definition.[103] In its publication *Towards a Common Language for Functioning, Disability and Health* WHO's framework for health and disability, the International Classification of Functioning, Disability and Health (ICF) explains that previous thinking puts the disabled into a separate category since it held that 'disability began where health ended'.[104] The ICF believes that on their own neither the medical model nor the social model is adequate 'although both are partially valid' since 'disability is a complex phenomena that is both a problem at the level of a person's body, and a complex and primarily social phenomena'.[105] Instead, the ICF offers an integration of the medical and social models, the 'biopsychosocial model' that takes account of both health conditions and contextual factors such as environmental and personal factors.[106] The ICF considers it is making a 'radical shift' in moving to a focus on health and functioning. Every human being, it argues, can experience a 'decrement in health' and therefore disability so it is not an issue for the minority. Rather disability is a universal human experience. In order to enhance the performance of health systems in member states the ICF recommends looking at an individual's level of functioning not only physically but also in society, employment and education 'at the level of the whole human being in day-to-day life' and plan treatments or interventions that can maximise that functioning.[107] Whilst disability does involve 'dysfunctioning'[108] the ICF says it 'mainstreams' the experience of disability by arguing that their classification of functioning is applicable to everyone irrespective of their condition and so 'should not become a tool for labelling persons with disabilities as a separate group'.[109] Moreover the ICF call for parity so that there is no distinction between health conditions that are, for instance, physical and those that are mental.

Of course even the biopsychosocial model cannot escape the criticism that it is a model used and interpreted by people with abilities who determine what is dysfunction and how to manage that problem. It retains the difficulty of thinking about ability rather than disability and how to assist in functioning instead of helping people with disabilities to deal with their lives on their own terms. It seems to be about people as active and functioning rather than as human beings in their own right.

A life like any other?

Despite attempts to level out the differences between people with disabilities and people who are able-bodied discriminatory attitudes seem to be entrenched. Such attitudes and behaviours have been set out clearly in the House of Lords Joint Committee on Human Rights Seventh Report of Session 2007-08 *A Life Like Any Other? Human Rights of Adults with Learning Disabilities*. The overwhelming evidence presented to the joint committee is encapsulated in a statement from the Director of People First (Self Advocacy), Andrew Lee. According to Lee

> at the root of the barriers we face is an idea that we are less good and less worthwhile than other people. Doctors try to stop us from being born in the first place when we are born our parents are given negative views about our chances in life. They are encouraged to mourn the fact that they have abnormal children, and their disappointment stays with us throughout our lives the extent to which society looks down on us contributes to the fact that throughout our lives people with learning difficulties do not get their human rights, and yet there is no public outcry, no-one up in arms about how little choice or control we have over our everyday lives.

The Report highlights a general 'culture of disrespect and ultimately abuse' where the intellectually disabled regularly have their rights infringed in all daily aspects from healthcare to liberty and freedom of choice and where professionals express the pervasive belief that such people are of less worth.[110] The Report further recognises the history behind dehumanising disabled people so that it remains possible for some to think it is acceptable to treat the disabled in a discriminatory way including the practice of social exclusion and the ignoring of anti-social or criminal behaviour directed against disabled people. More significantly the Report states that this goes beyond a general cultural perception into areas where the disabled are not given equal medical treatment, they are not fed properly and DNR (Do Not Resuscitate) notices are regularly placed on hospital notes.

A Report that influenced the House of Lords was compiled in 2007 by MENCAP and its title, *Death by Indifference* reinforces the overall findings of the House of Lords. MENCAP's report came as a result of its earlier publication in 2004 *Treat me right!* That publication suggested that there are a disproportionately high number of early deaths among people with disabilities who are recognised as already vulnerable. It found that healthcare workers have low expectations for certain patients. Moreover staff are generally unresponsive to the needs of these patients. Furthermore healthcare workers expect parents or care home staff to provide basic care in hospitals that they would usually provide to 'normal' patients. As far as *Treat me right* is concerned discrimination involves value judgments by healthcare staff about the worth of a disabled patient's life such that for instance heart surgery was refused for a disabled patient but would have been offered to a 'normal' child, and staff place DNR notices on medical notes since they believed it to be in the best interests of the patient and carers for the patient to die. This already damning publication was given more cause by the responses it provoked including the revelation that six people had died in NHS care through poor practice. MENCAP's follow up publication, *Death by Indifference* highlights the 'widespread ignorance and indifference' that exists throughout healthcare services and the lack of response at governmental levels. It uncovers a 'shocking level of ignorance' and 'institutional discrimination' among healthcare professionals who seem ignorant about how to feed some patients so do not bother, and about pain thresholds so proper pain relief is denied those who cannot complain. It identifies a general viewpoint among healthcare professionals that it is not worth treating certain patients when in cases of 'normal' patients they would not hesitate to treat or that it is better for everyone to allow certain patients who would otherwise be saved to die.

More evidence of indifference and inferior care has been brought to public attention by the National Confidential Enquiry into Patient Outcome and Death, *An Old Age Problem* published in November 2010 and the Patients Association publication *Listen to patients, speak up for change* produced in December 2010. Both of these documents highlight systemic failures in the care of the vulnerable elderly, care on the basic level of good nutrition and adequate pain management. Despite the publication of these reports and the initial outcry they produce evidence of the failure to care whether in institutions or in a person's own home, of serious neglect, of depersonalising attitudes, continue to mount.[111] Arguably it is the fear of being treated as less than a person rather than the fear of inadequate pain relief or crippling illness that fuels the call for assisted suicide and assisted dying.

Unfortunately in 2012 MENCAP found the need to update its 2007 report *Death by Indifference*. MENCAP's new report, *Death by Indifference: 74 deaths and counting* points to a lack of sufficient progress and continued discrimination in the care of the disabled.

Summary: the 'signs of the times'

An exploration of the signs of the times is vital to set into context the thinking of Pope John Paul so that the standpoint he takes can be fully appreciated. It demonstrates that the dignity of some human beings is under serious attack not only by indifference or lack of respect but also by the failure to acknowledge that all human beings are persons. The frequent appeal to the notion that 'we all think' in a particular way about human beings and human persons illustrates the insidious nature of this attack. Even if the separation between human beings and persons, between biological life and biographical life, exists only in academia it seems that there is a widespread implicit assumption that there are certain human beings who do not live lives that are worth living. Even if this does not take the form of explicit discrimination it seems that a culture of indifference to persons with profound disability exists, particularly to those with intellectual disability including the vulnerable and confused elderly. In the healthcare setting this means that these people receive a different and lower level of care from other patients.

It seems that behind some academic bioethical literature and behind the kinds of contemporary thinking that implicitly judges the lives of certain categories of people as not worthwhile lie the assumption that some people do not act out their lives on the world's stage in the same way as 'normal' persons. Perhaps they are passive, non-acting in the sense that they do not formulate desires or hopes for the future or they do not appear to have interests that require protecting or they do not exhibit the kind of independence and perhaps communication skills that some naturally associate with acting persons, or they are too confused to appear to be acting rationally. Some profoundly disabled people do not appear to be capable of making even the simplest choices and choice is often regarded as the most obvious sign of the acting person.

As professor of ethics and as pastor Pope John Paul constantly refutes the notion that there are some human beings who are not persons and he situates his thinking squarely in the Christian tradition. Moreover, and simply put, for Pope John Paul there cannot be a living human being who is a 'non-acting' person. As for the issue of indifference to those who are profoundly disabled, Pope John Paul's pastoral approach addressed to real people who came to meet him at his many gatherings witnesses to the concrete ways in which he deals with some of the most challenging of human situations. In this he shows himself to be at the cutting edge of much work that has been done to see the profoundly disabled human being as a person in his or her own right with full human dignity and not simply as the subject for differing models of disability.

Still, whilst some models of disability point out discrimination or injustice and argue for full participation of the disabled into society, Pope John Paul does something more. He demonstrates that the profoundly disabled in particular have a vital part to play in God's plan of salvation for humanity.

The Acting Person, Karol Wojtyła's seminal work as a professor of ethics, is an exploration of human beings and their capacity to make and shape their lives through their action. It is a significant contribution to the study of ethics and anthropology. However, in the light of the separation some make between apparently acting human beings, the 'person' as one who has a biographical life, and apparently 'non-acting' human beings, the human being with 'merely' biological life, and the general indifference to injustices perpetrated against those whose lives are judged to be of lesser value because they cannot take part on the world stage there seems to be a case for explaining precisely what Pope John Paul means by the 'acting person'. This is not merely an academic exercise. The 'signs of the times' clearly indicate the gravity of the situation and the high stakes involved. They demand an outspoken and decisive stand. Pope John Paul makes such a stand and it has its foundation in rigorous theological and philosophical thinking.

Notes

1. K. Wojtyła, 'The Person: Subject and Community' (1976) in *Catholic Thought from Lublin Vol.IV Person and Community* (New York: Peter Lang, 1993), p. 220.

2. B. Maier, W.A. Shibles, *The Philosophy and Practice of Medicine and Bioethics: A Naturalistic-Humanistic Approach* (London: Springer, 2011), pp. 113–117.

3. House of Commons Science and Technology Committee (19 January 2005), Ev. 177. <http://www.publications.parliament.uk/pa/cm200405/cmselect/cmsctech/7/7ii.pdf > [accessed 3 April 2010].

4. Pope John Paul II, *Fides et Ratio*, 5.

5. *Ibid.*, 46.

6. *Ibid.*, 60.

7. This is his aim behind his book *Sources of Renewal* (London: Fount, (1975) 1980).

8. K. Wojtyła, *Sources of Renewal*, pp. 32–33.

9. Vatican II, *Gaudium et spes*, 21.

10. K. Wojtyła, *Sources of Renewal* p. 33.

11. Vatican II, *Gaudium et spes*, 2.

12. *Ibid.*, 3.

13. Pope John Paul II, *Redemptor Hominis*, 13.

14. As Pope Benedict XVI points out, *Homily on the Beatification of Pope John Paul II* (1 May 2011).

15. D. Jones, 'The end of bioethics' in *The Pastoral Review* 6/1 (2010), pp. 51–55 at p. 52.

16. Pope John Paul II, *Redemptor Hominis,* 10.

17. Vatican II, *Gaudium et spes,* 24.

18. Pope John Paul II, *Redemptor Hominis,* 8.

19. Pope John Paul II, *Evangelium vitae,* 1.

20. *Ibid.,* 4.

21. *Ibid.,* 11–12.

22. A. Verhey, *Reading the Bible in the Strange World of Medicine* (Grand Rapids: Eerdmans, 2004), p. 72.

23. J. Fletcher, *Situation Ethics: the new morality* (London: Westminster John Knox Press, 1997), pp. 40, 42.

24. *Ibid.,* p. 26.

25. J. Fletcher, *Humanhood: essays in biomedical ethics* (Buffalo New York: Prometheus Books, 1979), p. 16.

26. J. Fletcher, *Humanhood: essays in biomedical ethics* pp. 19–20.

27. P. Ramsey, *The Patient as Person* (Yale: Yale University Press, 1970), p. xiii.

28. See G. Meilaender, '*Terra es animata*: On having a Life', in S. Lammers, and A. Verhey (eds.), *On Moral Medicine* (Grand Rapids: Eerdmans, 1998), p. 390.

29. See for instance H.T. Engelhardt, *The Foundation of Bioethics* (Oxford: Oxford University Press, 1986), p. 108; J. Rachels, *The End of Life: Euthanasia and Morality* (Oxford: Oxford Unversity Press, 1986), pp. 5, 25; K. G. Gervais, *Redefining Death* (New Haven: Yale University Press, 1986); P. Singer, *Rethinking Life and Death* (Oxford: Oxford University Press, 1995), pp. 64ff; N. Biggar, *Aiming to Kill* (Cleveland: The Pilgrim Press, 2004).

30. D. Dennett, 'Conditions of Personhood', in A.O. Rorty (ed.), *The Identities of Persons* (London: University of California Press, 1976), pp. 175–176.

31. S. Toulmin, 'How medicine saved the life of ethics' in *Perspectives in Biological Medicine* 25/4 (1982), pp. 736–750.

32. W. Ruddick, 'Biographical Lives Revisited and Extended' in *Journal of Ethics* 9/3–4 (2005), pp. 501–515 at p. 514.

33. The definition provided by J. Glover in *Causing Death and Saving Lives* (London: Penguin, 1990), p. 41 appears to cover Fletcher's understanding.

34. J. Rachels, *Created from Animals: The Moral Implications of Darwinism* (Oxford: Oxford University Press, 1990), p. 199.

35. *Ibid.,* Chapter 2.

36. *Ibid.,* Chapter 3.

37. *Ibid.,* Chapter 4.

38. *Ibid.,* Chapter 3.

39. J. McMahan, *The Ethics of Killing: Problems at the Margins of Life* (Oxford: Oxford University Press, 2002), p. 439.

40. J. Fletcher, 'Four Indicators of Humanhood—the Enquiry Matures' (1975), in S. Lammers, and A Verhey (eds.), *On Moral Medicine: Theological Perspectives in Medical Ethics* (Grand Rapids: Eerdmans, 1998), pp. 376–380 at p. 377.

41. R. Veatch, 'The dead donor rule: true by definition' in *The American Journal of Bioethics* 3/1 (2003), pp. 10–11.

42. M. Green and D. Wikler, 'Brain death and personal identity' in *Philosophy and Public Affairs* 9/2 (1980), pp. 105–133 at p. 117.

43. M. Green and D. Wikler, 'Brain death and personal identity' in *Philosophy and Public Affairs* at p. 128; see also H.T. Engelhardt, 'Infanticide in a post-Christian age', in R. McMillan, H.T. Engelhardt, and S. Spicker (eds.), *Euthanasia and the Newborn* (Boston: D. Reidel, 1987), p. 83.

44. D. Wikler, 'Not Dead, Not Dying? Ethical Categories and Persistent Vegetative State' in *Hastings Center Report* 18/1 (1988), pp. 41–47.

45. M. Lockwood, 'The moral status of the human embryo: implications for IVF' in *Reproductive BioMedicine Online* 10/1 (2005), pp. 17–20 at p. 18 <http://www.rbmonline.com/Article/1613> [accessed 1 February 2010].

46. J. McMahan, *The Ethics of Killing* p. 451.

47. Apollinarius, 'Apodeixis' in St Gregory of Nyssa, *Antirrheticus: Treatise against Apollinarius*; St Gregory of Nazianzus, *To Cledonius Against Apollinarius, Epistles 101* and *102*.

48. B. Brody, 'On the humanity of the fetus', in M. Goodman (ed.), *What is a person?* (Clifton New Jersey: Humana Press, 1988), pp. 248–249.

49. J. Lizza, 'Persons: natural, functional or ethical kind?' in *American Journal of Economics and Sociology* 66/1 (2007), pp. 195–216.

50. J. McMahan, *The Ethics of Killing* p. 6.

51. N. Biggar, *Aiming to Kill* p. 39.

52. R. Rakestraw, 'The Persistent Vegetative State and the Withdrawal of Nutrition and Hydration' in D. Clark and R. Rakestraw (eds.), *Readings in Christian Ethics Vol.2 Issues and Applications* (Grand Rapids: Baker Publishing, 1996), pp. 126–127.

53. R. Cranford, 'The case of Mr Stevens' in *Issues in Law and Medicine* 7/2 (1991), pp. 199–211 at pp. 205–206 quoting with apparent approval R. Wennberg, *Terminal Choices* (Grand Rapids: Eerdmans, 1989), p. 176.

54. R. Cranford and D. Smith, 'Consciousness: the most critical moral (constitutional) standard for human personhood' in *American Journal of Law and Medicine* 13 (1987), pp. 233–248 at p. 237.

55. J. Harris, 'On the moral status of the embryo', in A Dyson and J. Harris (eds.), *Experiments on Embryos* (London: Routledge, 1991), p. 79.

56. J. Harris, *Enhancing Evolution* (Princeton: Princeton University Press, 2007), p. 96.

57. J. Harris, *The Value of Life: An Introduction to Medical Ethics* (New York: Routledge, 1985), p. 8.

58. J. Harris, 'Euthanasia and the Value of Life', in J Keown (ed.), *Euthanasia Examined* (Cambridge: Cambridge University Press, 1995), pp. 8–9.

59. Lord Goff in *Airedale NHS Trust* v *Bland* [1993] 2WLR p. 366.

60. Lord Brown in *Airedale NHS Trust* v *Bland* [1993] 2WLR p. 833.

61. See for instance comments at <http://www.guardian.co.uk/commentisfree/2010/jun/03/disabled-people-assisted-suicide>.

62. P. Cavalieri and P. Singer, 'The Great Ape Project', in H. Kuhse (ed.), *Unsanctifying Human Life* (Oxford: Blackwell, 2002), pp. 132–136.

63. P. Singer, *Practical Ethics* (Cambridge: Cambridge University Press, 1997), p. 13.

64. P. Singer, *Practical Ethics* p. 57.

65. See also J. Glover *Causing Death and Saving Lives* pp. 50–51; J. Harris 'On the moral status of the embryo' in *Experiments on Embryos* pp. 69–70; P. Singer, *Practical Ethics* p. 156; D. DeGrazia, *Taking Animals Seriously* (Cambridge: Cambridge University Press, 1996), p. 272 and D. DeGrazia, 'Must we have full moral status throughout our existence?' in *Kennedy Institute of Ethics Journal* 17/4 (2007), pp. 297–310 at p. 305.

66. D. DeGrazia, *Taking Animals Seriously* p. 272.

67. P. Singer, *Rethinking Life and Death* Ch.9.

68. *Ibid.*, p. 206.

69. P. Singer, *Practical Ethics* p. 78.

70. *Ibid.*, p. 78.

71. P. Singer, *Writings on an ethical life* (London: Fourth Estate, 2001), pp. 44–45.

72. P. Singer, *Practical Ethics* pp. 51–54.

73. *Ibid.*, pp. 188–189.

74. *Ibid.*, pp. 99–100.

75. *Ibid.*, p. 101.

76. *Ibid.*, pp. 104–105.

77. P. Singer, *Rethinking Life and Death* pp. 52, 207.

78. T. Shakespeare and N. Watson, 'The Social Model of Disability: an Outdated Model?' in *Research in Social Science and Disability* 2 (2002), pp. 9–28 at p. 26.

79. H-J Stiker, *A History of Disability* (USA: University of Michigan Press, 1999), pp. xi–xii.

80. R. Descartes, 'The World' (1629–1633), in R. Ariew (ed.), *Philosophical Essays and Correspondence. The World or Treatise on Man; Passions of the Soul; Discourse on method; Meditations* (Indiana: Hackett, 2000), Ch.18.

81. R. Descartes, 'Passions of the Soul' (1649), in *Philosophical Essays and Correspondence. The World or Treatise on Man; Passions of the Soul; Discourse on method; Meditations* Part 1.6.331.

82. T. Hobbes, 'Philosophical Rudiments Concerning Government and Society' (1650/1651) in *The English Works* Vol.III (W. Molesworth, London, 1839), ppix–xii.

83. R. Descartes, 'To More' (1648/1649), in *The Philosophical Writings of Descartes* Vol.III, translated by J. Cottingham, R. Stoothoff, D. Murdoch, and A. Kenny (Cambridge: Cambridge University Press, 1997), p. 366.

84. J. Branson and D. Miller, *Damned for their Difference* (Washington: Gallaudet University Press, 2002), pp. 23–25.

85. A. Young, *Theology and Down Syndrome* (Waco: Baylor University Press, 2007), p. 34.

86. J. Locke, *An Essay Concerning Human Understanding* (1689), K. Winkler (ed.) (Cambridge: Hackett Publishing, 1996), III.VI.23.

87. *Ibid.*, IV.IV.16.

88. *Ibid.*, III.VI.22.

89. *Ibid.*, IV.IV.16.

90. B. Woll and P. Ladd, 'Deaf Communities', in M. Marschark, and P.E. Spencer (eds.), *Deaf Studies, Language and Education* (Oxford: Oxford University Press, 2003), p. 156.

91. D. Braddock and S. Parish, 'An Institutional History of Disability', in G. Albrecht, K. Seelman, and M. Bury (eds.), *Handbook of Disability Studies* (London: Sage Publications, 2001), p. 39.

92. *Ibid.*, p. 42.

93. B. Woll and P. Ladd, 'Deaf Communities' in *Deaf Studies, Language and Education* p. 156.

94. A. Jonsen, *The Birth of Bioethics* (Oxford: Oxford University Press, 2003), p. 17.

95. M. Saxton, 'Disability Rights and Selective Abortion', in L. Davis (ed.), *The Disability Studies Reader* (New York: Routledge, 2006), p. 107.

96. WHO, Document A29/INFDOCI/1, Geneva, Switzerland.

97. See N. Messer, 'Human Genome Project, Health and the Tyranny of Normality', in C. Deane-Drummond (ed.), *Brave New World?* (London: Continuum, 2003), pp. 97–98.

98. T. Shakespeare and N. Watson, 'The Social Model of Disability: an Outdated Model?' in *Research in Social Science and Disability* at p. 24.

99. *Ibid.*, at p. 27.

100. *Ibid.*,, at p. 24.

101. *Ibid.*, at p. 26.

102. *Ibid.*, at p. 24.

103. See O. Garin et al 'Validation of the "World Health organization Disability Assessment Schedule, WHODAS–2" in patients with chronic diseases' in *Health and Quality of Life Outcomes* 8/51 (2010) <http://www.hqlo.com/contents/8/1/51> [accessed 7 September 2011].

104. International Classification of Functioning, Disability and Health (ICF), *Towards a Common Language for Functioning, Disability and Health 2002.* <http://www.who.int/classifications/icf/training/icfbeginnersguide.pdf> [accessed 3 September 2011] p. 3.

105. ICF, *Towards a Common Language for Functioning, Disability and Health* 2002, pp. 8–9.

106. *Ibid.*, pp. 9–10.

107. *Ibid.*, pp. 5–7.

108. *Ibid.*, p. 10.

109. *Ibid.*,., p. 13.

110. Oral evidence from Jo Williams Chief Executive of MENCAP in House of Lords Joint Committee on Human Rights Seventh Report of Session 2007–08 *A Life Like Any Other? Human Rights of Adults with Learning Disabilities.* <http://www.bild.org.uk/humanrights/docs/A life like any other vol 2 pdf> [accessed 2 August 2011].

111. See <http://www.bbc.co.uk/news/health-13813460>.

2

A HUMAN BEING AND A PERSON BY

NATURE: THE ACTING PERSON

As Pope, John Paul is noted for his juxtaposition of the culture of life and the culture of death. However, in his earlier academic career he focuses on a different juxtaposition: that between the philosophy of being and the philosophy of consciousness. Both the acting and the apparently 'non-acting' person can be situated in this context. Whereas for some modern thinkers some human beings are deemed 'non-acting' because they do not act in purposeful ways, in Karol Wojtyła's philosophy of being there is no such thing as a non-acting person. According to Karol Wojtyła, all living human beings are acting persons. However, in some philosophies of consciousness there are also no non-acting persons but for a different reason: such apparently non-acting subjects are indeed non-acting since they do not demonstrate the kinds of thought processes that qualify them to act as persons. But, according to these philosophies they are not non-acting *persons*: they are not persons they are merely non-acting human beings.

Although in *The Acting Person* Karol Wojtyła associates philosophies of consciousness with phenomenology, philosophies of consciousness seem to encompass much of the analytic philosophy that characterises contemporary bioethical thinking. With its focus on mental states, consciousness and conscious human experiences philosophies of consciousness seem to represent the person as something insubstantial. In the frequently made separation of biological from biographical life such philosophies do not take account of the concrete reality of the human being who is at the same time a spiritual and corporeal being. And in their concentration on rationality they cannot cater for vulnerable and fragile embodied human beings.

Similarly the concrete reality of the human person seems to be disregarded by those who regard the profoundly disabled with indifference or who implicitly judge them as living lives that are not worth living since their lives are not characterised by what many would term a 'normal' mental life. Those who see disability in terms solely of social barriers and attitudes may not necessarily embrace a philosophy of consciousness. However they also seem to forget this particular disabled person with his or her particular impairment since impairment is not seen as part of daily experience but rather it is completely bracketed out.[1]

Instead Pope John Paul offers a renewed metaphysics and philosophy of being that is built upon lived experience and that includes the real experience of what some may see as the 'non-acting' person, the human being who exists in radical dependence. His own lived experience perhaps offers a starting point for his interest in ethics.

Karol Wojtyła: the professor interested in acts

Undoubtedly the extreme heroism and the extreme evil demonstrated during the Second World War had great influence on the young Karol Wojtyła who was still a student at the outbreak of the conflict that changed Europe. Pope John Paul himself says that his priestly and pastoral vocation took 'definitive shape' during the war.[2] The objective reality of war, showing what people are capable of and what they suffer placed the focus sharply on the acts of human beings. Hence perhaps Karol Wojtyła's interest in the acting person that seems perhaps inevitably to have taken root in his formative years and the key role that philosophy of the human being occupies in his thinking. A collection of Karol Wojtyła's essays and lectures charting this thinking from the early 1950s to his election to the papacy in 1978 was published in 1993 as *Person and Community*. Notably most of these early works were written before the rise of bioethics and its emergence as the battleground for the human person.

In his 1959 lecture *Human Nature as the Basis of Ethical Formation* Karol Wojtyła explains that his concern for ethics took shape in the light of reflection on two questions: firstly, what makes the human being and human actions good and what makes them bad? Secondly, what gives the human being complete goodness, that is happiness?[3] From his pastoral experience as a priest Karol Wojtyła recognises what had been documented at least as far back by Aristotle and explored by St Thomas Aquinas that in order to act well people need to acquire skills and virtues. This holds true for the disabled as well as for the able. As Pope, John Paul says 'for disabled people, as for any other human being, it is not important that they do what others do but that they do what is truly good for them, increasingly making the most of their talents and responding faithfully to their own human and supernatural vocation'.[4]

Certainly Pope John Paul sees that co-operation with grace is at the heart of this vocation. However he also notes that in suffering and impairment 'there is concealed a particular power that draws a person interiorly close to Christ'.[5] Moreover he sees that suffering 'clears the way for the grace which transforms human souls'.[6] Pope John Paul's thinking is far from the modern view that sees the profoundly disabled human being as less than a person or indeed not even a person. For Pope John Paul even when a person is 'almost incapable of living and acting' his or her 'spiritual greatness' becomes evident. Whereas this modern view dismisses the profoundly disabled Pope John Paul points out that the disabled offer a 'touching lesson to those who are healthy and normal' and the foundation for this spirituality is that 'Christ acts at the heart of human suffering'.[7]

So for Pope John Paul the idea of growing in virtue is deeply rooted in the Christian tradition and for the Christian growth in virtue is inextricably linked to theology and grace. To a certain extent it is found in the distinction made by the Patristic Fathers in the Genesis account of the creation of human beings, created in God's image and likeness.[8] According to many of the early Fathers human beings are made in the image of God and grow into the divine likeness through virtue or away from it through sin: being is followed by action. Moreover the Fathers are also adamant that even if it is obscured the image of God in human beings can never be lost.[9] Unlike its pagan counterparts the Christian perspective as presented by the Church Fathers rejects the notion that perfection can be attained only by the elite through some form of rarefied knowledge as apparently claimed by the Gnostics[10] and it refutes the idea put forward by the Platonists and Stoics that perfection can be reached through a human being's own powers of philosophy.[11] As St Clement of Alexandria explains, the grace of baptism and a life in Christ brings illumination and salvation[12] and a life of virtue can only be achieved through grace and by following Jesus as model and teacher.[13]

This strong link between image and likeness found in the writings of the early Church Fathers seems to have faded out during the Christological debates, possibly because a stress on likeness to Christ might have implied that Christ himself in his turn is only 'like' God in the sense of similarity (*homoiousios*) rather than of one being (*homoousios*). Nevertheless, it seems that in much the same way as for the early Church Fathers, for Karol Wojtyła there is an intimate connection between action, exercise of the virtues and the person: human beings shape themselves, for a human being is formed through his or her morally good acts and deformed through his or her evil ones.[14] The experience of war perhaps reinforced the notion that if a person acts with justice it is easier to act again with justice and, conversely, acting with injustice allows a person more easily to do injustice. So, according to Karol Wojtyła 'activity most fully reveals the human being as a person'.[15] However this also implies that human 'being' has priority in relation to activity.[16] Moreover when it comes to the apparently 'non-acting' person just as in the distinction of image and likeness action follows being Karol Wojtyła gives priority to being over activity even though as professor of ethics his interest lies in human activity.

The danger of modern culture, as Karol Wojtyła sees it, is that human beings cease to have priority for who they are and they become valuable for what they have or what they can achieve or for their usefulness. Activity and having takes precedence over being and, as in the utilitarian framework, the value of an act is judged solely on the basis of its effects in the world and not on how it shapes the very being of the actor.[17] In his 1977 paper *The Problem of the Constitution of Culture Through Human Praxis* Karol Wojtyła places this move away from the priority of the human being to his or her activity in the clash with atheism which rejects the relation of human beings to God and the clash with systems that propose a 'collective form of existence'.[18]

Karol Wojtyła identifies two approaches in order to come to some understanding of the human person, human activity and of the priority of being.[19] The first focuses on the individual functions and structure of the human being in a 'purely phenomenal way' meaning that it rests on description rather than explanation. Although this may be a useful approach, Karol Wojtyła considers it is limited and cannot explain the subjectivity of the human being in a complete way. The second approach then looks at the 'whole experience of the human being' which reveals him or her as someone who exists and acts. And it is here that Karol Wojtyła brings in what for him is a significant Latin tag enabling him to identify the relation between existence and activity: *operari sequitur esse,* action follows being.

Operari sequitur esse

As a teacher at the Jagiellonian University and the Catholic University in Lublin Karol Wojtyła had the opportunity to develop his interests in anthropology, metaphysics, ethics and philosophy. He adopts as his main theme the classical saying *operari sequitur esse.* As Karol Wojtyła puts it the activity of a being is 'an extension', 'a continuation' of its existence.[20] This is perhaps in contrast to some Enlightenment thinking that seems to pursue *esse sequitur operari,* the kind of thinking that sees the being of a thing mechanistically as nothing else than all of its activities and functions. Instead Karol Wojtyła is interested in the acting person because a person's acts express who he or she is. Activity externalises a being's essence or nature. For Karol Wojtyła 'nature' is 'a thing's essence, understood as the basis of the thing's activity'.[21] Of note here is the idea that what is internal, the being of the person, is externalised, made manifest.

Karol Wojtyła understands *operari sequitur esse* as the act of personal existence that has its direct consequence in the activity of the person: action is the basis for disclosing and understanding the person.[22] Moreover, he is clear that *operari* include the whole human dynamism, what merely happens in the human being as well as everything the human being does.[23] The importance then of action for Karol Wojtyła is that it has 'the most basic and essential significance for grasping the subjectivity of the human being'.[24] Its foundation lies in the concrete experience the person has of being a subject of experiences. This is why he is so interested in ethics and the acting person. Nevertheless, Karol Wojtyła is equally clear that 'from the very beginning the human being is someone who exists and acts, although fully human activity [*actus humanus*] or action, appears only at a certain stage of human development'.[25] A full quote situates the apparently non-acting person firmly within Karol Wojtyła's thinking on the acting person:

> the human being is a person 'by nature'. The subjectivity proper to a person also belongs to the human being 'by nature'. The fact that the human *suppositum,* ['the whole experience of the human being'[26]] or metaphysical subjectivity, does not display traits of personal subjectivity in certain cases (that is in cases of psychosomatic or purely psychological immaturity in which either the normal human self has not developed or the self has developed in a distorted way) does not allow us to question the very foundations of this subjectivity, for they reside within the essentially human *suppositum.*[27]

Certainly for Karol Wojtyła 'consciousness and especially self-consciousness is an indispensable condition for the constitution of the human self' and he underlines its significance in his insistence that we are 'authors' of our own lives through the exercise of our freedom, will and responsibility.[28] However, Karol Wojtyła takes issue with those who reduce the person to a subject of consciousness by seeing consciousness as an independent subject. Karol Wojtyła makes it plain that consciousness always reflects the existence and activity of the self: 'human beings exist "in themselves"'.[29]

To clarify this focus on activity and nature Karol Wojtyła explains that even if some human activity has 'a certain similarity' to the activity of non-human animals saying 'an animal acts' means something different to saying 'a human being acts' because 'a different nature lies at the basis of the one activity and the other'.[30] He further describes human activity that is similar to but not the same as non-human animal activity as *actus hominis* to distinguish this from *actus humani,* human actions that are the concern of ethics. As professor of ethics Karol Wojtyła says he is interested principally in human actions, *actus humani,* and only perhaps indirectly in *actus hominis.*[31] The distinction between *actus humani* and *actus hominis* is classic in the field of ethics and Karol Wojtyła clearly follows in the Thomistic tradition. At first sight it may seem that a distinction between *actus hominis* and *actus humani* bears a significant similarity to the distinction made by some bioethicists between human being and person. In fact this is not the case: in the bioethical distinction the human being may never have been a person or may gain or lose personhood; there is a definite separation between the two ideas. In the distinction between *actus hominis* and *actus humani* both are the acts of the human person; the being of the human person remains intact in its priority over activity.

Actus hominis and actus humani

Certainly Pope John Paul notes the usefulness of the descriptive and experiential methodology of phenomenology, indeed his book *Person and Act* explores whether phenomenology can be assimilated into Christian thinking. However ultimately he rejects phenomenology as inadequate. Instead he relies on the thinking of St Thomas Aquinas who was writing some seven centuries before and he frequently attests to the influence of St Thomas in his own work though it is also enriched by elements of modern thinking.[32] For an appreciation of Karol Wojtyła's use of *actus hominis* and *actus humani* it is necessary to return to St Thomas, arguably the most important Catholic theologian.

In his *Summa Theologica,* a summary of sacred doctrine, St Thomas treats of God and all that is in relation to God. St Thomas's reflection on human beings and their relationship with God involves in part an exploration of moral philosophy, though for St Thomas there is no formal separation of theology and philosophy. This is why St Thomas can refer to Aristotle or 'the Philosopher', St Augustine, Boethius and Scripture in the same breath. However since St Thomas's discussion of the human being takes place in the context of our way to God it seems that for St Thomas the human person is most fully understood by reference to God. In considering human action and the moral order St Thomas modifies 'the philosopher' Aristotle to make a clear distinction in the acts of the one human person: between *actus humani*, a human act, and *actus hominis*, an act of a human being. In an *actus humani* the act (or failure to act) proceeds from the person's free will in the light of the end of the act itself so such an act has a moral dimension and carries with it responsibility for that action.[33] Here the distinctively human capacities of will and intellect make up a complete act when these capacities are exercised or deliberately not exercised. So, according to St Thomas, if a ship sinks because the helmsman stops steering when he could and should have steered then the helmsman can be held responsible for his human action or in this case deliberate inaction. In contrast an *actus hominis* is any action performed by a human being and this includes involuntary action like coughing or breathing, reactions to pain and emotions. Merely being present on the deck of the ship is an *actus hominis* of the helmsman. If, then, the helmsman decided to fail to steer out of premeditated controlled revenge that act of revenge would be an *actus humani*. If he experienced a sudden burst of uncontrolled anger that act might be an *actus hominis*. What then distinguishes an *actus humani* from an *actus hominis* is the contribution of reason and will. But both *actus humani* and *actus hominis* are acts of the human person.

This explains why for Karol Wojtyła there is in fact no such thing as a living but 'non-acting person': both the activity that is the subject of ethics, the kind of activity whereby I am the efficient cause of my actions, and the activity that happens within me are human acts. They are human acts because they are acts belonging to a human being, a being with a rational human nature destined for friendship with God. Again concentrating on the person acting in the ethical sphere, Karol Wojtyła explains 'to say that the human being is a rational being is also to say that the human being is a person. The human being is a person by nature'.[34] As the title of this section of *Person and Community* indicates human nature is the basis of ethical formation.

Of course as a professor of ethics Karol Wojtyła is interested in the idea that reason as the ability both to form judgments and to come to know the truth is the basis of morality[35] and so much of his work is on reason, freedom and the will in relation to the true and the good. However, since some thinkers challenge the notion of 'person' when applied to human beings who do not actually seem to use reason, freedom or will it is worthwhile looking at what Karol Wojtyła means by the person. Although as a theologian Karol Wojtyła recognises that the foundation of the person lies in the Genesis account of human beings made in the image and likeness of God, in his early philosophical writings he locates its philosophical starting point in the thought of the sixth century Roman writer Boethius.

Boethius is perhaps best known for his book *Consolation of Philosophy* a reflection on the purpose of life. However, realising that a working knowledge of Greek was in decline among his contemporaries Boethius also set about translating the works of Plato and Aristotle into Latin. Boethius's execution by the Arian ruler Theoderic meant that much of Aristotle's work and all of Plato's remained untranslated until the twelfth and thirteenth centuries when Greek texts became available to the West from Constantinople. Nevertheless St Thomas refers extensively to Boethius from the *Consolation of Philosophy* to Boethius's work on the Trinity and on goodness and so it could be said that Boethius stands as an intermediary between the ancient world and the world of the Middle Ages. Moreover St Thomas begins his discussion on the Divine Persons with the archetypal definition provided by Boethius 'a person is an individual substance of a rational nature' and Karol Wojtyła takes up the first objection put by St Thomas: 'it would seem that the definition of person given by Boethius is insufficient'.[36] Karol Wojtyła begins this exploration by analysing some modern conceptions of 'person' and 'nature'.

Karol Wojtyła on person, nature and Boethius

In his 1970 paper *The Human Person and Natural Law* Karol Wojtyła points out that there are various understandings of 'nature' and he draws attention to two of these understandings in particular: one offered by thinkers like the phenomenologists the other offered by those who operate out of the Thomist school. According to Karol Wojtyła those who come from a similar perspective as phenomenologists place 'person' in opposition to 'nature'. Since they focus on mental states and the definitive characteristics of conscious human experiences these thinkers make a distinction between the person and what merely happens in the person by nature. This, he says, means that in the concrete reality of the human being the person is excluded: he or she is not the author of what happens in him or her. A similar move is made by those bioethicists who clearly separate the biographical life of a human being from his or her biological life and who locate personhood in mental states or consciousness. This quasi spiritualism that places the 'real person' in the mind or consciousness perhaps mirrors the materialism of some forms of Darwinism that recognise matter as the only reality and deny the spiritual aspect of the human person. For Karol Wojtyła neither the view that the person is the mind nor the view that the person is a mechanism of atoms fully corresponds to the common human experience that we are at one and the same time corporeal and spiritual beings.

In contrast Thomists such as Karol Wojtyła himself take 'nature' in its 'traditional sense, the metaphysical sense'.[37] According to Karol Wojtyła and in keeping with the tradition human nature is a possibility for a certain kind of life and it does not exist apart from its actualisation in the human person. Everything in that nature such as the body and soul, and the capacity for thinking and willing, is found in this human being. Reason attaches to the person as an entity with a rational nature it is not simply affirmed 'in the intellectual plane'.[38] As Pope, John Paul explains in depth what he had demonstrated as professor of ethics, that those who place 'person' in opposition to 'nature' also risk distorting the significance of freedom and the moral act for the acting person. In his encyclical letter on moral theology *Veritatis Splendor* Pope John Paul underscores the unity of the human person as an ensouled body where the soul is the form of the body. He draws attention to some theories of human freedom which end up treating the human body as 'raw datum, devoid of any meaning and moral values until freedom has shaped it in accordance with its design'. Under these theories human nature and the body appear to be 'extrinsic to the person'. Pope John Paul explains that this understanding of the human being and the moral theories that accompany it do not correspond to 'the truth about man and his freedom'. Referring to the Ecumenical Council of Vienne, the Fifth Lateran Ecumenical Council and to the Second Vatican Council document *Gaudium et spes* Pope John Paul affirms the 'unity of the human person, whose rational soul is *per se et essentialiter* the form of his body': 'the spiritual and immortal soul is the principle of unity of the human being, whereby it exists as a whole—*corpore et anima unus*—as a person'.[39]

Certainly in his 1974 paper *The Personal Structure of Self-Determination* Karol Wojtyła does make a distinction between the ethical and the ontological aspects of human beings. In the ethical aspect self-determination and freedom reveal the acting person as a person and give a unique insight into that person as a person. This is because acts of the person's will are directed to particular objects or values. In this way the person becomes either good or bad, he or she determines himself or herself as well as directing his or her activity. So 'through self-determination the human being becomes increasingly more of a "someone" in the ethical sense'.[40] However, Karol Wojtyła is equally clear that 'in the ontological sense the human being is a "someone" from the very beginning.'[41] Such a statement is obviously significant when it comes to considering the embryo and the foetus. However it is also crucial for those people who will never exhibit acts of self-determination, the apparently non-acting person. Unlike some modern notions that suggest personhood or being a 'someone' can be gained and lost as certain capacities or abilities emerge and disappear, or indeed notions that claim certain human beings are not persons, for Karol Wojtyła the profoundly disabled person is a 'someone' from the first moment of his or her existence and remains a 'someone' even if his or her potential is never realised.

Given what is at stake it seems worthwhile labouring the point that Karol Wojtyła further clarifies in his 1975 paper *Participation or Alienation?*. As he explains 'action is what most fully and profoundly reveals the human being as an I'.[42] Being has priority over activity since the already existing person is revealed by his or her activity. This revelation of the person takes place through participation. In Karol Wojtyła's understanding participation is a rich concept that goes beyond merely empowerment or inclusion. Participation, he says, involves an awareness of the other human being as 'another I', 'my neighbour'.[43] Karol Wojtyła adds that this awareness is not gained principally through the categorical knowledge that 'we share like humanity' and so presumably it does not rely on the satisfaction of a list of characteristics. This is because the neighbour relationship does not emerge from some kind of universal concept of the human being. Rather, Karol Wojtyła says, the relationship is 'always interhuman, unique and unrepeatable in each and every instance'.[44] Certainly for Karol Wojtyła the universal concept of human being opens up the way for each person to experience the other as another I and, he adds, every human being is included in this concept. Still, participation, that 'call to experience another human being as another I' is a task to be actualised in the case of every human being before us.[45]

The discernment that the person before us is another 'I' is critical for any true interaction with people who have profound disabilities, who do not appear to be acting or reacting in ways commonly associated with human interaction. Those who do not communicate in recognisable ways, those who react unpredictably or indeed not at all, suffer most acutely from the risk of alienation. However, the simple acknowledgment of the humanity of people who are profoundly disabled remains inadequate. It plays into the separation some make either explicitly or implicitly between human beings and human persons. Instead Karol Wojtyła's understanding of participation calls for the recognition that each human being is, like me, unique and unrepeatable: a person, another 'I'. Moreover, it is a matter of being with the other person as subject to subject.

The unrepeatablity of each human being is central for Karol Wojtyła and it is in the context of this uniqueness that he explores the thinking of Boethius and Aristotle. Karol Wojtyła begins with Aristotle's definition of human beings: man as rational animal, *homo est animal rationale*. As he points out this definition fits in with Aristotle's aim to define species, in this case human being, in relation to genus, living being, and the feature that apparently distinguishes the species in that genus, endowed with reason.[46] Karol Wojtyła notes that this definition may be useful. However he thinks that it also implies a reductive view of the human being: it sees the human being as mainly an object among other objects in the world. Yet, he observes, this approach to the human being became the dominant view in metaphysical anthropology up until Descartes[47] hence perhaps Karol Wojtyła's interest in attempting to combine experiential philosophies with metaphysics.

Turning to Boethius, Karol Wojtyła thinks that Boethius's definition falls short since it does not fully reflect the uniqueness of the human person and still centres on objectivity. Moreover, the definition is open to misinterpretation. John Crosby, an American professor of philosophy influenced by Karol Wojtyła's personalism, attempts to cut through possible misinterpretation.[48] He explains that although it seems that Boethius is following Aristotle Boethius speaks of person both in the Trinitarian context where he confirms that Persons do not indicate three individual gods, and in the context of the unique person of Christ. So Boethius's notion of person as an individual implies not so much an individual instance of a human nature but rather a uniquely irreplaceable being: a Cicero or a Plato unlike any other of that name. Moreover Crosby explains that Boethius takes Aristotle's notion of the human being as '*a* rational animal' and develops it further to an individual substance of rational nature precisely so that he can include incommunicability in contrast to Aristotle's individuality. Similarly Karol Wojtyła's concern over common misinterpretation of Boethius's definition leaves him determined to build on Boethius's ideas through 'lived experience' and he urges a recovery of this equally venerable tradition of uniqueness and irreducibility of the human being since 'this belief stands at the basis of understanding the human being as a person'.[49]

From this lived experience Karol Wojtyła develops a 'personalistic understanding' as he attempts to account for the human being 'inwardly'.[50] He suggests that the irreducibility of the human being refers not only to the concrete subject but also to 'everything in the human being that is invisible and wholly internal and whereby each human being, myself included, is an "eyewitness" of his or her own self—of his or her own humanity and person'.[51] In this way Karol Wojtyła wants to explore how each person experiences themselves as a person, a subject, through their own lived experience of self-possession and self-governance. He is adamant that this lived experience can only be 'disclosed' or 'revealed', it is not just some kind of descriptive cataloguing of the contents of an individual's sense perception. True to his calling as a professor of ethics Karol Wojtyła is interested in this lived experience since he believes it is through self-possession and self-governance that a person shapes his or her life and so becomes good or bad. However, what is significant is that Karol Wojtyła understands the person to be disclosed or revealed through his or her acts. This is significant because even where there is no possibility of the actualisation of self-possession and self-governance the underlying structure of the human being is that of a person but it is that of a person who has not been able to disclose or reveal himself or herself.

As is perhaps now clear Karol Wojtyła's focus on the person has its roots in a philosophy of being. This is in contrast to a philosophy of consciousness which claims, he says, to be the first philosophy to discover the human subject.[52] Karol Wojtyła explores this contrast in his 1976 lecture *The Person: Subject and Community*. He thinks that not only does a philosophy of being predate a philosophy of consciousness it also offers an earlier account of the human person as subject; meanwhile a philosophy of consciousness leads inevitably to 'an annihilation of the subject'.[53] This is because a philosophy of consciousness relies on pure subjectivity and it forgets that the person is a concrete self, it is both a subject and object, for in human experience 'the human being is given to us as someone who exists and acts' and all human beings have this in common.[54] The reason why Karol Wojtyła can claim that all living human beings exist *and* act is because he sees in the acting person more than actions of the immaterial subjective self. It is all the things going on in the living subject that contribute to his or her being an acting person. And each of these concrete selves is 'in every instance unique and unrepeatable'.[55] One aspect of this uniqueness is perhaps best described when he explains that each person experiences his or her own self as existing and acting differently from how they experience others, as does every other concrete self,[56] a description of human subjectivity that has been noted by practitioners in intensive interaction therapies as applying significantly to people with profound disabilities. As Pope John Paul later explains in his famous *Theology of the Body* human beings exist in solitude, alone in his or her self 'in the midst of the visible world',[57] surely a poignant guide to the life of the profoundly disabled person even if it is not directed specifically to disability. However, Karol Wojtyła thinks that it is important to stress another aspect of human existence: he points to the biblical account of the creation of human beings to indicate that they also exist in community, *communio*, with others.[58]

I and Thou and We

The experience of the Second World War marked a whole generation of thinkers, not merely the young Karol Wojtyła. For many philosophers the Holocaust was a watershed for philosophical ethics: the Holocaust seemed to prove that the good are not rewarded, the bad are not punished, that duty based ethics can fail. Yet the atrocities perpetrated by the Nazis also gave rise to a new philosophical appreciation. The 'subject who thinks' now recognises not only his or her own thoughts and the 'I' that does the thinking. He or she also is aware of the domination and exploitation of others. Rather than fostering a philosophy of power where the other is seen in terms of what he or she has in common with other beings thus reducing the other to the same, there emerges a philosophy of relationship which accepts the absolute otherness of the other.

Karol Wojtyła demonstrates as a fact of human reality that human beings coexist and cooperate.[59] 'I-Thou relationship' and 'we relationships' are part of human experience. The I-Thou relationship contains within it both the separateness of the human being and his or her connection with the other where that other is seen as another I.[60] Moreover, Karol Wojtyła sees in this relationship a self-affirmation of the 'I' as well as a confirmation of the person of the other.[61] Ideally this is, he says, a relationship where human beings mutually reveal themselves so that an 'authentic subjective community' takes place. This revealing involves trust since it is a giving of oneself and so alongside this giving there is a mutual responsibility for one another.[62]

However, Karol Wojtyła sees the other not simply as 'an other' but as 'neighbour' where neighbour has gospel connotations. He

expresses the 'distinctive character' of 'neighbour' as 'to participate in the humanity of another human being' which means 'to
be vitally related to the other as a particular human being and not
just related to what makes the other a human being'.[63] It is not,
then, a relationship of human being to human being. Rather it is
a mutual relationship of a person to a person.

Karol Wojtyła explains that the interpersonal dimension
of I-Thou becomes the community of 'we' in its social dimension. Although he thinks that this 'we' is best expressed in the
relationships in marriage and its *communio personarum* it is not
restricted to marriage.[64] The 'we' dimension, this *communio personarum*, seems to centre on the 'common good'.[65] However Karol
Wojtyła clearly distinguishes the 'common good' from utilitarian
or totalitarian concepts. Of note perhaps here is that the care
of people with profound disabilities cannot be merely a social
or community enterprise or a way of dealing with problematical
human beings. For Karol Wojtyła the 'common good' is indeed
'superior' to the individual good of each separate 'I' but this is
because the good of each 'I' is 'more fully expressed and more
fully articulated' in the common good.[66] Unlike utilitarian and
totalitarian systems the 'we' does not entail the diminution of
the 'I' and the 'I' is not subordinated to the 'we'. Rather 'we' relationships exist to facilitate and promote the 'I'. Clearly for Karol
Wojtyła the focus of this is not simply the promotion of individual autonomy. Such individuality seems to alienate the person
from the other. Instead the focus is on the person's self-fulfilment
and, following *Gaudium et spes,* Karol Wojtyła says this can only
be achieved through the gift of self. It is both the 'I' of the cared
for and the 'I' of the carer that are the subjects of the 'we' relationship. Moreover both are gifts for each other: the apparently
non-acting person making a gift of his or her humanity and pre-
senting him or her self to the other as a person so enabling the
other to make a gift of self.[67]

Certainly it is a common apprehension that in the situation
of people with profound disabilities it is the carer who gives and
the cared for who receives. However, it is the experience of many
who are carers that what they give is more than matched by what
they themselves receive from the person they care for so that
the relationship becomes truly interpersonal and truly mutual.

Nevertheless, as significant as this undoubtedly is, this mutual relationship is not simply an activity a person shares in common with another person, nor is it completely encapsulated in the idea that each is a gift for the other and indeed their relationship is itself a gift. It is not even reducible to a question of friendship, as profound as such a relationship may be or of recognising a common humanity. After all, relationships of interdependence do not rule out the possibility of domination or exploitation. Since persons are gifts for each other the gospel neighbour relationship becomes a matter of justice and *agape*. It also becomes a matter of solidarity. As a virtue and so grace from God solidarity, the 'firm and persevering determination' that 'we are all really responsible for all',[68] calls each to bear the burdens of others, to recognise and address sinful structures and barriers, to be alive to the possibilities of personal conversion. Above all it requires us to discern anew the other not as a subject with rights but as an image of God, part of a greater mystery, destined for friendship with God, unique and irreplaceable.

Karol Wojtyła adds that alongside this renewed discernment we need to recover the experience of 'wonder and awe' at reality and rediscover a sense of the world and its relation to truth, goodness and beauty.[69] In this way we can move beyond seeing value merely in the useful and beyond a culture that focuses on consumption, both of which are, he says, bound up with what is being used up and destined to die,[70] with what he later calls the culture of death. A renewed focus on what cannot be used up, on truth, goodness and beauty, on fostering human dignity, community and freedom is, for Karol Wojtyła, making present the Kingdom of God on earth[71] and is an opening to a culture of life.

Karol Wojtyła's request to rediscover wonder and awe goes beyond simply being more observant or attentive to the world around us. Notably, people with the profoundest disabilities, particularly those who appear to live radically in the present, often seem more open to the simple beauty of the world around them. Theirs is an activity of contemplation rather than objective analysis. Arguably this is where people with profound disabilities become valuable teachers since they do not necessarily view the world in terms of scientific observation. Rather they demonstrate that it is more a matter of being opened up to the spiritual. Certainly the Church is keen to foster knowledge about the world. As Pope John Paul explains, new scientific knowledge raises new questions and the better the Church's knowledge the more the Church can understand the impact of these new questions.[72] However, he also notes that some scientific theories particularly those that think the spiritual aspect of human beings merely emerges from living matter or is simply a by-product of matter do stand in opposition to the truth about human beings.[73] It is, he argues, a matter of epistemology[74] and here perhaps he is challenging the positivist view that it is only science that can provide valid knowledge or indeed the possession of a level of actual rationality that makes a person. As Pope John Paul says the science of observation describes and measures but the moment of the transition to the spiritual cannot be an object of this kind of scientific observation. Rather it is a matter for philosophical analysis and reflection where theology brings out its ultimate meaning.[75]

Certainly Scripture and theology underpin Pope John Paul's anthropology. Nevertheless as professor of ethics Karol Wojtyła makes much use of philosophy especially in his dialogue with philosophies of consciousness. Arguably this focus on philosophy reflects his teaching remit and his audience rather than a reliance solely on philosophy for his anthropology. Furthermore, it appears that his presentation of the Christian view from a philosophical perspective may have been a necessary approach in the light of Communist government censorship existing in Poland after World War II and government refusal to allow a religious approach in academic institutions.[76] Still, even as professor of ethics Karol Wojtyła does not accept any real break between philosophy and theology, indeed, quoting the Second Vatican Council decree on the training of priests he recalls the injunction from the Conciliar Fathers for a 'more effective coordination of philosophy and theology so that they supplement one another'.[77] Moreover he suggests that theology, philosophy and other sciences advance knowledge in the Church and are permeated and 'given form' by Scripture.[78] As Pope and speaking to the faithful John Paul's anthropological focus is on scripture aided by theology, philosophy and science.

Summary

Karol Wojtyła follows in the patristic tradition of seeing all human beings as persons on account of their underlying structure of a rational nature. This means that every human activity, even somatic activity is the activity of a particular human being who is a person. Thus there is no such entity as a living non-acting human person. There can be no separation between biological and biographical life because it is the one concrete human person that is living and living with his or her own story. In keeping with tradition Karol Wojtyła gives priority to being over activity and he says that the being of a person as unique and unrepeatable awaits discovery. The subjectivity of a human being cannot be brought into question simply because it has not been discerned. Moreover, such discernment takes place through participation and solidarity, recognising the other as another 'I' and not merely as another human being. Such recognition is not one person attributing 'I' to another. Rather it is an acknowledgment of a truth. Failure to recognise the other in this way risks alienation, an experience all too frequently felt by people with profound disabilities. However, the alienation also applies to the other person who stands in opposition to the other and not only misses out on the opportunity of relationship but also loses out on the chance of growing as a person through that relationship.

The priority that Karol Wojtyła gives to being over activity takes concrete expression in the rediscovery of awe and wonder at creation and in particular at the dignity that has been bestowed on humanity. This expression is often found in the gift that people with profound disabilities may have of an openness and simplicity towards the world and other human beings. That receptiveness to a spirituality that is not reliant on knowledge or perhaps clouded by the complexity of day to day living is a reminder that no human individual should be subordinated 'as a pure means or a pure instrument', as merely an object of care, for each has 'a value per se'; each human being 'is a person'[79] with his or her unique perspective on the world. To explore this value more deeply requires the move from philosophy to theology and a consideration of the human being as created in the image of God.

Notes

1. T. Shakespeare and N. Watson, 'The Social Model of Disability: an Outdated Model?' in *Research in Social Science and Disability* 2 (2002), pp. 9–28 at p. 11.

2. Pope John Paul II, *Gift and Mystery* (London: CTS, 1996), p. 34.

3. K. Wojtyła, 'Human Nature as the Basis of Ethical Formation' (1959) in *Catholic Thought from Lublin Vol. IV Person and Community* (New York: Peter Lang, 1993), p. 95.

4. Pope John Paul II, *On the Occasion of the International Symposium on the Dignity and Rights of the Mentally Disabled Person* (5 January 2004), 4.

5. Pope John Paul II, *Salvifici Doloris*, 26.

6. *Ibid.*, 27.

7. *Ibid.*, 26.

8. *Gn* 1:26.

9. See for instance Tertullian *On Baptism*, V; St Augustine *On the Trinity*, XIV, 8.11.

10. St Clement of Alexandria *Instructor*, I, IV.

11. St Clement of Alexandria *Stromata*, II, XII.

12. St Clement of Alexandria *Instructor*, I, VI.

13. St Clement of Alexandria *Exhortation to the heathen*, XI.

14. K. Wojtyła, 'Human Nature as the Basis of Ethical Formation' (1959) in *Catholic Thought from Lublin Vol. IV Person and Community* p. 98.

15. K. Wojtyła, 'The Problem of the Constitution of Culture Through Human Praxis'(1977) in *Catholic Thought from Lublin Vol. IV Person and Community* p. 266.

16. *Ibid.*

17. K. Wojtyła, 'The Problem of Catholic Sexual Ethics' (1965) in *Catholic Thought from Lublin Vol. IV Person and Community* p. 294.

18. K. Wojtyła, 'The Problem of the Constitution of Culture Through Human Praxis' (1977) in *Catholic Thought from Lublin Vol. IV Person and Community* p. 265.

19. K. Wojtyła, 'The Person: Subject and Community' (1976) in *Catholic Thought from Lublin Vol. IV Person and Community* pp.222ff.

20. K. Wojtyła, 'Human Nature as the Basis of Ethical Formation' (1959) in *Catholic Thought from Lublin Vol. IV Person and Community* p.96.

21. *Ibid.*

22. K. Wojtyła, 'The Person: Subject and Community' (1976) in *Catholic Thought from Lublin Vol. IV Person and Community* p. 223.

23. *Ibid.*, p. 224.

24. *Ibid.*

25. *Ibid.*, p. 225.

26. *Ibid.*, p. 223.

27. *Ibid.*, p. 225.

28. *Ibid.*, p. 229.

29. *Ibid.*, p.227.

30. K. Wojtyła, 'Human Nature as the Basis of Ethical Formation' (1959) in *Catholic Thought from Lublin Vol. IV Person and Community* p. 96.

31. *Ibid.*

32. See, for instance, Pope John Paul II, *Crossing the Threshold of Hope* (London: Jonathan Cape, 1994), p.31; *Fides et Ratio,* 83, 105; *Memory and Identity* (London: Weidenfeld & Nicolson, 2005), p.13.

33. St Thomas Aquinas, *Summa Theologiae* (London: Spottiswoode, 1970), I.II.q.1, a 3.

34. K. Wojtyła, 'Human Nature as the Basis of Ethical Formation' (1959) in *Catholic Thought from Lublin Vol. IV Person and Community* p. 97.

35. *Ibid.*

36. St Thomas Aquinas, *Summa Theologiae* I.29; K. Wojtyła, 'Human Nature as the Basis of Ethical Formation' (1959) in *Catholic Thought from Lublin Vol. IV Person and Community* p. 97.

37. K. Wojtyła, 'The Human Person and Natural Law' (1970 paper) in *Catholic Thought from Lublin Vol. IV Person and Community* p. 182.

38. *Ibid.*, p. 185.

39. Pope John Paul II, *Veritatis Splendor,* 6.

40. K. Wojtyła, 'The Personal Structure of Self-Determination' (1974 paper) in *Catholic Thought from Lublin Vol. IV Person and Community* pp. 190–192.

41. *Ibid.*, p. 192.

42. K. Wojtyła, 'Participation or Alienation?' (1975 paper) in *Catholic Thought from Lublin Vol. IV Person and Community* p. 198.

43. *Ibid.*, p. 200.

44. *Ibid.*, p. 201.

45. *Ibid.*, p. 203.

46. *Ibid.*, p. 210.

47. *Ibid.*, p. 211.

48. J. Crosby, *The Selfhood of the Human Person* (Washington: Catholic University of America Press, 1996), p. 59.

49. K. Wojtyła, 'Subjectivity and the Irreducible in the Human Being' (1975 paper) in *Catholic Thought from Lublin Vol. IV Person and Community*, p. 211.

50. *Ibid.*, p. 213.

51. *Ibid.*, p. 214.

52. K. Wojtyła, 'The Person: Subject and Community' (1976) in *Catholic Thought from Lublin Vol. IV Person and Community*, pp. 219–220.

53. *Ibid.*, p. 220.

54. *Ibid.*, p. 221.

55. *Ibid.*

56. *Ibid.*

57. Pope John Paul II, *Theology of the Body: Human Love in the Divine Plan* (Boston: Pauline Books, 1997), pp. 36–37.

58. Pope John Paul II, *Theology of the Body*, p. 46.

59. Wojtyła, 'The Person: Subject and Community' (1976), p. 239.

60. *Ibid.*, p. 241.

61. *Ibid.*, p. 243.

62. *Ibid.*, p. 246.

63. *Ibid.*, p. 237.

64. *Ibid.*, p. 247.

65. *Ibid.*, p. 247.

66. *Ibid.*, pp. 250–251.

67. See K. Wojtyła, 'Parenthood as a Community of Persons' (1975) in *Catholic Thought from Lublin Vol. IV Person and Community* p. 333.

68. Pope John Paul II, *Sollicitudo Rei Socialis*, 53.

69. K. Wojtyła, 'The Problem of the Constitution of Culture Through Human Praxis' (1977) in *Catholic Thought from Lublin Vol. IV Person and Community*, p. 270.

70. *Ibid.*, p. 272.

71. *Ibid.*

72. Pope John Paul II, Pontifical Message *To the Pontifical Academy of Sciences: On Evolution* (22 October 1996), 2.

73. *Ibid.*, 5.

74. *Ibid.*, 4.

75. *Ibid.*, 6.

76. See J. Sheets, 'The Spirituality of Pope John Paul II', in J. McDermott (ed.), *The Thought of Pope John Paul II* (Rome: Editrice Pontificia Universita Gregoriana, 1993), p. 104.

77. Vatican II, *Optatam totius*, 14.

78. K. Wojtyła, *Sources of Renewal* (London: Fount, (1975) 1980), p. 257.

79. Pope John Paul II, *To the Pontifical Academy of Sciences: On Evolution*, 5.

3

HUMAN BEINGS: PERSONS MADE IN

THE IMAGE OF GOD

According to Pope John Paul one of the 'key points' in the thinking of the Church Fathers at the Second Vatican Council is that 'the revelation of the mystery of the Father and his love in Jesus Christ reveals man to man, and gives the ultimate answer to the question, "What is man?"'.[1] The answer to this question encompasses not only human identity but also the vocation of every human being. It has at its foundation one of the central tenets in the Christian tradition: that human beings are made in the image of God and that through the Incarnation the solidarity of Christ with humanity sharpens, as it were, that image. Writing in the second century Tertullian, one of the earliest Latin theologians, explains 'in whatever way the clay was pressed out, He was thinking of Christ, the Man who was one day to be: because the Word, too, was to be both clay and flesh'.[2] Pope John Paul develops this reflection and brings it to bear specifically on the mentally disabled: he explains that 'when God turns his gaze on man, the first thing he sees and loves in him is not the deeds he succeeds in doing, but his own image'.[3]

Although he is better known for his use of *Genesis 2* in his *Theology of the Body* Pope John Paul roots his early reflection on human beings in the account of the creation of the first man and woman in *Genesis* 1:26–31. He is not alone in this for like many of the early Church Fathers Pope John Paul sees the Genesis passage referring to human beings created in the 'image and likeness' of God as constituting the 'immutable basis of all Christian anthropology'.[4] Indeed, the *imago Dei* has proved to be a rich source of reflection in the theological tradition even though there are notably few references to it in the Old Testament[5] and its most well-known reference in *Genesis* 1 sets the idea of humans as image of God in a very broad context.

Nevertheless for some modern commentators the image of God in human beings appears to be expressed in terms solely of rational capacity[6] as if it is the actual possession of rationality that sets human beings apart from the rest of creation. If this reflects the thinking of Pope John Paul then it would seem to have serious repercussions for the apparently 'non-acting' person: it might suggest that indeed it is the acting person who is in the image of God leaving the apparently non-acting person, the human being who is not able to exercise rational capacities, lacking that image. However Pope John Paul stands firmly in the early Christian tradition that embraces a rich and profound understanding of the *imago Dei* rather than a reductive version. Moreover the idea that human beings are made in God's image does not remain in the creation tradition. For a fuller anthropological understanding Pope John Paul locates the foundation of the image and also the dignity of every human being in his trilogy of encyclicals on the Trinitarian God: *Redemptor Hominis* 1979, *Dives in Misericordia* 1980 and *Dominum et Vivificantem* 1986.

Created in the image and likeness of God

Many early theologians explain that when God made human beings in his image this meant that he constituted human beings as a particular kind of animal, animals of a rational nature. Whilst this is a starting point, for Pope John Paul this raises the concern that human beings may be seen merely as objects among other objects in the world or even entities simply classified by their possession of rationality.[7] Instead Pope John Paul is interested in looking at the human being 'inwardly' in order to focus on his or her uniqueness and incommunicability.[8]

Certainly some early theologians also explore the 'inner man' though it seems this is not so much in order to stress uniqueness but rather in response to particular concerns and challenges. The second century Greek theologian Origen answers one such challenge raised by Celsus who had produced a polemic against the Christians in 178 AD. According to Origen Celsus had claimed that there are no differences in the souls of any species be they human or ant. In reply Origen argues that irrationality is the mark of non-human creatures whilst reason is 'the common possession of men, and of divine and heavenly beings, and perhaps of the Supreme God himself, on account of which man is said to have been created in the image of God, for the image of the Supreme God is his reason (*logos*)'.[9] Whilst Origen appears to be saying that all human beings have a rational nature it seems to be but a short step to claim that actually to be rational and to exhibit this quality is the mark of the image of God. Hence perhaps the ease with which the notion of image of God can be reduced to the exercise of reasoning capacities.

St Augustine is another theologian who addresses certain concerns and his response has allowed some to think he places the image of God purely in rationality. St Augustine seeks to answer those who claim that God is a body in the context of those who argue that women do not share in the image and likeness of God to the same extent as men. St Augustine says that man (a human being) is made in God's image according to his (her) rational mind, that is, not any part of the mind but where the knowledge of God can exist. Renewal of the mind, a return to likeness to God, takes place at baptism and women are 'fellow-heirs' in this.[10] St Augustine takes pains to point out that it is not a question of seeing women in bodily terms and men in terms of the mind for they share both aspects.[11] Rather he sees the image of God in that aspect of the person that seeks to understand and behold God.[12] That image, he argues, may be obscured or defaced but it always remains.[13]

Some have interpreted St Augustine's perspective as pure intellectualism and even charged him with bequeathing the 'baneful legacy' of rationalism, intellectualism and individualism that is the mark of the modern concept of the person.[14] However, for St Augustine and for early thinkers the fact that God does not have a body does not mean that his image can only reside in the rational mind. In Christian thinking the body and soul are not two parts of the human being bolted together. Rather human beings are embodied souls or ensouled bodies: the rational soul as form of the body constitutes the human being as a human being. The Christian belief in the unity of each human being as neither a soul without a body nor a body without a soul but rather 'a being composed out of the union of soul and body into one form of the beautiful'[15] in addition to belief in the resurrection of the body seem to confirm that the body, the material, shares in the beauty of creation in the image of God. Resurrection of the body moreover gives future likeness with the Son.[16]

Moreover St Augustine says that he will not stay silent on one particular claim. He responds vehemently to the belief expressed by some of his more Platonically minded contemporaries that souls who in a previous life had sinned 'with a special amount of enormity' fell into bodies and so 'are born with faculties akin to brute animals'. St Augustine notes the actual and effective witness of many such profoundly disabled people to God. He believes that they are 'brought into being' to demonstrate God's grace, that grace blows where God chooses, and grace 'does not pass over any kind of capacity'. Indeed such a person may have a 'preference in the award of the grace of Christ over many men of the acutest intellect'.[17]

Certainly Pope John Paul shares St Augustine's conviction that the disabled are profound witnesses to God's grace. He also follows St Augustine in seeing the image of God theologically in terms of the relationship human beings have with God. With reference to Boethius and to St Thomas Aquinas Pope John Paul explains in traditional terms the likeness to God that all human beings bear within themselves from the beginning by the 'fact that - unlike the whole world of other living creatures, including those endowed with senses *(animalia)*—man is also a rational being *(animal rationale)*'.[18] He expands this idea of a rational being to confirm that 'every individual is made in the image of God, insofar as he or she is a rational and free creature capable of knowing God and loving him' and this helps us to understand 'even more fully what constitutes the personal character of the human being'.[19] John Paul as Pope and as professor of ethics interested in the person who acts with freedom and rationality stands firmly in the traditional position. This position recognizes the importance of intellect, will and freedom as an 'outstanding manifestation of the divine image'[20] but where this is taken to be a significant aspect of human nature rather than a required criterion of each and every human being who is said to be created in God's image. Thus Pope John Paul makes clear that 'the whole man, not just his spiritual soul, including his intelligence and free will, but also his body share in the dignity of "the image of God"'.[21] So for Pope John Paul human beings are 'to an equal degree' created in God's image and this image is passed on to their descendants with the injunction to be stewards of creation. All human beings then 'derive their dignity and vocation from the common "beginning"'.[22] In his address to the Pontifical Academies Pope John Paul may speak of the concept of the person as 'the unique and unrepeatable centre of freedom and responsibility whose inalienable dignity must be recognized'.[23] But in the same speech he also calls each human being 'a microcosm of the world and an icon of God'[24] echoing the thought of the fourth century Cappadocian theologian St Gregory of Nyssa.[25] In the footsteps of St Gregory for Pope John Paul true greatness does not refer to the highest biological existence or greatest rationality. Rather it refers to each person's unique and unrepeatable perspective, the person as a new world.

However, for early thinkers this notion of the human being as a microcosm is not individualistic or isolating. Early thinkers also acknowledged from the second account of the creation of human beings in *Genesis* 2:4-25 that human beings exist in relationship: man, Adam, is made complete only by the creation of woman. That the final redactor of the *Book of Genesis* allowed the two accounts of the creation of human beings to stand together even though they are apparently contradictory perhaps indicates that the writers of *Genesis* and later the Patristic Fathers understood human beings to be not simply biological creatures but also theological beings and the truth about human beings does not merely reside in the individual's natural capacities or qualities.

According to Pope John Paul since the likeness to God involves the Triune God, 'a living unity in the communion of the Father, Son and Holy Spirit' and since the *Genesis* account sees human beings not as existing alone but as existing in relation to others, 'being a person in the image and likeness of God also involves existing in a relationship, in relation to the other "I"'. So each human being is 'individually like God, as a rational and free being' and each 'in their common humanity' is called to mirror the 'communion of love that is in God'. [26] Furthermore in his influential series of catechetical lectures that became *The Theology of the Body: Human Love in the Divine Plan*, Pope John Paul adds that 'original man', the generic Adam, becomes the image of God not so much in the moment of solitude, that is when he becomes aware of himself as a person and different from all the other animals, it is not when he is self-aware or actually rational. Rather this image is concretised in the moment of communion, when 'man' is created male and female. The two exist in 'double solitude' since each are unique and unrepeatable persons but also in *communio*, a community and so 'an image of an inscrutable divine communion of persons'.[27]

Nevertheless Pope John Paul is clear that there are difficulties with any analogy between the Creator and creatures and that in particular any suggestion that there is a likeness to the divine communion can only be approximate, 'a certain likeness'. This approximation is implied in the biblical text itself since its imprecision on the content of 'image and likeness' expresses the limitations both of human language and of analogies.[28] This language echoes St Augustine's thinking. For St Augustine the belief that human beings are created in the image of God means that they show vestiges of the Trinity though 'not an adequate image, but a very distant parallel'.[29] St Augustine considers that love holds the key: in loving one's neighbour one loves God since if one loves one knows love and God is love, 'you see the Trinity if you see love'.[30] He then identifies as a trace of the Trinity three things in love: the one that loves the beloved and love.[31] The Holy Spirit is 'gift' of both Father and Son and signifies the unity of love between them. Moreover human beings are called to imitate this action of self gift.[32]

Pope John Paul develops this call to love and to self-discovery through discovery of the other as another 'I' in his exegesis of *Genesis* 2:18-25.[33] For Pope John Paul the meaning of help in this passage is precisely the helping of each to discover their humanity through their 'interpersonal communion', a task that can be accomplished by 'the very fact of their "being human persons"'. Although Pope John Paul uses this *Genesis* text to root his teaching on marriage, 'the first and, in a sense, the fundamental dimension of this call' to interpersonal communion, he says that it is also a call for every human being. For Pope John Paul, 'to be human means to be called to interpersonal communion'.[34]

Human beings and Image of the Image

It would be impossible to consider the thinking of Pope John Paul on the human person without taking into account the two texts from the Second Vatican Council to which he most frequently refers: *Gaudium et spes* 22 and 24. Both these texts hinge on the central theological point that 'it is only in the mystery of the Word made flesh that the mystery of man truly becomes clear'.[35]

Whilst accepting that various meanings have been, are and will be read into the historic events of the Second Vatican Council as a bishop Karol Wojtyła took an active part in its proceedings and so believed that he could offer a particular perspective on this 'exceptional and deeply felt experience'.[36] Firm in the conviction that the Council was Spirit led, Karol Wojtyła was equally firm in the belief that the Council proceedings demanded a response in faith, as 'a debt we have to pay'.[37] This response by the now Cardinal Wojtyła took the shape of a study on the implementation of the Second Vatican Council for the Pastoral Synod of the archdiocese of Kracow. Arguably, a continuation of this implementation of the Council has framed the whole of Pope John Paul's pontificate as can clearly be seen in his approach to the human person that he bases solidly in *Gaudium et spes* and its focus on the dignity of each and every human being. The mystery of the Word made flesh speaks of the paradox of strength in weakness, of total self-giving, as the Word empties Himself and takes on human littleness in order to raise humanity up to God. The apparent littleness and vulnerability of people with the profoundest of disabilities in a particular way images that littleness and weakness assumed by the Word. *Gaudium et spes* 22 seems to encapsulate the principal motif of Pope John Paul's thinking, brought out in his first encyclical *Redemptor Hominis*.

Redemptor Hominis, *the Redeemer of Man and the raising of humanity*

Firmly planted in the earliest Christian tradition Pope John Paul explains in his encyclical that creation is good however it is also subject to futility because of sin that broke the link between it and God. But Christ has reforged that link. Moreover, as the intricately argued Christological disputes of the early centuries come to grasp, in the Incarnation the Second Person of the Trinity assumed human nature he did not absorb it and in this taking he raised our human nature to a dignity beyond compare.[38] Furthermore, this taking of human nature does not entail a relationship with humanity in the abstract but rather it involves real and concrete human beings. As Pope John Paul adds 'in a certain way' Christ has united himself with each human being, 'each one is included in the mystery of the Redemption' and every human being 'has become a sharer from the moment he is conceived'.[39] And for Pope John Paul this holds even where a human being is unaware that he or she has been redeemed and united to Christ[40] so it applies equally to all human beings whether disabled or able.

This reflection on union in Christ holds out two significant aspects: on the one hand all are one in Christ and on the other hand we have a 'deep wonder' at ourselves because through Christ's redeeming act humankind is newly created and rediscovers the greatness, dignity and value that belong to our humanity.[41] Once we have grasped this truth then we cannot remain indifferent to what threatens the true welfare of human beings and we have a responsibility to ensure that progress in the world makes human life 'ever more human'.[42] For this progress to be more worthy of human beings, to be 'truly better' it must lead each human being to becoming 'more mature spiritually, more aware of the dignity of his humanity, more responsible, more open to others, especially the neediest and the weakest, and readier to give and to aid all'.[43]

Following *Gaudium et spes* Pope John Paul calls the Church 'a sign and a safeguard of the transcendence of the human person' since the Church is a witness to the 'surpassing dignity' of every human being.[44] Pope John Paul sees that the Church, as the body of Christ, has been entrusted with the care of each human being in his or her 'unique unrepeatable human reality, which keeps intact the image and likeness of God himself'.[45] Moreover, every human being is an 'unrepeatable reality' because every human being is a person so has 'a history of his life that is his own and, most important, a history of his soul that is his own',[46] or in the words of the Patristic Fathers each human being is a whole new world.[47] Pope John Paul adds, from the first moment of his or her existence a human being 'writes this personal history' through, notably, not only his or her general activity and contracts with others but also through social structures, the family and his or her own bodily needs.[48] In contrast to some secular bioethical thinking that separates biological life from biographical life Pope John Paul thinks that every human being has a biographical life. Moreover, every human being whatever his or her condition has his or her 'supreme calling' and is given by Christ the 'light and the strength' to measure up to it[49]. Pope John Paul demonstrates the source of this surpassing dignity of every human being in his second encyclical *Dives in Misericordia*.

Dives in Misericordia, *God rich in mercy calls human beings for love*

Using the account of the creation of human beings in *Genesis* 1:26 Pope John Paul affirms that love is 'the fundamental and innate vocation of every human being', it has been inscribed into humanity, since God created human beings in his own image and likeness and God himself 'lives a mystery of personal loving communion'.[50] This call to love involves every aspect of the human being, body and soul, and not simply the mind since the human being is 'an incarnate spirit' whose soul 'expresses itself in a body' and whose body is 'informed by an immortal spirit': 'the body is made a sharer in spiritual love'.[51] This of course still raises the issue of the relationship of the apparently 'acting' person and the apparently 'non-acting' person and how they can answer this call to love.

Pope John Paul perhaps recognises this issue when he describes the practice of mercy, 'love's second name'[52] in the spirit of love towards one's neighbour.[53] Mercy for Pope John Paul is a richer concept than some 'common' notions of mercy.[54] Such popular notions of mercy as magnanimity or pity through benevolence often seem to place the object of mercy on a lower plane than the giver of mercy. This may lead to a perception of mercy as a humiliation, a pitying or as an offence against personal dignity. To a certain extent this commonly held view is reflected in some models of disability, notably the tragic or charitable models. In contrast Pope John Paul explains that mercy is based on the common experience of human dignity and goodness: mercy is 'the most perfect incarnation of equality between people' because through it the dignity owed to every human being is recognised and affirmed.[55] Continuing with the link between mercy and love he points out that the practice of mercy as 'a whole lifestyle, an essential and continuous characteristic of the Christian vocation' consists in 'the constant discovery and persevering practice of love as a unifying and also elevating power'. Nevertheless he also notes the psychological and social difficulties involved. His thinking on this bears full quotation:

> In reciprocal relationships between persons merciful love is never a unilateral act or process. Even in the cases in which everything would seem to indicate that only one party is giving and offering, and the other only receiving and taking (for example, in the case of a physician giving treatment, a teacher teaching, parents supporting and bringing up their children, a benefactor helping the needy), in reality the one who gives is always also a beneficiary. In any case, he too can easily find himself in the position of the one who receives, who obtains a benefit, who experiences merciful love; he too can find himself the object of mercy.[56]

It would seem that his examples where apparently one gives and the other receives can be extended to cases where one party seems to act and the other appears to be passive: the case of the 'non acting' person. So, the question remains, what according to Pope John Paul is involved in this reciprocity?

Even as professor of ethics, when his focus is on morality and the acting person Karol Wojtyła is clear that the likeness human beings have to God 'is based not only on having a rational and free nature… but also on being a person, a personal being' and 'by reason of their capacity for community with other persons'.[57] This 'fact of being a person', he says, presupposes reason and freedom, the 'spiritual nature' of the human person.[58] Moreover every human being although 'formed from the dust of the earth' is, says Pope John Paul, 'a manifestation of God in the world' because of the intimate bond that unites each human being to his or her Creator.[59] The significance of each and every human being as an image of God indicates that every person presents him or her self as a gift to others and nowhere is such a gift more complete than where a person entrusts him or her self to another in total dependency on that other person, where a person makes a gift of his or her humanity.[60] And this call to self-gift and to love finds its completion in the call to friendship with God as described in Pope John Paul's encyclical *Dominum et Vivificantem*.

Dominum et Vivificantem, *Lord and giver of the fullness of life*

Pope John Paul points out that the life given to human beings 'cannot be reduced to mere existence in time'.[61] In his encyclical *Dominum et Vivificantem* on the Holy Spirit, Pope John Paul explains that against the 'background' of the image and likeness of God the gift of the Spirit 'ultimately means a call to friendship'.[62] This notion of becoming a 'friend' of God can be found in the *Book of Wisdom* and some early Christian thought.[63] Friendship first and foremost involves the initiative of God whereby 'the transcendent "depths of God" become in some way opened to participation on the part of man'.[64] For Pope John Paul this seems to be chiefly the work of God in the sense that God provides and human beings participate as far as they are able. This understanding can be found in St Gregory of Nyssa's treatise on the premature death of foetuses. St Gregory explains that a life of friendship with God is 'a heritage of humanity' and that God comes into each of us as is appropriate for each and that includes, it seems, the embryo.[65] This 'capacity of having a personal relationship with God', as, Pope John Paul says, '"I" and "you"', is constitutive of human nature and thus held from the very beginning of the human being.[66] This personal relationship is also the 'capacity of having a covenant' which is perhaps in some sense similar to the biblical covenant that God made with the Israelites. Unlike those thinkers who seem to place the focus on the ability of a human being to respond to a covenant as constitutive of the image of God in that person[67] for Pope John Paul this covenant takes place again chiefly through God's work in his 'salvific communication with man'.[68] Destined for unity with God all human beings achieve their full greatness and dignity in the covenant with God.[69]

Certainly Pope John Paul sees that rationality and freedom and the response each human being is called to make to God's initiative do express 'the greatness and dignity of the human subject'. However, at the same time Pope John Paul points out the littleness and need of human beings for 'this personal subject is also always a creature: in his existence and essence he depends on the Creator'.[70] Furthermore, it is through God's own gracious initiative that the whole of humanity has been '*elevated* from the beginning through the eternal choice of God in Jesus' and this applies to 'each and every one without exception'.[71] So Pope John Paul sees that all human beings are destined for this friendship with God. As he notes, 'just as all are included in the creative work of God "in the beginning," so all are eternally included in the divine plan of salvation, which is to be completely revealed, in the "fullness of time," with the final coming of Christ'.[72]

Whilst every human being has 'his own share in the Redemption' Pope John Paul also recognises that at the same time every one is called 'to share in that suffering through which all human suffering has also been redeemed'.[73] As common experience shows, some human beings endure more sufferings than others but, in contrast to those who even deny them personhood, for Pope John Paul those who suffer are especially near to Christ. This is not to glory in suffering in itself. Rather it is because Christ has 'raised human suffering to the level of the Redemption'[74]. Undoubtedly in the human condition there will always be tears but in the *Book of Revelation's* final analysis 'He will wipe away all tears from their eyes; there will be no more death, and no more mourning or sadness or pain':[75] the cross of suffering is always seen in the light of the glory of the resurrection.

Pope John Paul's often repeated reliance on the *Gaudium et spes* text that the human being 'is a person and therefore "the only creature on earth which God willed for its own sake"; and at the same time this unique and unrepeatable creature "cannot fully find himself except through a sincere gift of self"'[76] is also often placed in the context of the first sin that disturbed the relationships between people and 'obscured' but did not destroy the image of likeness of God in people.[77] In his letter to women and in the context of marriage Pope John Paul speaks of the inequality of the relationship between man and woman that has resulted from the Fall where domination takes the place of sincere gift of self. He argues that this inequality not only disadvantages the woman but it also 'diminishes the true dignity of the man'.[78] Perhaps it is in the area of discrimination of the disabled that the disruption of relationships between equal persons can be most acutely felt hence the need for a consideration of discrimination and liberation theologies. However first it seems necessary to explore interpersonal relationships. Pope John Paul's appreciation of this disruption in relationship and the need to overcome it through proper and graced relationships is a theme of his *Theology of the Body*, his catechetical reflection intended for everyone included the disabled and the subject of the next chapter.

Summary

In keeping with early theological tradition Pope John Paul's anthropology is built upon the scriptural revelation that human beings are made in the image of God, redeemed through Christ and destined for a sharing in eternal life in friendship with God. Moreover each human being has a calling to witness and to glorify God as a result of this image. Pope John Paul does not place the dignity of human beings in their own capacities or qualities, including their apparent rational abilities. Rather, for Pope John Paul following in the early Christian tradition it is the elevation of humanity by God to eternal friendship with him that is the grounding for the dignity of each human being: each human being is created to be 'a son in the Son'.[79] If it is a question of being a 'helper', of seeing the other as an other and in so doing gaining a deeper awareness of self as well as affirming and confirming the self of the other then how this can be made relevant for the radically disabled and dependent person becomes a crucial issue. Such an affirmation can be found in Pope John Paul's *Theology of the Body*.

Notes

1. K. Wojtyła, *Sources of Renewal* (London: Fount, (1975) 1980), p. 75.
2. Tertullian, *On the Resurrection of the Flesh*, 6, referenced also in Vatican II, *Gaudium et spes*, 22.
3. Pope John Paul II, 'Mentally Ill Are Also Made in God's Image' in *L'Osservatore Romano* (11 December 1996), 4.
4. Pope John Paul II, *Mulieris Dignitatem*, 6.
5. *Gn* 1:26–27, *Gn* 9:6, *Ps* 8:5–6 (the psalm does not use the term 'image' but it does echo the image and dominion themes of Genesis), *Si* 17:3 *Ws* 2:23, 7:26.
6. See for instance T. Shannon, 'Grounding human dignity' in *Dialog A Journal of Theology* 43(2) (2004), pp. 113–117; R. Rakestraw, 'The Persistent Vegetative State and the Withdrawal of Nutrition and Hydration', in D. Clark and R. Rakestraw (eds.), *Readings in Christian Ethics Vol.2 Issues and Applications* (Grand Rapids: Baker Publishing, 1996), pp. 126–127.
7. K. Wojtyła, 'Subjectivity and the Irreducible in the Human Being' (1975) in *Catholic Thought from Lublin Vol.IV Person and Community* (New York: Peter Lang, 1993), p. 210.
8. K. Wojtyła, 'Subjectivity and the Irreducible in the Human Being' (1975) in *Catholic Thought from Lublin Vol.IV Person and Community* p. 213.
9. Origen, *Against Celsus*, Book IV, 85.
10. St Augustine, *On the Trinity*, XII,7.12.
11. *Ibid.*, XII,13.20.
12. *Ibid.*, XIV,4.6.
13. *Ibid.*, XIV,4.6; XIV,8.11.
14. C. Gunton, *The Promise of Trinitarian Theology* (London: T&T Clark, 1997), pp. 33–43.
15. St Methodius, *From the Discourse on the Resurrection*, Part III,1–4; Tertullian *On the Soul*, IX; St Irenaeus, *Against Heresies*, V,6,1; St Gregory of Nyssa, *On the Making of Man*, XXIX.
16. St Augustine, *On the Trinity*, XIV, 18.24.
17. St Augustine, *On the Merits and Remission of Sins*, I,32.
18. Pope John Paul II, *Mulieris Dignitatem*, 6–7.
19. *Ibid.*, 7.

20. Vatican II, *Gaudium et spes*, 17.

21. Pope John Paul, II, 'Mentally Ill Are Also Made in God's Image' in *L'Osservatore Romano* (11 December 1996), 3.

22. Pope John Paul, *Mulieris Dignitatem*, 6.

23. Pope John Paul II, 'Incarnation Inspires Christian Genius: Address to the joint session of all the Pontifical Academies', in *L'Osservatore Romano* (4 December 1996), 3.

24. Pope John Paul II, Address to the joint session of all the Pontifical Academies, 5.

25. St Gregory of Nyssa, *On the Making of Man*, XVI.

26. Pope John Paul II, *Mulieris Dignitatem*, 7.

27. Pope John Paul II, *Theology of the Body: Human Love in the Divine Plan* (Boston: Pauline Books, London: Fount, 1997), pp. 45–48.

28. Pope John Paul II, *Mulieris Dignitatem*, 7, 8.

29. St Augustine, *City of God* XI, 26; *Sermon*, 2, 17; *On the Trinity*, IX,2.2.

30. St Augustine, *On the Trinity*, VIII, 8.12.

31. *Ibid.*, VIII, 10.14.

32. *Ibid.*, V,11.12; VI, 5.7.

33. Pope John Paul II, *Mulieris Dignitatem*, 7; see also Pope John Paul II, *The Theology of the Body: Human Love in the Divine Plan* pp. 35–37.

34. Pope John Paul II, *Mulieris Dignitatem*, 7.

35. Vatican II, *Gaudium et spes*, 22.

36. K. Wojtyła, *Sources of Renewal*, p. 9.

37. *Ibid.*, p. 10.

38. Pope John Paul II, *Redemptor Hominis*, 8.

39. *Ibid.*, 8, 13.

40. *Ibid.*, 14.

41. *Ibid.*, 10.

42. *Ibid.*, 13.

43. *Ibid.*,15.

44. *Ibid.*, 13.

45. *Ibid.*

46. *Ibid.*, 14.

47. St Gregory of Nyssa, *On the Making of Man*, XVI.

48. Pope John Paul II, *Redemptor Hominis*, 14.

49. Ibid., 14.

50. Pope John Paul II, *Familiaris Consortio*, 11.

51. *Ibid.*

52. Pope John Paul II, *Dives in Misericordia*, 7.

53. *Ibid.*, 14.

54. *Ibid.*, 6, 14.

55. *Ibid.*

56. Pope John Paul II, *Dives in Misericordia*, 14.

57. K. Wojtyła, 'The Teaching of the Encyclical Humanae Vitae on Love' (1968) in *Catholic Thought from Lublin Vol.IV Person and Community* (New York: Peter Lang, 1993), pp. 317–318.

58. *Ibid.*, p. 318.

59. Pope John Paul II, *Evangelium vitae*, 34.

60. K. Wojtyła, 'Parenthood as a Community of Persons' (1975) in *Catholic Thought from Lublin Vol.IV Person and Community* p. 333.

61. Pope John Paul II, *Evangelium vitae*, 37.

62. Pope John Paul II, *Dominum et Vivificantem*, 34.

63. *Ws* 7:27; see for instance St Gregory of Nyssa, *On infants' early deaths*, a treatise dealing with the death of foetuses.

64. Pope John Paul II, *Dominum et Vivificantem*, 34.

65. St Gregory of Nyssa, *On infants' early deaths*.

66. Pope John Paul II, *Dominum et Vivificantem*, 34.

67. See R. Cranford, 'The case of Mr Stevens' in *Issues in Law and Medicine* 7/2 (1991), pp. 199–211; N. Biggar, *Aiming to Kill* (Cleveland: The Pilgrim Press, 2004), p. 47.

68. Pope John Paul II, *Dominum et Vivificantem*, 34.

69. Pope John Paul II, *Mulieris Dignitatem*, 9.

70. Pope John Paul II, *Dominum et Vivificantem*, 36.

71. Pope John Paul II, *Mulieris Dignitatem*, 9: his italics.

72. Pope John Paul II, *Redemptoris Mater*, 7.

73. Pope John Paul II, *Salvifici Doloris*, 19.

74. *Ibid.*

75. *Rev* 21:4.

76. Pope John Paul II, *Mulieris Dignitatem*, 10.

77. *Ibid.*, 9.

78. *Ibid.*, 10.

79. Pope John Paul II, *On the Occasion of the International Symposium on the Dignity and Rights of the Mentally Disabled Person* (5 January 2004).

4

THE PERSON AND PROFOUND

DISABILITY: A THEOLOGY OF THE BODY

Whilst Karol Wojtyła is known principally for his book *The Acting Person* and his Lublin lectures *Person and Community* as Pope John Paul he is perhaps most associated in the popular mind with his catechetical audiences that became the *Theology of the Body*. In these weekly audiences between September 1979 and November 1984 Pope John Paul gave teaching on the bodily dimension of human personhood and on sexuality and marriage in the light of biblical revelation. Although his focus is on the complimentary vocations of marriage and celibacy both directed towards the Kingdom of God and he notes that marriage and procreation in particular give 'a concrete reality' to the meaning of the body he adds that they 'do not determine definitively the original and fundamental meaning of being a body or of being, as a body male and female'.[1] According to Pope John Paul, whilst the 'meaning of being a body' is obviously connected with marriage, fatherhood and motherhood, 'the original and fundamental significance of being a body and, in particular, being male and female—that is precisely that nuptial significance—is united with the fact that man is created as a person and called to a life in *communione personarum*'.[2] Pope John Paul's *Theology of the Body* is a theology for all human beings, including people with disabilities. Notably, what is often forgotten or neglected is that the disabled are, like every other human being, sexual beings.

Certainly the *Theology of the Body* is aimed at the acting person since one of Pope John Paul's goals is to demonstrate that in the context of marriage and celibacy a truly human act is one that involves the whole person. This is expressed in terms of his or her bodily actions under the influence of self control, self mastery, and the exercise of virtue and freedom yet also in the knowledge that the person is created, fallen, redeemed and destined in hope for an eternal life with God. Still, in analysing how human beings act in a truly human way Pope John Paul explores the person as a personal subject and integrates what that person does with what happens in him or her: he translates *operari sequitur esse*, that acts disclose the person, into 'the language of the body'. At first sight it may seem that Pope John Paul's focus on rational control, will and intention represented in the 'language of the body' is at variance with the apparently 'non-acting' human being (in modern terms), the person who does not exhibit rational, willed and intended activity. To be sure that person is unable to express the person he or she is or even more likely it is we who are unable to grasp the subjectivity of that person because we have not fathomed how to engage successfully with him or her. Nevertheless, Pope John Paul offers some deep insights into aspects of human existence that are common to all human beings and his reflection on solitude and *communio*, two key terms in the *Theology of the Body*, can speak volumes to the experiences of the person with profound disabilities.

In particular Pope John Paul identifies as a major concern the tendency to make the other person into an object 'for me' rather than seeing him or her as a personal subject, as unique and unrepeatable with full human dignity. Although Pope John Paul discusses this objectivising of the other in terms of sexual relationships he locates the basis of making the other into an object in more general human attitudes. So his analysis of this is clearly of relevance as it seems to be reflected in many contemporary attitudes towards the person with profound disabilities.

People with profound disabilities are particularly vulnerable to objectivisation and the domination of others as well as loneliness on at least four accounts. Firstly they are often voiceless when it comes to reporting mistreatment or abuse so the full extent of this remains in silence. Secondly, and perhaps more intractable, many people with profound disabilities are even more open to the interaction of others through their own innocence and guilelessness and so they may inadvertently subject themselves to the dominance of others. Jean Vanier's experience in living with the disabled attests to this particular vulnerability. He describes people with disabilities as 'those who live essentially by their hearts', seeking personal relationship, where the 'opening of the heart implies vulnerability and the offering of our needs and weaknesses'[3]. In contrast he says that 'the powerful' see the heart as a 'place of weakness' and so fear it or take advantage of it.[4]

Thirdly, and perhaps less well recognised is the loneliness of those who seem to live only a hidden interior life. This may make them even more susceptible to the promise of companionship with others and if this companionship becomes dominance then loneliness may be increased. The loneliness of all human beings has long been recognised by mystic and spiritual writers indeed it is seen as essential to humanity as part of the 'restlessness' that St Augustine talks about in the person's search for something beyond themselves.[5] However, as Jean Vanier points out, most people can cover up their sense of loneliness by action, seeking recognition and success. But for the disabled and the elderly who cannot actively deal with it loneliness often manifests itself as depression or confusion, 'agony, a scream of pain'.[6] In a 'life turned in upon itself'[7] the promise of companionship is compelling yet where companionship becomes overbearance, without true charitable love, loneliness is doubled. Loneliness, as Jean Vanier puts it, is 'a feeling of not being part of anything, of being cut off….loneliness is a taste of death'.[8]

Fourthly, as Alice Maynard the chairman of Scope, a charity that supports disabled people and their families, explains when commenting on the prevalence of discrimination and abuse suffered by people with disabilities travelling to and from work, they need to build a 'shell' around themselves to cope with the abuse.[9] On the one hand this shell is it seems a cause of additional loneliness as some strive to protect themselves against the hurt caused by the other. On the other hand some severely disabled people are not even able to build a protective shell. People with profound disabilities are unguarded in every sense of the word.

Both the search for companionship and this vulnerability to loneliness seem to be aspects of human existence that are common to all human beings. As common human experiences Pope John Paul explores both of these aspects in his *Theology of the Body* through his analysis of *communio* and solitude but in a deeper sense than simply friendship and loneliness. His understanding of each person becoming a gift for the other has resonance with Jean Vanier's experience of the disabled. The 'language of the body' and the metaphor of the enclosed garden from the *Song of Songs* not only provides reflection for those in personal relationships it also contributes to an appreciation of the interior life of the person with profound disabilities.

Theology of the Body: in context

Pope John Paul originally considered the theology of the body to be a 'working term' because as he says he is concerned principally with exploring the redemption of the body in the context of the sacramentality of marriage and celibacy and not with broader issues such as suffering, disability and death. His other possible titles, 'Human love in the divine plan' or more precisely 'The Redemption of the Body and the Sacramentality of Marriage' bear this out.[10] Nevertheless, as a title *The Theology of the Body* appears to have captured the public imagination. Even though he does not deal specifically with disability Pope John Paul offers an anthropological account of the human person that also encompasses the situation of the person with profound disability. This can be found in particular in his analysis of the main 'modern' anthropological problem and in his identification of 'solitude' and '*communio*' in his focus on biblical and personalistic aspects of this theology of the body.

To begin with, Pope John Paul follows St Thomas Aquinas in recognising that we cannot reach the truth merely empirically or rationally without the risk of mistake so we need Revelation. However, by reference to the conversation Jesus has with the Sadducees about the levirate law on the duty of a man to marry his dead brother's wife[11] Pope John Paul also acknowledges that mere literal knowledge of scripture is not enough; 'the Scriptures are above all a means to know the power of the living God who reveals himself in them... to reread the Scriptures correctly... means to know and accept with faith the power of the Giver of life, who is not bound by the law of death which rules man's earthly history'.[12] So when Pope John Paul follows Jesus in returning to the significance of *Genesis* by going back to the beginning he does so in the conviction that this is the 'threshold of the revelation of historical man'.[13] Furthermore, Pope John Paul makes this move with the overarching theme that the human being is the only creature on earth that God has willed for its own sake; he can fully discover his true self only in sincere giving of himself.[14]

Notably this overarching theme addresses all human beings whatever their state in life. Moreover, Pope John Paul uses *Ephesians* 5 as pivotal to his understanding. In *Ephesians* 5 the author, reputedly St Paul, reminds his readers that in God's plan of salvation Christ loves the Church and gives himself totally up for her so he confers on his redemptive love a spousal character and meaning. However, Pope John Paul adds that the author of *Ephesians* is not speaking directly of the sacrament of marriage rather the sacramentality of the whole of Christian life and in particular marriage indirectly.[15] Thus the theology of the body encompasses 'the meaning of being a body, on the sense of being, as a body, man and woman' and so is relevant for all human beings.[16]

In setting the context for his theology of the body Pope John Paul analyses the main problems he sees in modern anthropology. He notes that 'modern man' tends towards dualism and the domination of forces of nature rather than self mastery. This shows up, he says, in modern science where biological knowledge manifests itself in a separation of what is corporeal in man from what is spiritual so that the body is treated as an object of manipulations. Pope John Paul argues that now that human beings have lost sight of the fact that the body is proper to the person the body has been deprived of its meaning and dignity rooted in that fact and so human beings cease to identify themselves subjectively with their own bodies. This leads, he says to a 'Manichaean mentality': 'in the whole Manichaean myth there is only one hero and only one situation which is always repeated: the fallen soul is imprisoned in matter and is liberated by knowledge' and matter is 'an evil instinct for pleasure';[17] body and sex have an anti-value.[18] From this he concludes that in this modern Manichaeistic way of thinking the problem becomes the physical body becomes rather than the problem being located in the 'lust in the heart', or the interior attitudes people take towards the body.[19]

It seems that this Manichaean mentality that condemns the body as 'the real source of evil'[20] is evident in some models of disability that locate the 'problem' of disability in the body and then seek to reform the body until it meets some kind of norm. Similarly it can be found in models where disability is seen in terms of external barriers and the reality of the person with disabilities is taken to be disembodied. This mentality is perhaps best summed up by those who see the person with disabilities as a self imprisoned in a broken body or, as in the case of profound intellectual disability, as merely a human body lacking the component of 'person'. It mirrors the separation some make between biological and biographical life. The 'problem' of disability easily becomes indifference, discrimination or even hostility to one who seems so unlike 'us' so that the person with disability him or herself becomes the problem rather than the problem lying in the interior attitudes of others. However, according to Pope John Paul theology has corrective insights to offer on the body and attitudes to it precisely because of the Incarnation when 'the body entered theology through the main door':[21] the body, as part of God's creation and redeemed through Christ is good.

The Manichaean way of thinking that saw everything as a mixture of good and bad also embraced a deterministic view of the inevitability of personal evil and Pope John Paul finds traces of this in modern thinking influenced by and developed from Freud, Marx and Nietzsche.[22] Since Pope John Paul is trying to reestablish the truths of freedom, self-mastery and right action in the field of marriage he critiques those like the phenomenologists (and it also applies to physicalists) who say 'nature' is to do with natural impulses and responses (what happens in man, *actus hominis*) and nothing to do with rationality and freedom (what man does *actus humani*). This distinction has, of course, bearing on the subject of the acting person and the 'non-acting' person (in the modern sense). 'Nature' according to phenomenologists seems to be in conflict with the 'free person' and the 'person' is somehow above nature. Of course for Pope John Paul both *actus hominis* and *actus humani* are human acts therefore he sees it as vital to explain and keep together the 'exterior' and 'interior' of the human being, so that the body remains proper to the person. As what happens in the body is an aspect of the person those people with the profoundest disabilities who only appear to have what some would say merely bodily life still have a personal life.

Moreover, it cannot be said that a person with mere bodily life is not in some way in relationship with his or her Creator. To suggest otherwise is to despair of the power of God to act in all areas of life. Since it is the case that body and person belong together then both are called in the one human being to imitate Christ as far as is possible in total self-giving to others, what Pope John Paul calls the 'nuptial meaning' of the body, a meaning he anchors in the texts critical for his thinking, *Gaudium et spes* 22 and 24 and in the *Book of Genesis*.

Starting points for the Theology of the Body

It is important to realise that Pope John Paul's return to the text of *Genesis* for his anthropology is not simply a matter of chronology. Pope John Paul is in fact taking as his starting point Jesus's teaching.[23] However Jesus remains the centre point for Pope John Paul: it is Jesus who looks back to *Genesis* and then forward to the resurrection of the body. As Pope John Paul further explains, the new sacramental economy based on the spousal gracing of the Church by Christ differs from the original economy because it is directed not to the 'man of justice and original innocence' but to 'man burdened' with original sin and a state of sinfulness.[24] This revelation is also intimately related to human experience and since, Pope John Paul says, 'corporeal man' is perceived by us mainly by experience, experience too is an 'indispensable point of reference'.[25]

Although Pope John Paul concentrates on the story of the creation of human beings in *Genesis* 2 since he sees it as speaking of humanity's universal experience he notes that the origins of humankind lie both in anthropology and in theology because humanity is bound up with the idea of the image of God found in *Genesis* 1.[26] Pope John Paul's identification of 'original solitude' and 'original unity' lie in the context of 'man's original innocence' and his 'original happiness' all of which are aspects of the mystery of his existence before he broke the first covenant with his Creator: before original sin.[27]

Taking the account of the creation of humankind in *Genesis* 2 Pope John Paul explains that from the beginning there is a clear boundary between the world of animals and human beings created in the image and likeness of God. Moreover, he says, human beings are well aware that they are not merely beings among other beings.[28] This is reflected in the experience of 'original solitude': as God brings the animals to Adam, generic 'man', so that he can name them Adam realises that 'he' is aware of 'himself' as a person and a being in the world. 'He' has a consciousness of 'his' own body and its meaning as well as an awareness of choice and self-determination. This means that he is both a subject and an object and he is also different from the visible world: he is 'alone before God'.[29] Continuing the generic story of human beings in *Genesis* Pope John Paul explains that it is 'not good' for man to be alone so there is a 'second creation': he becomes male and female, a unity of the two.[30] In this solitude (where he is revealed to himself as a person) he opens up to a being like himself, also a person in solitude, so that the 'original unity' of the first couple overcomes solitude and this leads to joy, enrichment and *communio*, a communion of persons.[31] According to Pope John Paul, and focusing on his principal task of exploring marriage, man and woman are two different ways of the human 'being a body' in the unity of the image of God.[32]

Moving away from the generic 'man' of *Genesis* Pope John Paul speaks about every human being as 'historical man', meaning 'each one of us' separated from the mystery of original innocence by original sin[33]. This of course includes the disabled. Nevertheless, he also understands from *Genesis* that this break in original innocence and consequent state of sin is not simply the 'lost horizon of human existence'. It is also the 'first promise of redemption' as demonstrated by the passage that tells 'he shall crush your head, you shall bruise his heel'.[34] So, historical man participates not only in the history of human sinfulness that is both hereditary and personal but also in the history of salvation. The human person is at the same time closed to original innocence and open to redemption.[35]

Solitude and communio in 'historical man'

Following the pattern of *Genesis* 2 Pope John Paul sees that all human beings are 'in solitude', alone in the visible world that expresses what he or she 'is not'. Nevertheless, the person is at the same time in search of a definition of him or herself such that in solitude and in the awareness of being a person he or she discovers his or her transcendence. Thus there remains an orientation towards relationship, *communio*.[36]

It is important to note the significance that both solitude and communion have for Pope John Paul. Pope John Paul explains that solitude never ceases to be a personal dimension of everyone's nature since fundamentally every human being, including those with the profoundest of disabilities, is alone and stands alone before God. However, solitude is not simply to be equated with loneliness. Indeed the dimension of loneliness seems to have entered into human history at the Fall when Adam no longer naturally sees Eve as an other but instead tends towards objectivising her.[37] Rather, the term solitude, found from the beginning before the Fall, expresses what is unique and unrepeatable about each and every human being. Solitude then seems to express the relationship of a human being, wanted by his or her Creator for his or her own sake. Being 'wanted for one's own sake' is an affirmation of every human being no matter what his or her condition. It is to regard each human being as particularly loved by God and sent out and accepted as a gift to others. Moreover, each person is constantly being called towards a 'new and even fuller form of intersubjective communion with others', and in the last analysis in the community of saints. This communion is, says Pope John Paul, an authentic development of human beings created in God's image and likeness in its Trinitarian meaning, that is, as a communion of Persons.[38] For human beings this Trinitarian meaning embraces the unity of all yet also maintains the distinctive uniqueness of the person.

Although Pope John Paul speaks about *communio* in reference to the marital relationship and in terms of how the couple are an 'image of God' not only through their humanity but also through this communion of persons that reaches out in procreation[39] it seems to be worthwhile exploring what Pope John Paul means by *communio*. Pope John Paul sees that the relationship in marriage is a *communio* and not simply a community: it is formed from a double solitude since both husband and wife are separate from the animal world and each are unique and unrepeatable but they exist for each other as 'help', that is, as person beside person.[40] Of course for Pope John Paul this special reciprocity found in marriage requires self-knowledge and self-determination[41] since it concerns freedom and choice made in the marriage vows. Moreover it involves complementarity: they are man and woman and a 'gift for each other', they accept and receive each other with what Pope John Paul calls 'interior innocence', that is, purity of heart, so that the other is not seen as an 'object for me'.[42] Pope John Paul describes this 'disinterested gift of oneself' as the 'nuptial meaning of the body'. Key for 'gift' in this nuptial meaning is that a human being only realises his or her essence completely by existing with and for someone in the original truth of masculinity and femininity.[43] This involves not only fruitfulness and procreation but also the gift of self and affirmation of the other who is also willed by God for his or her own sake.[44] Thus it concerns knowing the other as a unique, unrepeatable 'self'.[45]

Extrapolating from the marriage relationship it can be said that the person with profound disability and his or her companion are each in solitude that is they are unique and unrepeatable subjects, who can also form a relationship of person beside person. Clearly in the case of the most profoundly intellectually disabled this does not entail a sexual element so in that it is unlike the deep *communio* of marriage. Indeed any such element would seem to be an abuse of the person if he or she did not have capacity truly to consent. However, in the companionship of a disabled person with an 'abled' person there is always the danger that the 'person' of the first is lost through the dominance of the other. Moreover, the sexuality of the person with profound disabilities is often overlooked if he or she is seen only in terms of his or her diminished mental capacities instead of being a man or woman. Pope John Paul's theology of the body is relevant here as he points out that 'particular attention must be given to the emotional and sexual dimensions of disabled persons' precisely because these are 'constitutive dimensions' of the human being. He reminds that the disabled have the same need 'to love and to be loved, they need tenderness, closeness and intimacy'. However this entails 'authentic relationships in which they can find appreciation and recognition as persons'.[46] It requires treatment and rehabilitation that takes into account 'a complete vision of the human person'.[47]

In discussing the relationships between the disabled and the non-disabled terms become complicated. For Jean Vanier in such a relationship it is not 'a question of performing good deeds for those who are excluded but of being open and vulnerable to them in order to receive the life that they can offer':[48] friendship is the goal. Jean Vanier also explains that 'accompaniment' is always necessary for everyone at all stages of life since the one who accompanies 'is not there to judge us or to tell us what to do, but to reveal what is most beautiful and valuable in us, as well as to point towards the meaning of our inner pain'.[49] Notably a companion can mean both someone who accompanies another, travels with them and someone employed to assist, live with or travel with another. It also can carry a notion of complimentarity that expresses not equality in terms of sameness but equality in terms of difference. These senses seem to resonate when discussing people with disabilities and those they encounter. Moreover, 'companion' comes, in part, from the Latin *com* + *panis*, together + bread. Not only does this suggest 'one who eats bread with another' it may by extrapolation also have connotations of feeding another. Perhaps then it better expresses the complexities of the relationships of the person with disabilities and others than other notions. Again as Jean Vanier puts it the one who accompanies helps us 'to come to life, to live more fully' and he adds that the 'accompanier receives life also'. Moreover, 'they do not clutch on to each other but give life to one another and call each other to greater freedom'.[50]

No doubt Pope John Paul has Jean Vanier's example in mind when the Pope commends 'certain Christian communities' and their work with the mentally disabled. Like Jean Vanier, Pope John Paul also appreciates both the demands and the reciprocity that can be found in companionship with the disabled. As the Pope explains the mentally disabled require 'attentive listening, understanding of their needs, sharing of their sufferings, patience in guidance' so that they can be introduced into 'a human relationship of communion, to enable them to perceive their own value, and make them aware of their capacity for receiving and giving love'. After all, for Pope John Paul the disabled, like all human beings are 'called from the outset to find fulfillment in the encounter with others and in communion'.[51]

However Pope John Paul is also well aware of the vulnerability of the disabled, particularly the mentally impaired. He accepts that they need 'perhaps more attention, affection, understanding and love than any other sick person: they cannot be left alone, unarmed and defenceless, as it were, in the difficult task of facing life'.[52] This reflects a central concern for Pope John Paul and it can be found in Jean Vanier's experience as well. In relationships between the disabled and non-disabled there is a danger that the strong take advantage of the weak. There is the risk that in their relationships human beings are tempted to reduce the other person to a mere object instead of discerning that person as a unique and unrepeatable boy or girl, woman or man.

Persons as objects: interior attitudes to people

The notion that the other is reduced to a mere object is described by Pope John Paul as seeing each other in a limited way merely with the eyes of the body where personal intimacy and the peace of the 'interior gaze' is disturbed.[53] Pope John Paul, the ethicist, is primarily thinking here of possessive relationships between men and women with concupiscence as lust of the flesh, the eyes, and pride all of which are the fruit of the breaking of the first covenant, broken in man's heart.[54] In summing up this situation of 'historical man' Pope John Paul says the original capacity of communicating to each other has been shattered and diversity is now felt as mutual confrontation.[55] Undoubtedly he is speaking of the man-woman relationship and the pull of lust. However, what is going on here, the seeing of the other as *not* an other, the limited way of looking indeed the attitude of pride of those who see themselves as strong, intelligent and capable speaks volumes when it comes to reflecting on the relationship and attitudes of others to the person with profound disabilities. It is a loud comment on the negative attitudes some people hold towards the disabled from seeing them as objects of pity, discomfort or embarrassment to treating them with prejudice and hostility. Perhaps the ultimate objectifying of the disabled person is the current push for assisted suicide where some able bodied people would rather be dead than live a life of dependence. As Richard Hawkes, the chief executive of the disability charity Scope explains in the charity's opposition statement to weakening the law on assisted suicide, 'sadly some people assume disabled people's lives aren't worth living. And not every disabled person is in a position to argue that it is'.[56]

Again in terms of the relationship between men and women Pope John Paul says that Christ addresses 'historical man' (every man) in his heart, that interior aspect of man. In doing so he 'shifts the point of gravity of sin' to the heart.[57] When a man (and for Pope John Paul it is usually the man) looks lustfully at a woman the cause of the lust lies not with the woman's body rather it lies in what is in the man's heart: *operari sequitur esse* a man acts according to what he is.[58] Something similar seems to occur where the 'problem' of disability is located in the disabled body in front of us rather than in the attitude we hold towards disability. So it is not only institutions and structures that may need to change. In the healthcare context a call to better training, closer supervision, more staff, more careful recruitment, a shake-up of institutions may be necessary but the central focus of change must be people themselves and their attitudes. This need for a change in attitudes is growing more pressing as reports and surveys have routinely found that attitudes to the disabled are getting worse.[59]

Pope John Paul roots this call for constant conversion in Jesus's words in the Sermon on the Mount. Pope John Paul notes that Jesus does not invite a return to the state of original innocence: because of the Fall humanity has irrevocably left this state behind. Instead, he says that Jesus calls human beings to rediscover 'on the foundation of the perennial and indestructible meanings of what is human—the living forms of the new man'.[60] Pope John Paul has in mind here 'the ethos of the redemption of the body' that is realised through self-mastery and temperance so that what is done becomes a truly personal act. It involves a call to the human heart rather than an accusation. However, he says the 'indispensable condition' of this call to purity of heart is a consciousness of sinfulness.[61] Once a person with the help of grace has confronted his or her distorted attitudes then with the help of grace he or she can grow in purity of heart and so begin to see with clear vision the dignity and the person of the other. He or she becomes a 'new person' in seeing the other anew.

As for the person with profound disability he or she may already be living a 'new life', new because it may be a different kind of life to the one we expect. Whilst for the most part human beings now regard activity, functionality, purpose and efficiency as the marks of a worthwhile life the person whose life does not reflect this may indeed help others to rediscover some of the meanings of what it is to be human. For many who are profoundly disabled the key to unlocking and making sense of the world is found in sensory experience. Using sight, hearing, touch, taste and smell is not a new way of living but it is one that is often forgotten in the busyness of daily life. Staying still, being apparently passive and allowing experience to come is a profoundly human activity.

Nevertheless, for Pope John Paul the 'new man' has a further and deeper significance that is found in the eternal future for which each person waits in hope.

The eschatological future of human beings

Pope John Paul still has the marriage relationship in mind when he considers the eschatological, eternal future of human beings. However his words have significance for people with disabilities. He thinks that in the 'new condition of the human body in the resurrection' bodies will keep their masculinity or femininity but 'the sense of being a male or a female in the body will be constituted and understood in that age in a different way from what it had been from the beginning, and then in the whole dimension of earthly existence'.[62] By taking this line already found in St Augustine Pope John Paul means that every human being will keep his or her authentic subjectivity. By implication this seems to include disability where a person feels it to be a defining aspect of his or her identity. Notably and in keeping with his conviction of the goodness of the body and its place in the resurrection Pope John Paul speaks of a 'spiritualization of man' where the human being which was subject to death is now restored to real life in his or her psychosomatic nature so that it is a bodily restoration not simply a new creation 'like the angels'.[63] He is adamant that this is not a 'disincarnation' but 'a new submission of the body to the spirit'[64] and this is not just spirit dominating body but spirit fully permeating body: 'the perfect participation of all that is physical in man in what is spiritual in him....the perfect realisation of what is personal in man' instead of man being at war with himself.[65] This realisation in glory will reveal the definitive value of what was to be from the beginning and although it will be new it will not be alien.[66] According to Pope John Paul resurrection indicates the end of the historical dimension and ushers in the eschatological dimension which will be perfectly personal and communitarian at the same time.

The language of the body

Pope John Paul develops two further ideas in his theology of the body that are directed specifically towards marriage yet also have bearing on disability. The first of these is his understanding of the 'language of the body'. Pope John Paul uses this idea in order to convey the essential truth that the body is not merely an organism that has certain reactions. Pope John Paul sees a sacramental dimension to the body. Just as, he says, a sacrament is a visible sign the body also signifies what is visible so that, albeit 'in the most general way', the body enters the definition of sacrament being 'a visible sign of an invisible reality', that is 'of the spiritual, transcendent, divine reality.'[67] This is why for Pope John Paul the 'language of the body' has such significance particularly in marriage. It is represented in the wedding vows as an intentional expression on the level of intellect and will, consciousness and heart to become a mutual gift for each other in the communion of persons.[68] The spouses also 'speak' when carrying out 'the conjugal dialogue proper to their vocation and based on the language of the body', that is in the marital act, and they form life and living together as a communion of persons on the basis of that language.[69] The demands of the commitment to married life, the level of intent and exercise of intellect and will seems to place many people with profound disability outside marriage and the marital union. However disabled people still belong to families and that communion of persons formed through marriage. The 'language of the body' remains a way for parents to respond to the gift of a disabled child particularly in the contemporary technological age where some forms of genetic engineering seek to remove the problem of disability by engineering out disabled embryos or where abortion is seen as the solution to problematical individuals. Moreover a challenge can be made to the notion that some people with profound disability, especially perhaps the patient in persistent vegetative state or the anencephalic infant, are simply organisms with purely somatic or automatic reactions. The idea that the body is a visible sign of an invisible reality is a truth for the person with profound disability even where it seems impossible for the body to express that reality in ways that can be understood by another.

Pope John Paul suggests that the human being is aware of him or herself as subject on the basis of his or her own body, that is to say that he or she is the author of truly human activity. In this way the body expresses the person, the visible expresses the invisible hence in ethical terms the task of dominion over self or self-mastery.[70] When it comes to the person with profound disabilities following the first part, that the body expresses the person, it seems that Phoebe Caldwell, one of the principal practitioners of intensive interaction therapy identifies a similar pattern in the internal 'conversation' of repetitive behaviour. She says that this behaviour appears to be part of a communication system. However instead of it being used to communicate with others, this communication is with the self and one of the tasks of therapy is to make sense of this communication.[71] Often the profoundly disabled do have their own language that expresses themselves and it requires will on the part of others to recognise this. As for the second part, Pope John Paul adds that this self-consciousness and self-knowledge develops with knowledge of the world such that the person realises that he or she is a subject of the covenant that he or she must discern between good and evil, life and death. It is at this point perhaps that the activity of a person with intellectual disabilities remains on a primary as opposed to an ethical level. However, the fact that he or she is a human being made in the image of God signifies that he or she is also the subject of a covenant with God. Thus it is important to acknowledge that even the most profoundly disabled person has spiritual needs.

The garden

The second idea is the 'enclosed garden' metaphor that Pope John Paul explores through the richness of the language of the body in the *Song of Songs*. For Pope John Paul this metaphor is a reflection on the person as master of his or her own mystery. It encompasses the personal dignity of the person who as a spiritual subject is in possession of his or herself and can decide not only on the metaphysical depth but also on the essential truth and authenticity of the gift of self.[72] Pope John Paul also points to the 'interior inviolability' of the person[73] and 'the near impossibility of one person's being appropriated and mastered by the other'.[74] This seems to indicate the incommunicability of every human being, that each person is unique and unrepeatable. What perhaps has resonance here with the life of a person with profound disability is that we can never know the full mystery of another person whatever their capacity to express themselves. Moreover, we simply do not know what dreams or thoughts a person with profound disability has or indeed the graced relationship he or she has with God. Even a person in persistent vegetative state enclosed in his or her own garden may dream.

Summary

It should come as no surprise that Pope John Paul's *Theology of the Body* has something to say to people with profound disability. The deep loneliness perhaps felt by people who cannot fully express themselves or who open themselves up unwittingly to becoming merely an object for others and the longing for companionship seem to be extensions of a primordial human experience even if such extreme experiences are not commonly felt by those who are able to build a shell of protection around themselves or actively search for fuller relationships. Nevertheless Pope John Paul's interpretation of human experience allows us to reflect on all human beings, whatever their situation, as created by God who has wanted each one just for his or her self in his or her uniqueness. This standing before God in solitude may be where the most profoundly disabled person is. But it is not a Godfor-saken place.

Pope John Paul's *Theology of the Body* focuses on the dignity of every human being as a personal subject who is never an object for the other. This also means that the person is never the object of pity where pity comprises a looking down on the other. It is this kind of pity that liberation theologies of disability seek to challenge. As another of those 'signs of the times' liberation theologies of disability bring both risk and promise so the Chapter 5 outlines these theologies in the broader context of liberation theology. This allows a clearer response to be made by Pope John Paul in Chapter 6 specifically in his work in Catholic Social Teaching.

Notes

1. Pope John Paul II, *Theology of the Body: Human Love in the Divine Plan* (Boston: Pauline Books, 1997), p. 247.
2. *Ibid.*, p. 247.
3. J. Vanier, *Becoming Human* (London: Darton, Longman and Todd, 1998), p. 63.
4. *Ibid.*, pp. 46, 78.
5. St Augustine, *Confessions,* I.1.
6. J. Vanier, *Becoming Human*, pp. 7–9.
7. *Ibid.*, pp. 8–9.
8. *Ibid.*, p. 33.
9. A. Maynard in a report by A. Asthana, 'Disabled face rising levels of abuse, says charity boss' in *The Times* (11 June 2011), p. 1.
10. Pope John Paul II, *Theology of the Body,* pp. 419–422.
11. *Mt* 22:23–33.
12. Pope John Paul II, *Theology of the Body,* p. 236.
13. *Ibid.*, p. 109.
14. Vatican II, *Gaudium et spes* 22, 24.
15. Pope John Paul II, *Theology of the Body,* p. 342.
16. *Ibid.*, p. 353.
17. *Ibid.*, pp. 185–186 footnote 62.
18. *Ibid.*, p. 164.
19. *Ibid.*, pp. 165–166.

20. *Ibid.*, p. 162.

21. *Ibid.*, p. 88.

22. *Ibid.*, pp. 165–166.

23. *Mt* 19.3ff; *Mk* 10.2ff.

24. Pope John Paul II, *Theology of the Body*, p. 340.

25. *Ibid.*, p. 34.

26. *Ibid.*, p. 47 and p. 102 corrigenda.

27. *Ibid.*, p. 67.

28. *Ibid.*, p. 282.

29. *Ibid.*, pp. 37–39.

30. *Ibid.*, pp. 42–45.

31. *Ibid.*, pp. 45–48.

32. *Ibid.*, p. 58.

33. *Ibid.*, p. 106.

34. *Ibid.*, p. 33.

35. *Ibid.*, p. 33.

36. *Ibid.*, p. 46.

37. *Ibid.*, p. 41.

38. *Ibid.*, p. 273.

39. *Ibid.*, p. 47.

40. *Ibid.*, pp. 45–46.

41. *Ibid.*, p. 46.

42. *Ibid.*, pp. 69–71.

43. *Ibid.*, pp. 60–63.

44. *Ibid.*, p. 63.

45. *Ibid.*, p. 79.

46. Pope John Paul II, *On the Occasion of the International Symposium on the Dignity and Rights of the Mentally Disabled Person* (5 January 2004), 5.

47. Pope John Paul II, Homily *Jubilee of the Disabled* (3 December 2000), 5.

48. J. Vanier, *Becoming Human*, p. 84.

49. *Ibid.*, p. 129.

50. *Ibid.*, pp. 129–130.

51. Pope John Paul II, *On the Occasion of the International Symposium on the Dignity and Rights of the Mentally Disabled Person* (5 January 2004), 5.

52. *Ibid.*, 4.

53. Pope John Paul II, *Theology of the Body*, p. 58.

54. *Ibid.*, p. 109.

55. *Ibid.,* p. 118.

56. R. Hawkes, *Scope comment on assisted suicide debate in Parliament.* <http://www.scope.org.uk/news/assisted-suicide-debate-parliament> [accessed 28 March 2012].

57. Pope John Paul II, *Theology of the Body,* pp. 142–144.

58. *Ibid.,* p. 147.

59. See <http://www.scope.org.uk/news/latest-attitudes-survey> [accessed 9 September 2011].

60. Pope John Paul II, *Theology of the Body,* p. 175.

61. *Ibid.,* pp. 176–177.

62. *Ibid.,* p. 239.

63. *Ibid.,,* p. 239.

64. *Ibid.,* p. 240.

65. *Ibid.,* p. 241.

66. *Ibid.,* pp. 246–249.

67. *Ibid.,* pp. 305–306.

68. *Ibid.,* p. 356.

69. *Ibid.,* p. 364.

70. *Ibid.,* pp. 40–41.

71. P. Caldwell, *Finding you finding me* (London: Jessica Kingsley Publishers, 2006), p. 121.

72. Pope John Paul II, *Theology of the Body,* pp. 368–372.

73. *Ibid.,* p. 372.

74. *Ibid.,* p. 374.

5

DISABILITY AND LIBERATION

THEOLOGIES

Many of Pope John Paul's writings follow the methodology established by the Fathers of the Second Vatican Council in *Gaudium et spes*, the Pastoral Constitution on the Church in the Modern World. This involves looking first at the 'signs of the times' to contextualise reflection in what is actual and concrete before offering a reflective response. By considering the 'joy and hope, the grief and anguish' of people in today's world the Church shows itself 'in solidarity' with 'the whole human family'.[1] However in relation to the situation of the profoundly disabled, to the precarious position of human beings at the earliest stages of life, to the perilous circumstances of the person in vegetative state there appears to be more grief and anguish than joy and hope in the signs of the times.

In contemporary disability studies the 'signs of the times' incorporate the explicit discrimination inherent in the separation some make between the human being and the person as well as the implicit discrimination that surfaces in certain attitudes towards the disabled. In response to experiences of discrimination a new branch within disability studies has emerged that is distinctly theological. This branch is associated in particular with liberation theologies, which concentrate on actual lived experience. Undoubtedly many liberation theologies take new and invigorating approaches to the signs of the times. However, whilst they offer a renewed perspective some liberation theologies also risk losing focus. Given that liberation theologies of disability are becoming more prevalent it seems worthwhile flagging up some of the problems that may accompany some liberation theologies and applying these to certain interpretations of liberation theologies of disability.

Certainly Pope John Paul has always been interested in the concrete situation and experiences of human beings though this is in the context of the truth of the human being in relation to God. According to Karol Wojtyła's analysis of the Second Vatican Council the human being is 'at the centre of religion… in all his reality and with all his specific problems'. This is because Christianity lives by and proclaims the reality of creation and of redemption and these 'divine realities' lead human beings away from what in modern terms is 'alienation' into a more profound reflection of the whole truth about his or her humanity.[2] So Karol Wojtyła is convinced that the dignity of the human person is inevitably the central concern for the Church. Indeed, in his first encyclical as Pope, John Paul explains that the object of the Church's care is every real and concrete human being 'in his unique unrepeatable human reality, which keeps intact the image and likeness of God himself'.[3]

Church tradition has always seen that respect for all human beings is fundamental and that it is the duty of the Church to witness to this respect especially when human dignity and integrity is threatened or under attack.[4] Moreover the Church follows scripture in its specific concern for the poor, marginalised and vulnerable, recognising that they are specially loved by God. However the 1970s saw the rise of new theologies of liberation that have at their heart the awakening of the experience of these particularly marginalised people. Perhaps coinciding with the development of the social model of disability there has been a flourishing of literature on disability seen through the prism of liberation theologies and individual experience.

A clear connection between the two can come as no surprise since the social model seems to fit smoothly with the premises of liberation theologies. Liberation theologies look to the concrete experience of those who are struggling against marginalisation and oppression perpetrated on them by those in positions of power; for those who hold to a strong version of the social model of disability is redefined by the disabled as 'the social barriers, restrictions and/or oppressions they face' where 'professional interventions have come to be seen as often adding to these problems rather than seeking to deal with them.[5] Liberation theologies seek to allow the voices of the oppressed to be heard so that liberation comes from within their own activity; in a liberation theology of disability what is significant is the conviction that if those who are not disabled write the account of disability on which professional practices and interventions are based then such an account will inevitably be a distortion: it must be written and spoken of by people with disabilities so that it arises from personal experience.[6] In disability studies literature this enabling experience seems to come through a raised consciousness of disability issues. This is often linked to a former attitude of denial that gradually becomes a 'collective embracement of disabled people' so that 'the personal is the political.[7]

Liberation theologies and liberation theologies of disability

Liberation theology was brought to the attention of the world by the work of Gustavo Gutierrez, a Dominican priest and theologian born in Peru in 1928 most notably through his book *A Theology of Liberation* published in 1971. Early liberation theology focused on the people in South America who experienced extreme poverty. Moreover their situation of oppression seemed to be shored up by political and social institutions. Gustavo Gutierrez explains that the 'name and reality' of liberation theology came into existence during his series of lectures at Chimbote, Peru in July 1968 as a way of preaching the Gospel for a new historical situation,[8] at a moment of *kairos*, a crisis moment of opportunity.[9] He then coined the term 'preferential option for the poor' as the appropriate Christian attitude to this *kairos* and this came out of discussions of the Latin American Catholic bishops in the CELAM (Consejo Episcopal Latinamerico) conferences a few months after Chimbote in Medellin in 1968 and Puebla in 1979. The 'poor' are not only the economic poor but also the marginalised and those who suffer social injustice. As Gustavo Gutierrez acknowledges there is no good definition of the 'poor' and he offers an approximate explanation: 'the poor are the nonpersons, the "insignificant ones", the ones that don't count either for the rest of society, and—far too frequently—for the Christian Churches'.[10]

Undeniably the roots of the principle of a preferential option for the poor are biblical. Notably, in the Old Testament the 'poor' included the marginalised and oppressed, the resident alien, widows and orphans, since they presumably did not have protection of their clan, were vulnerable and often economically disadvantaged.[11] Reference to this option for the poor can be found in the Pentateuch, the first five books of the Old Testament known as the Law or *Torah*. This body of law differs from other ancient legislation since it is motivated by religious considerations so that civil, criminal and religious precepts are all set within the context of the covenant with Yahweh. As a collection of codes inserted into the narrative of the Pentateuch there is some variation as different concerns and conditions and other neighbouring cultures influenced legislation. There is the early legal code of the Covenant dating to around 1500 BC and found in *Exodus* 20:22-23:33. This seems to be later than the Decalogue or 'Ten Words' inscribed on the tablets at Sinai since it deals with a settled way of life of farmers, peasants and shepherds rather than nomads. Then there is the still later code in *Deuteronomy* 12:1-26:15 that also concerns itself with debt and the situation of slaves. Finally there are the regulations in *Leviticus* 17-26 that is itself a collection of laws going back perhaps to nomadic times, certainly before the Exile and inserted into the Pentateuch by its priestly editors. However, all these codes offer a measure of protection to the poor and the marginalised. The poor are permitted to take the gleanings from the fields.[12] Any loans or assistance were for the purpose of alleviating distress, not for profit hence the injunction not to lend on interest in case the lender makes his brother poorer.[13] There was to be no taking in pledge the tools of someone else's trade in case that prevented him from earning his living[14] and no exploitation of poor and needy wage-earners whether 'brothers' or foreign residents.[15] Moreover, if anyone took as a pledge another's cloak, the outer garment that protected him from the cold as a blanket, then he was called to return it at sunset.[16] Significantly Yahweh gives the poor his special protection from oppression and hears their appeal against injustices.[17] After these injunctions to be mindful of the poor and marginalised the constant refrain to the Israelites takes the form of a reminder from God who says 'I am Yahweh your God who brought you out of Egypt' where you were an alien, a stranger, a slave, oppressed.[18]

Liberation theologies are, then, particularly aware of the Exodus story with its theme of freedom from slavery and oppression as a point of reference. This awareness further involves theology in the actual activity of human beings in history: it is the 'struggle to construct a just and fraternal society where persons can live with dignity and be agents of their own destiny'; a struggle where 'human beings transform themselves'.[19] This appreciation of events and historical situations means that liberation theologies are concerned more with actual praxis than abstract theory. And the viewpoint it begins from is that of the poor, the ones who are in fact suffering in those situations. As Gustavo Gutierrez explains, liberation theology is 'the irruption of the poor', the 'new presence' of those who used to be absent, of little importance, who have no opportunity to express their sufferings.[20] Arguably the methodology of liberation theology differs considerably from traditional Catholic theology since, before any other theological considerations liberation theology gives primacy to reflection on liberating praxis and it demands social change that is to be brought about by those intimately involved in this praxis: the poor themselves.[21]

Given that liberation theology focuses on the lived experience of people who are marginalised or oppressed and aims at enabling the 'absent ones' to turn themselves into 'active agents of their own destiny'[22] it is necessary to point out that there is no one liberation *theology*: these are *theologies* of liberation. Each group has its own particular experience and so there can be a liberation theology of disability in the same way as, say, a feminist liberation theology, a black liberation theology and indeed a black feminist liberation theology of disability. This appeal to personal experience and to liberation from oppressive structures through social change clearly has resonance with those who argue for the social model of disability, that it is precisely attitudes and structures that constitute any disadvantage and that a stand is to be made alongside those who are suffering from this oppression and injustice.

However those who appeal to liberation theologies of disability have to contend with the fact that whilst in scripture the 'poor' seem specially favoured by God this does not seem to be always the case with the disabled. Of particular note is the text of *Leviticus* 21:17-24 which seems to exclude from priestly service those who suffer from various deformities, disabilities and general defects. In ancient thought it appears that holiness was transmissible: Yahweh, as the Holy One, sanctifies people and things so that, for instance, anyone who touched the holy altar was made holy[23] and all things that are holy are excluded from profane use. These things are not holy in themselves rather they are holy in relation to Yahweh. So, for example a communion sacrifice that has been offered but instead of being eaten on the same day has been allowed to rot is no longer an acceptable sacrifice and offends against Yahweh's holiness.[24] Similarly, although as a rule the priesthood was a hereditary office it seems that physical disfigurement was thought to profane the sanctuary.[25] However, this does not necessarily imply that a disabled priest was ritually unclean since, after all, the disabled person continued to live with the priestly family and eat holy food.[26]

Still it seems that physical defects also excluded any person from participation in worship, so for instance eunuchs were not admitted to the assembly.[27] Although this was later reversed[28] it seems exclusion remained the norm so when Jesus cures the leper he sends him to the priest to be declared clean and to offer the relevant sacrifices for purification as required by the Mosaic law.[29] Undoubtedly the situation in ancient times was complex: it seems that practical measures took on a life of their own such that what appears to have begun as diagnostic and precautionary measures to prevent the spread of diseases, the identification of a serious skin disease as opposed to a trivial one, seems to have taken on religious significance since the task was entrusted to priests and restoration to the community took the form of a ritual sacrifice. Moreover, this wariness towards disability may have been influenced by other ancient notions of disability as a sign of God's displeasure or the result of evil spirits, notions found among, for instance the Babylonians.[30]

Certainly for some writers some Christian theology and the *Leviticus* passage are problematic on many levels. Four prominent female writers, Nancy Eiesland, Sharon Betcher, Hannah Lewis and Jennie Weiss Block, use their own lived out experience of disability to inform their liberation theologies and to challenge more traditional theology. They argue that this lived experience gives them a privileged position from which to comment on disability and theology. Possibly foremost of these four is Nancy Eiesland who died in 2009 aged forty four from possible lung cancer. She lived her life with a congenital bone defect that, she said, made her who she was and in this way she perhaps speaks for many disabled people who write on theologies of disabilities: her disablity defined her identity and character so much so that she hoped that in the next life she would still be disabled; she does not want to be 'fixed' in heaven.[31] This is why in her writings she takes issue with the idea that theology seems to equate disability with moral impurity, a view that she feels persists in theology today. She feels that theology mistakenly promotes disability as virtuous suffering and the passive acceptance of social barriers; she is perturbed by the idea that tackling disability is seen as a matter of charity.[32]

These four writers identify a tendency in Christianity to see hope in the next life for a 'fixed' body and they see the miracle cures of Jesus as a foretaste of this. As Sharon Betcher argues, in Christianity's notion of 'world brokenness' the Fall has something to do with the body and the body is treated as defective needing to be made whole.[33] Hannah Lewis explores the way in which healing miracles are linked to wholeness and so holiness and she suggests that the link made between sin and disability is like the medical model of disability in that it does not take account of the actual person.[34] Hannah Lewis considers the episode where the disciples of John the Baptist come to ask if Jesus is the one who is to inaugurate the Kingdom of God and Jesus replies with the evidence that the blind see and the lame walk.[35] Her interpretation is that this encounter carries the implication that 'all people with disabilities will be physically healed, that if you are not healed, you cannot be a member of the kingdom of God'.[36]

In response these writers explore how Scripture and Church have contributed to oppression and how Scripture may be reinterpreted usually through the focus on discipleship.[36] As Hannah Lewis explains in her book *Deaf Liberation Theology*, from her own experience 'Deaf people' see themselves as members of a minority group who are being oppressed by a Church unconscious of its oppression. Hannah Lewis draws a distinction between culturally Deaf people, the focus on the capital 'D' and people who are deaf, that is have significant hearing loss but who do not necessarily identify themselves as culturally deaf.[38] Jennie Weiss Block, an advocate for the disabled, perhaps sums up the position of a liberation theology of disability: there is nothing wrong with being disabled and people with disabilities do not want sympathy or pity but rather equality, independence and inclusion;[39] 'people with disabilities must tell their own stories, recover their own histories and claim their own voice and language';[40] and they want to formulate their own theology from their history and culture.

It appears that this theology can be characterised by the way in which God is re-imaged.[41] Such a re-imaging that has perhaps become iconic is Nancy Eiesland's vision of a disabled God. In seeking to reconceptualise disablement and rethink what is 'normal' Nancy Eiesland takes the image of the resurrected Christ who shows his wounds, God who is disabled, as a new model of wholeness. She explains that this Jesus is neither an imperial Lord nor a suffering servant: he is not cured or made whole and his injuries remain with him; he is a survivor. Jennie Weiss Block offers 'an accessible God' through her 'theology of access',[42] a God who through disability reminds us that his 'ways are not our ways'.[43] The Gospel message is of a God who welcomes everyone and who obliges everyone to put an end to oppressive structures and attitudes; hearing the voice of people with disabilities is part of this message of inclusion.

Undoubtedly liberation theologies of disabilities present a strong case: as Gustavo Gutierrez points out the most important part in liberation is played by the people themselves who belong to marginalised groups to make their voices heard, to emerge from invisibility.[44] And the 'ultimate commitment' to these people is found 'in the God of our faith'.[45] He adds that a preference for these 'absent ones'[46] is not some radical, progressive theology.[47] Rather it is 'an essential element in the understanding that the Church as a whole has of its task in the present world'.[48]

Still, what remains problematic is the situation of people with intellectual disabilities: Nancy Eiesland's disabled God has physical wounds; it seems more challenging to envisage a God with mental impairment. Moreover, given that the commitment of liberation theologies of disability, along with liberation theologies in general involves reflecting the experience of the oppressed, the disabled themselves, so that they become the agents of their own destiny and thus the danger of imposing 'foreign categories' on them is avoided[49] it is difficult to see how those people with the profoundest of intellectual disabilities can achieve this.

Further problematic issues that arise from the commitment of liberation theologies are those of conflict and exclusivity. Gustavo Gutierrez calls these issues liberation theology's 'painful moments' with the Church and he mentions especially liberation theology's singular homing in on the preferential option for the poor.[50] Still, Gustavo Gutierrez considers the ensuing difficult debate to have been 'an enriching experience'.[51] Certainly it seems that both liberation theology's methodology and critique of what many saw as oppressive Church structures created much tension within the Church. Nevertheless liberation theologies have been influential. Indeed Pope John Paul remarks that 'liberation theology is not only timely but useful and necessary'.[52] However he adds that its true significance and influence emerge when it remains consistent with the teachings of the Gospel, the living tradition of the Magisterium and in company with the reflection of the Church's Social Teaching: 'it should be seen as a new stage, closely connected with earlier ones in the theological reflection that began with the apostolic tradition and has continued in the great fathers and doctors, the ordinary and extraordinary exercise of the Church's teaching office, and more recently, the rich patrimony of the Church's social teaching'.[53] Taken with this broader connection Pope John Paul thinks that the Church's mission to the marginalised, the poor and the suffering demonstrates not an exclusive love, that is one that excludes those who are not poor, but a preferential one.[54]

A preferential option for the poor and the disabled: conflict and exclusivity?

Although the language of 'preferential option for the poor' comes out of the South American liberation theology experience it seems equally important to point out that traces of the option for the marginalised predate the CELAM conferences albeit in at times a radically different form. It has already been noted that concern for the poor and marginalised permeates Scripture. Still in more modern times the idea of option for the poor emerges in *Rerum novarum* written in 1891 by Pope Leo XIII and this document is the first of what are referred to as the Church's social encyclicals. Even though the focus is on the poor, much of what is said is translated in subsequent Church documents to those who are marginalised and the disabled.

In *Rerum novarum* Pope Leo XIII is particularly concerned with poverty, abject working conditions and the apparent appeal of Marxism with its class struggle as the solution. In perhaps stark contrast to the approach of liberation theologies Pope Leo does not intend to alter substantially the structures of capital and labour, indeed he believes that both should live in harmony,[55] and it seems that he takes this view out of concern for the devastation and misery that revolution brings in its wake. Furthermore, unlike many liberation theologians for whom Marxist analysis became a useful tool, Marxism and socialism for Pope Leo cannot have any place in Christian thought since they are fundamentally atheistic, materialistic and their basis in conflict is a threat to the stability of society.[56] Instead Pope Leo's response is to promote charity and mercy[57] as well as a just wage[58] to alleviate poverty, misery and exclusion. Furthermore he calls on states to improve the common good and the life of the poor so that the whole community flourishes. He recognises that all are citizens and that since all contribute to the common good even though in different ways all are entitled to a share in that good.[59] In view of the concerns of some liberation theologies of disability that refuse any sympathetic concern as an exercise in charity not equality, at the outset it is important to note that Pope Leo's option for the poor is not simply to be characterised as charitable handouts under a different disguise. Pope Leo is keen to point out that poverty in itself is not a disgrace and that God always inclines himself more to the poor who are particularly blessed. According to Pope Leo true human dignity lies not in wealth but in righteous living[60] and the poor are blessed because they are close to God. Moreover dignity is given to them by Christ who was himself a poor carpenter.[61]

Similarly in 1959 Pope John XXIII spoke of the Church and those 'particularly dear to us in the intimate love of Christ'. He includes those who suffer from misery, anxiety, who are sick and infirm, weak and fragile and the poor.[62] In answer to those who suggest that the option for the poor is an exclusive principle Gustavo Gutierrez himself refers to Pope John XXIII's pronouncement that the Church is 'for all, and in particular the Church of the poor'[63] thus assuring the universality of God's love. Moreover, in his maxim 'look, judge, act' Pope John XXIII offered a practical approach to social ethics that aims at putting teaching into practice.[64] 'Knowing how to look' and praxis are central according to Gustavo Gutierrez.[65] This 'knowing how to look' may be the starting point for addressing the ignorance and indifference that seems to blight the care of people with disabilities and the elderly where it is not so much an evil intention as an inability to see the other as an other that is at issue.

Whilst Pope Paul VI appears to agree with liberation theologians that each local community has to respond to its own particular situation[66] thus suggesting that the methodology begins from experience and praxis rather than abstract theory, like his predecessors Pope Paul VI expands the 'poor' to adapt to new social problems. Given the new problems of urbanisation, loneliness and alienation[67] Pope Paul VI now identifies the 'new "poor"' as the disabled and marginalised and those subject to discrimination.[68]

Meanwhile Liberation theologies themselves came under severe criticism from the Vatican for being overly influenced by Marxism, for encouraging class conflict in their focus on the oppressed poor and for portraying Christ as a political figure with the Kingdom of God placed similarly in a political light. Moreover, some liberation theologians judged and condemned the 'institutional' Church whilst claiming that a 'new Church' was springing from the poor whose consciousness had now been raised.[69]

Having had first hand experience of Marxism in Poland and convinced that the truth of the Church is guaranteed as the Body of Christ, it is hardly surprising that Pope John Paul seems less than enthusiastic towards theologies that seem to espouse Marxist philosophy and reject as corrupt the 'official' Church even if he finds some of the ideas of liberation theologies timely. The writer Peter Hebblethwaite explains that at the CELAM conference in Puebla in 1979 Pope John Paul offers 'an alternative form of the theology of liberation' that affirms liberation theology's concern for social justice but does so by taking as the starting point the traditional perspective of the source of theology, Scripture and Tradition rather than starting with the local situation.[70] However, Peter Hebblethwaite also points out that Pope John Paul well understood certain notions of liberation in the secular context that lead to essentially an atheistic humanism, one that reduces the human being to his or her material aspect.[71] So, Pope John Paul counters it is the 'complete truth' about the human person, the unity of the human person as bodily and spiritual, that constitutes the foundation of the Church's social teaching and is the basis for true liberation.[72]

These references to the Church's social teaching indicate that the nearness of otherwise marginalised people to Christ and the Church is theologically grounded. It is important to note that 'preferential' does not denote merely 'more' or 'special' and 'option' does not indicate simply choice. Nor does 'option for the poor' suggest any exclusivity. This is because theology asks us to love first as Jesus loved and to move from love of the marginalised towards love for all people. Gustavo Gutierrez adds that a commitment to people who are marginalised and excluded means 'to enter this world of the poor'. The significance here is that 'this action brings about something important: friendship. There is no genuine solidarity with the poor if there is no friendship with them' and friendship is considering 'the other as equal'.[73] Critically for people who are disabled and who are often treated as invisible this friendship with the other as an equal is also giving the loved one an identity, bringing them out of anonymity.[74]

Summary

Liberation theologies of disability seek to enable the voiceless to be heard on their own terms and to foster equality and freedom from oppression. For liberation theologies of disability the notion of equality and friendship between all human beings whatever their condition is crucial. Some of these theologies also present a re-visioning of God as disabled and this provides both a powerful and a challenging image. However, whilst Pope John Paul is keen to work out of human experience as a source for reflection, as shown in his *Theology of the Body*, he also appears wary of either reducing that source to its purely materialistic aspect or of taking it as the only source of reflection.

The following two chapters address some of the issues that liberation theologies of disability raise. Firstly in what are commonly referred to as his social encyclicals Pope John Paul positions the experience of people with disabilities at the centre of Church teaching alongside the experience of all those who are marginalised by societies. Taking the perspective that is entirely grounded in the Second Vatican Council that 'man is the way of the Church and Christ is the way of man' Pope John Paul contributes decisively to Catholic Social Teaching in a way that includes all people whether with disabilities or not in the family of humankind: they do not and should not stand apart from other human beings. Moreover, as human beings who are often marginalised, people with profound disabilities become a particular concern of the Church. Secondly, in his writings on suffering Pope John Paul presents a deeply theological approach to disability that goes beyond the demands of liberation theologies.

Notes

1. Vatican II, *Gaudium et spes*, 1.
2. K. Wojtyła, *Sources of Renewal* (London: Fount, (1975) 1980), p. 273.
3. Pope John Paul II, *Redemptor Hominis*, 13.
4. See Vatican II, *Gaudium et spes*, 27.
5. M. Oliver, *Understanding Disability from Theory to Practice* (New York: Palgrave, 1996), p. 10.
6. *Ibid.*, p. 9.
7. *Ibid.*, pp. 11–13.
8. G. Gutierrez, *A Theology of Liberation: History, Politics and Salvation* (New York: Orbis, 1988), p. xviii.
9. *Ibid.*, p. xx.

10. G. Gutierrez, 'Renewing the option for the poor', in D. Batstone et al (eds.), *Liberation Theologies, Postmodernity and the Americas* (London: Routledge, 1997), p. 72.

11. See *Lv*19:10; *Dt* 24:14.

12. *Ex* 23:10–11; *Lv* 25:2–7; *Dt* 24:19–21.

13. *Ex* 22:24; *Lv* 25:35–38.

14. *Dt* 24:6.

15. *Dt* 24:14.

16. *Ex* 22:25; *Dt* 24:12–13.

17. *Ex* 22:20–22; *Dt* 24:15.

18. *Ex 22:20; 23:9; Lv* 25:38; *Dt* 24:22.

19. G. Gutierrez, *A Theology of Liberation: History, Politics and Salvation* Introduction.

20. *Ibid.*, p. xx.

21. C. Curran, *Catholic Social Teaching 1891–present. A historical, theological and ethical analysis* (Washington: Georgetown University Press, 2002), p. 185.

22. G. Gutierrez, *A Theology of Liberation: History, Politics and Salvation* p. xxi.

23. *Ex* 29:37; *Lv* 6:11.

24. *Lv* 19:7–8

25. E. Gerstenberger, *Leviticus: A Commentary* (London: Westminster John Knox Press, 1993), pp. 317–318.

26. *Lv* 21:22.

27. *Dt* 23:2.

28. See *Is* 56:3–4.

29. *Mt* 8:4; *Lk* 17:14; *Lv* 14:1–32.

30. E. Gerstenberger, *Leviticus: A Commentary* p. 318.

31. N. Eiesland, *The Disabled God: Toward a Liberatory Theology of Disability* (Nashville: Abingdon Press, 1994). See also J. W. Block *Copious Hosting: a theology of access for people with disabilities* (New York: Continuum International, 2002), pp. 17–18; S. Betcher, *Spirit and the Politics of Disablement* (Minneapolis: Fortress Press, 2007), p. 5.

32. N. Eiesland, *The Disabled God: Toward a Liberatory Theology of Disability* pp. 73–74.

33. S. Betcher, *Spirit and the Politics of Disablement* p. ix.

34. H. Lewis, *Deaf Liberation Theology* (Aldershot: Ashgate, 2007), pp. 65–67.

35. *Mt* 11:2–6.

36. H. Lewis, *Deaf Liberation Theology* p. 67.

37. See B. Patterson, 'Redeemed Bodies: Fullness of Life', in N. Eiesland and D. Saliers (eds.), *Human Disability and the Service of God. Reassessing Religious Practice* (Nashville: Abingdon Press, 1998), pp. 126–127; C. Grant 'Reinterpreting the Healing Narratives' in *Human Disability and the Service of God. Reassessing Religious Practice* Ch. 3; S. Horne, 'Those Who Are Blind See: Some New Testament Uses of Impairment, Inability and Paradox' in *Human Disability and the Service of God. Reassessing Religious Practice* Ch. 4; J. W. Block, *Copious Hosting: a theology of access for people with disabilities* Ch. 7.

38. H. Lewis, *Deaf Liberation Theology* p. x.

39. J. W. Block, *Copious Hosting: a theology of access for people with disabilities* pp. 17–18.

40. *Ibid.*, p. 97.

41. See D. Creamer, 'Theological Accessibility: The Contribution of Disability' in *Disability Studies Quarterly* 26/4 (2006) <http://dsq-sds.org/article/view/812/987> [accessed 8 March 2011].

42. J. W. Block, *Copious Hosting: a theology of access for people with disabilities* p. 11.

43. *Ibid.*, p. 91.

44. G. Gutierrez, *A Theology of Liberation: History, Politics and Salvation* p. xxiii.

45. *Ibid.*, p. xxvii.

46. *Ibid.*, p. xxi.

47. *Ibid.*, p. xxix.

48. *Ibid.*, p. xxviii.

49. G. Gutierrez, *A Theology of Liberation: History, Politics and Salvation* p. xxix; J. W. Block *Copious Hosting: a theology of access for people with disabilities* p. 97.

50. G. Gutierrez, *A Theology of Liberation: History, Politics and Salvation* p. xviii.

51. *Ibid.*, p. xviii.

52. Pope John Paul II, *Letter to the Bishops of Brazil* (9 April 1986), 5.

53. *Ibid.*

54. *Ibid.*, 3.

55. Pope Leo XIII, *Rerum Novarum,* 17.

56. Pope Leo XIII, *Quod Apostolici Muneris.*

57. Pope Leo XIII, *Rerum Novarum,* 30.

58. *Ibid.*, 25, 44–46.

59. *Ibid.*, 33, 34.

60. *Ibid.*, 30.

61. *Ibid.*, 24.

62. Pope John XXIII, *Christmas Message* (23 December 1959).

63. G. Gutierrez, 'Renewing the option for the poor' in *Liberation Theologies, Postmodernity and the Americas* p. 74. Although Gutierrez does not reference this it appears to be from a radio broadcast.

64. Pope John XXIII, *Mater et Magistra*, 236.

65. G. Gutierrez, 'Renewing the option for the poor' in *Liberation Theologies, Postmodernity and the Americas* p. 76.

66. Pope Paul VI, *Octogesima Adveniens*, 4.

67. *Ibid.*, 8–12.

68. *Ibid.*, 15–16.

69. P. Hebblethwaite, 'Liberation Theology and the Roman Catholic Church', in C. Rowland (ed.), *The Cambridge Companion to Liberation Theology* (Cambridge: Cambridge University Press, 2007), p. 214.

70. *Ibid.*, p. 213.

71. *Ibid.*, p. 214.

72. Pope John Paul II, Speech *To members of the 3rd General Conference of the Latin American Episcopate, Puebla* (28 January 1979), I.9.

73. G. Gutierrez, 'Renewing the option for the poor' in *Liberation Theologies, Postmodernity and the Americas*, pp. 72–73.

74. *Ibid.*, p. 75.

6

DISABILITY AND CATHOLIC SOCIAL

TEACHING

The very title of Pope Leo XIII's encyclical *Rerum Novarum* translated as 'Of New Things' perhaps indicates a new appreciation of the modern era and its particular problems. Starting with Pope Leo XIII Catholic Social Teaching begins to be built up more systematically through encyclicals, often written on the anniversary of *Rerum Novarum*, papal addresses and letters, and Bishops' statements and conferences in response to particular historical situations and pastoral issues. This corpus of teaching develops similar themes and offers deeper reflection on perennial subjects such as the true dignity of human beings, the option for the poor and marginalised, the promotion of the common good, justice, subsidiarity and solidarity. Inevitably, given his long pontificate and his concern with ethics Pope John Paul's contribution to Catholic Social Teaching is significant. Whilst the social encyclicals do not address themselves specifically to the issue of disability, the kinds of principles to which they appeal and the language they use are taken up by Pope John Paul in his dialogue with people with disabilities and those who suffer. The fact that the social encyclicals rarely single out people with disabilities is significant in itself: people with disabilities are simply spoken of as part of all people and principles such as justice, solidarity, vocation and participation apply to them as much as to any other person.

Although the term Catholic Social Teaching is usually applied specifically to the modern era since Pope Leo's encyclical marks the start of a more formal body of teaching, this teaching is also recognised to be a broad tradition of thought on social issues in the history of the Church with its roots in Scripture and Church tradition. The earliest Christian communities preached the coming of the Kingdom and developed even earlier Jewish teaching on the care of the poor, the sick, and the stranger. The collection taken by St Paul[1] and the possibility of living a life in common[2] witness to this social concern as does the call to living in right relationships with rulers.[3] Even discussion on the treatment of slaves, however culture bound it may be, and the role and work of laypeople demonstrates that the early Christian communities were concerned with matters of the world and society, with the 'signs of the times'. This concern continued in the writings of the early Church Fathers and their responses to particular pastoral situations. Often such responses reflected the perennial Christian paradox: the tension around the importance of working here-and-now for bringing about the Kingdom and a focus on the future Kingdom.

Pope John XXIII, whose vision it was to set up the Second Vatican Council, perhaps encapsulated the significance of this teaching tradition when he explained that 'the social doctrine of the Church is an integral part of its teaching about human life'.[4] The general ethos of the Second Vatican Council particularly expressed in its conciliar document *Gaudium et spes* maintains that a social ministry, works of justice, peace, and ecology are integral to the Church's mission and not an optional extra. Moreover, this is a theological enterprise serving the reign of God not merely the pursuit of good causes.

Certainly Pope John Paul is aware that the Christian anthropology expressed in Catholic Social Teaching differs from secular thought on the concept of the person. Not only is the person in Christian anthropology seen as both individual and social, the person is also both spiritually perfectible and sinful as well as being intrinsically valuable with an eternal destiny no matter what his or her earthy condition. The Christian person is specifically theological since he and she is made in the image of God. The Christian attitude to social action is also different from a secular perspective since it holds to a tension between the present reality and the eschatological end. Thus there may be unceasing imperatives to change and to ensure progress that is fully human but inevitably these are flawed since we live in the now-but-not yet.

Moreover, in his commentary on *Gaudium et spes* Pope John Paul agrees that a dichotomy affects the modern world and thus creates the 'modern dilemma': the world is 'at once powerful and weak, capable of doing what is noble and what is base, disposed to freedom and slavery, progress and decline, brotherhood and hatred. Man is growing conscious that the forces he has unleashed are in his own hands and that it is up to him to control them or be enslaved by them'.[5] This certainly seems to be the case in the area of disability. On the one hand the media reports instances of abuse and indifference and on the other hand there are clear examples of carers and healthcare workers dedicated to deepening the lives of those with profound disabilities. Technology is used to improve health and living yet some also propose to use it to eradicate certain groups of people by genetic engineering. The area of disability remains an area of ambiguity 'at once powerful and weak'. The Church Fathers at the Second Vatican Council go on to explain that this dichotomy is a symptom of a deeper dichotomy in human beings themselves who as the 'meeting point of many conflicting forces' are divided and confused and even convince themselves that their distorted views of reality are the truth.[6] For the Fathers the key to answering the deepest human questions lies in Christ and it is the task of the Church to rely on Christ in order to 'unfold the mystery that is man' and so tackle the world's problems.[7]

Analysis of the signs of the times over the modern period of Catholic Social Teaching demonstrates that secular ideologies exalt either liberty or equality or economic utility or a mixture of these yet at the same time marginalise solidarity, fraternity, person-in-community, and mutual responsibility. For theological reasons Catholic Social Teaching concentrates on what is so often neglected at the secular level and offers a combined focus on principles like justice, option for the poor, subsidiarity, principles that express what is being marginalised. However, it is not only what is being marginalised, more significantly it is who. So the demands of Catholic Social Teaching place the focus on the human person in his or her vulnerability and fragility and Pope John Paul returns the principle of a preferential option for the poor to beyond economic need. This means that people with disabilities are an integral part of this preferential option and this option reaffirms the inalienable dignity of every human being whatever his or her condition.

Human dignity and the person with profound disability

When the Fathers of the Second Vatican Council looked at the joys, hopes, fears and anguish of the world they saw that their foremost task was to guide people towards solutions that were 'fully human'.[8] To do that they first considered the question 'what is man' in the light of the difficulties, distortions and confusions of modern thinking. And they began from the perspective of the dignity of the human person as the foundation of Church teaching.

Whilst it appears easy to speak of inalienable dignity attempting to discuss it without being precise about it may lead to confusion. Certainly the notion of human dignity is problematic not least because there is disagreement on what it actually means and the complex relationship it has to other notions such as freedom and justice.[9] Moreover, the term dignity is often used on both sides of a debate and in the UK this was particularly apparent in the dispute between the Voluntary Euthanasia Society and the Association of Palliative Medicine.

'Dignity' was adopted by the Voluntary Euthanasia Society to champion their cause when the society changed its name to 'Dignity in Dying'. Vivid accounts of the failure to treat certain people with dignity no doubt fuel some of the calls for the legalisation of assisted suicide and euthanasia. Rather than fear of paralysis from severe illness, many supporters of a change in legislation are paralysed by fear: the fear of a loss of autonomy is cited as being the reason for choosing assisted death in ninety seven per cent of cases; being less able to engage in enjoyable activities eighty six per cent; and ninety two per cent of people said that loss of dignity was the main reason why they were choosing assisted death.[10] According to Deborah Annetts, Chief Executive of the Voluntary Euthanasia Society at the time of the name change, 'the word "dignity" emphasises, for me, that the dying person's wishes must be paramount'.[11] Of course to be pedantic it could be pointed out that people are not often dying until they embark upon an assisted dying programme nor is it an exercise of autonomy if a person requires assistance. Moreover, it is arguably difficult to claim, as does the Dignity in Dying website, that 'vulnerable groups of people have not been negatively impacted on by physician assisted dying or voluntary euthanasia' if the reasons put forward to support assisted death focus on 'patient control and quality of life rather than pain control and being a burden'[12] when loss of control means that the person will inevitably cross the threshold into one of those 'vulnerable groups' who may, as research shows, be treated as less than persons, a fate presumably worse than death. Nevertheless, Deborah Annetts's comments place dignity in the context of autonomy and control. In so doing it seems to move many profoundly disabled people, particularly the intellectually disabled, beyond the pale of dignity.

For many and certainly for the Association of Palliative Medicine this name change by the Voluntary Euthanasia Society in effect hijacked the concept of dignity. In a bid to persuade Alan Johnson, the then Trade and Industry Secretary, to oppose the change the Association of Palliative Medicine argued that people did indeed want 'dignity in dying'. But what they were asking for was good care not euthanasia or assisted suicide.[13] However the quarrel between the Association and the Voluntary Euthanasia Society did raise a common cause: both bodies call for people to be treated with dignity, to avoid being placed in undignified situations. It is just that 'dignity' bears different meanings: for the Association it refers to good and care-ful care, for the Society it refers to being in control and autonomy. Yet perhaps the major difference is that for Dignity in Dying, the Voluntary Euthanasia Society, once a person is in an undignified situation then that person has lost all dignity. In contrast the Association of Pallliatve Medicine is concerned to maintain the dignity of all its patients by attempting to avoid undignified situations. Nevertheless it also seems to recognise that all human beings retain their dignity no matter what their situation.

In the light of apparent disagreement on the import of dignity an exploration of its roots may prove insightful. According to the *Oxford English Dictionary* the term dignity derives from the Latin *dignitatem* and denotes merit or worth or a standard of excellence. In his historical account of the term Daniel Sulmasy, an American doctor, lecturer and Franciscan friar noted for his writing on spirituality and end of life care, points out that dignity does not seem to be an important word in Hebrew or Christian scriptures or in classical Western moral philosophy.[14] Daniel Sulmasy places the significance of *dignitatem* in Roman stoicism particularly the writings of Cicero, where it refers not to the subjective evaluation of others rather it involves the 'ability of everyone to recognize an instance of true human excellence'. Daniel Sulmasy contrasts this first Stoic interpretation with other interpretations of dignity: second, the Hobbesian notion that worth depends on one's value or price to the Commonwealth regardless of whether it is deserved because of one's excellence as a human being or one's nature as a human being; third, the Kantian notion linked to Kant's demand that a person should not be treated merely as an instrument of another's will, that the dignity of a person involves a worth that has no price and where humanity itself is a dignity. Whatever the differing interpretations, the notion of dignity seems to have been behind many significant events such as the abolition of slavery and the rise of human rights as well as the condemnation of actions of self-harm such as self-mutilation and drug addiction.[15]

Although as Daniel Sulmasy indicates dignity is a relative newcomer to debates on bioethical issues and economic justice and he adds, 'for almost two millennia, it was not an important theological term', the import it seems to carry seems to have a theological foundation in the understanding of human beings made in the image and likeness of God and therefore, unlike the status of other animals, created to be in a special relationship with their Creator. It seems then that the concept of dignity started out as a notion to denote some merit that publicly distinguished a person from others and so singling that person out as deserving of some honour. Then with Christianity's focus on human beings as images of God the attitude each human being is to take to the other is to see the other as another Christ so dignity now relies on solidarity rather than setting someone apart.

In order to ground human dignity Pope John Paul takes as his starting-point the special relationship human beings have with their Creator and he offers what he calls 'a precise biblical anthropology':[16] human beings are made in the image and likeness of God, they have fallen into sin but have been redeemed through the passion, death and resurrection of Jesus Christ. As destined to share eternal life in friendship with God, human beings journey towards this communion with Christ who is the perfect image of the Father. The dignity of the human being arises from this gracious gift whereby God has raised humanity to a supernatural level. Human dignity does not then rest upon a human being's abilities either of reason or of the practice of autonomy. Rather it is founded on his or her reality as a human person. This dignity 'remains the same to the last moment of one's life' no matter what the condition of a living person and neither is it lessened even in the most debilitating of disabilities nor reduced through problems in communicating with others.[17]

Just as it is with all human beings the dignity of a person with disabilities rests on his or her nature as a human person destined for friendship with God. As the document from the 1999 *Vatican Conference on the Family and Integration of the Disabled* adds, 'it is impossible even to entertain the hypothesis that God might have been "mistaken" when he created disabled children. On the contrary, we must say that God loves them personally, and that these children, thus conformed to the suffering Christ, are the object of his special tenderness'.

Pope John Paul's extensive writings on the human person demonstrate that he has taken the defence of the dignity of each and every human being to be a priority. Given contemporary attacks on the dignity of the most vulnerable in society a significant tool in this defence is the requirement of justice a principle in Catholic Social Teaching that presents the demands of the Gospel as deepening secular demands.

Justice

From the secular perspective justice is often conceived as to render what is due. Notions of justice can be found in ancient philosophy and the thinking of Aristotle seems particularly influential and has resonance with some modern views. In his *Nicomachean Ethics Book V* Aristotle draws attention to justice as either general or special. Aristotelian general justice seems to consider the man who is just, that is law abiding and fair in conduct as opposed to the man who is unjust, who is lawless, overreaching, or unfair. Justice for Aristotle is also the principal social virtue because it is enacted in relation to someone else and does not merely concern oneself. This special justice has two aspects: in its aspect of distributive justice it deals with distribution of honour or money or some other goods. Such goods are divisible among the members of the community and, for Aristotle, how these goods are distributed seems to depend on the person's contribution to the community. This appears to be according to merit so the virtuous citizen who makes a greater contribution to society can expect greater rewards in honour and respect. In its aspect of rectificatory justice attempts are made to correct the inequalities of an injustice that takes place over a transaction and both parties are treated as equal in order to achieve this aim; the issue here is not about whether the parties are virtuous or vicious. This develops into commutative justice where value is based on goods not on personal merit. Within Aristotle's understanding of justice there does not appear to be space for the person with disability who simply does not measure up to Aristotle's standard archetypal human being.

Arguably as a result of the development of the social model of disability there has been much recent debate about justice in relation to people with disabilities. Although the bioethicist and lecturer in ethics David Wasserman claims that 'in thirty years disabilities have gone from being seen as falling outside the scope of justice to being regarded as a central challenge for theories of justice'[18] it seems that appeal nevertheless is made principally to the notion of distributive justice.[19] This seems to fit in with the rather narrow view of the principle of justice as concerned principally with resource allocation articulated by the text book pioneers of Bioethics, Tom Beauchamp and James Childress though in the sixth edition of their seminal textbook they do consider justice in relation to vulnerability and exploitation.[20] In considering justice some argue that utilitarianism and its principle of equal respect offers a way of distributing resources according to the extent to which the disabled can benefit from these resources. Here the utilitarian principle works to help all those, whether disabled or not, who can most benefit whether or not they are worse off.[21] However, as Peter Singer admits equal consideration of interests 'does not dictate equal treatment' because overall equal treatment may not necessarily lead to a greater pleasure over pain ratio.'[22] Others point to justice in terms of the social model of disability and argue for the equalisation of social and economic environments and the removal of discriminatory attitudes.[23] However, the difficulty of approaches based on distributive justice is that they seem to require either a detailed and intrusive account of personal defects in order to justify some intervention, the conversation often carries undertones of charitable handout or by focusing on discriminatory situations they risk not taking the disability itself seriously.

Catholic Social Teaching has developed some of the Aristotelian notion of justice but has also extended it. To begin with Pope John Paul expresses a commonly held idea that is at risk of being forgotten in a world where autonomy and control is paramount. He reminds the world that 'only by recognising the rights of its weakest members can a society claim to be founded on law and justice'. The members of society that he has particularly in mind are those who appear to live lives that are ineffective, the apparently non-acting person, and he adds that 'discrimination on the basis of effectiveness is just as disgraceful as racial, gender or religious discrimination'.[24] Thus, in Catholic Social Teaching general justice has developed into social justice, the justice that regulates social relationships and the Church calls for commutative, distributive and legal justice to be respected.[25] Nevertheless Catholic Social Teaching makes use of a broader notion of justice that is built upon biblical justice. Whilst the 'golden rule' or ethic of reciprocity 'treat others as you would wish to be treated' is widely recognised in secular and religious societies Jesus's command to his followers in John's Gospel, 15:12 is to 'love one another as I have loved you'. This perhaps allows for a better understanding of justice that is not about treating everyone as equal since it is patently obvious that everyone is not the same. Rather it accepts that difference can become a matter of complimentarity where justice and love can see the disabled as 'differently abled'.[26]

However Pope John Paul also has full appreciation of the concrete situation of each person. He understands that there are some realities that require an appropriate response. So he also acknowledges that there is a 'subtle form of discrimination' in some political and educational projects that 'seek to conceal or deny the deficiencies of disabled people by proposing lifestyles and objectives that do not correspond to their reality'. Pope John Paul has at heart here the well being of disabled people because he realises that such proposals often lead to unjust and frustrating outcomes. Instead he calls for a fitting approach as a matter of justice, 'a continual and loving attention to the lives of others', so that the response takes account of 'the special and different needs of every individual, taking into consideration his or her abilities and limitations'.[27] In terms of what should be done Pope John Paul calls for a 'sincere commitment on the part of all to create practical living conditions, structures which provide support and legal protection' and the promotion of 'the integral good' of the disabled even, he adds, if this 'entails a greater financial and social burden'.[28]

In keeping with the drive of Catholic Social Teaching, conformation to Christ calls for a striving to bring about the Kingdom in the here-and-now. It cries out at the injustice of attacks against human life. It demands attention to the full needs of the disabled including their right to appropriate work, a just wage, the possibility of promotion and the elimination of obstacles.[29] It recognises the need to have just and authentic relationships.[30] It presses for doing what is 'truly good' for the disabled.[31] As Pope John Paul points out what is 'just' is determined by the identity of the human being who is not only an other but also an image of God and so is to be loved with the same love as Jesus loves him or her.[32] Thus, for Pope John Paul justice is opened up to the new horizon of love and solidarity.[33]

Solidarity and the foundation of a sensitivity to the needs of the disabled

For Pope John Paul solidarity is a leading principle not only because it deepens justice and so brings about peace but also because it is a virtue that contributes to the cohesion of society into a real community. He explains that through solidarity members of society 'recognise one another as persons'; it helps us to see the other as '"neighbour", a "helper" (cf Genesis 2:18-20) to be made a sharer, on a par with ourselves, in the banquet of life to which all are equally invited by God'.[34] Thinking in the context of the *Theology of the Body* helper is one who aids the development of the other so that he or she flourishes as a person. This is a mutual help so that each of the companions, no matter what their capabilities, help the other and each share the banquet, the bread, together. In this solidarity Pope John Paul says that the strong are responsible for the weak and the weak are not purely passive. Rather they do what they can for the good of all.[35]

In terms of the mission of the Church Pope John Paul believes that it is necessary to promote a 'spirituality of communion', *koinonia*, for without charity/love, *agape*, 'all will be in vain.[36] According to Pope John Paul the spirituality of communion, *koinonia*, has a double aspect: principally 'the heart's contemplation of the mystery of the Trinity dwelling in us' and then the light of the Trinity we see 'shining on the face of the brothers and sisters around us'[37] and so *koinonia* is an expression of the commandment to love God and to love our neighbour. Certainly the Church, as Body of Christ, is to form a 'profound unity' so that each member sees others as 'those who are a part of me' and consequently enables each to share their joys and sufferings, attend to their needs, 'to offer them deep and genuine friendship' so that each becomes 'gift' for the other and each bears the other's burdens.[38] Nevertheless, Pope John Paul sees the mission of the Church as witness to this love and as a going out into the world to bring this charity/love, *agape* to the marginalised. However, he is clear that this is not charity in the sense of what could be seen as 'a humiliating handout'. Rather it is a '"getting close" to those who suffer', a 'sharing between brothers and sisters' and a defence of 'the values rooted in the very nature of the human person'.[39] And this 'getting close' is not merely approaching the other. It is recognising the other as an other and it involves a 'being there' for the other person, seeking the good of the other.

According to Pope John Paul it is the 'fundamental fact' that the disabled person is 'a person, a human being' that in itself brings as awareness of his or her value and dignity. It is this fact of being a person and not the possession of 'secondary qualities' like strength or physical appearance that matters.[40] Pope John Paul explains that the demands of solidarity make it clear that there can be no discrimination against disabled people, particularly discrimination 'by the strong and healthy against the weak and sick'. In addition disabled people must be helped to take their place in society 'as far as is compatible with their capabilities' and members of society must foster their full integration.[41] Whilst recognising that there may be the need for a 'change of heart, a conversion' so that every person may accept every disabled person 'willingly and fraternally' in all areas of life[42] Pope John Paul makes a significant statement regarding the disabled themselves. They play he says 'an important part in creating a new civilization, the civilization of love, by removing social barriers and bringing in new values, the values not of force but of humanity'.[43] In itself this appears to be an interesting reversal of the social model of disability in the sense that Pope John Paul seems to be saying that it is not so much the abled who remove barriers thus removing disability, rather it is the disabled who remove the barriers so that the abled can come to realise that what they think is defining of personhood, strength and control is in fact a denial of the dependence of all human beings not only on others but more significantly on God. Moreover, they witness to Christ's message 'that has emphasized the absolute value of life and of the human person, who comes from God and is called to live in communion with God', a message that Pope John Paul explains can be found in Christ's own life of service and love for the sick and suffering and his call to his disciples to do the same.[44]

This refocusing of the part played by people with disabilities can be found in the Christian tradition. Confronted with the neo-platonic argument that bodily grossness or disability is determined by that person's past sins committed in his or her former celestial body St Augustine argues that people then commonly called *moriones*, the intellectually disabled, are in fact Christian witnesses who show that God's grace and the Spirit do not pass over any kind of capacity. Indeed St Augustine says they may have a preference of grace over people with a keener intellect.[45] This witness that the person with disabilities makes to the fundamental fact that he or she is fully a human person called to share the same destiny as all other human beings is an expression of his or her human dignity.

In the Christian tradition not only do all human beings have 'a transcendent vocation that goes beyond history and time'[46] they also have a vocation in the here-and-now.

Vocation

Certainly the Church sees all human beings including the weak and suffering, as gifts of God and as expressions of God's goodness.[47] Indeed, the weak and suffering are particularly close to God and so the Church sees in every human life 'the splendour of that "Yes", that "Amen", which is Christ himself'.[48] Moreover, as a consequence of the transcendent vocation of every human being, this call to friendship with God, no human being can be considered redundant, inconvenient or unproductive. However, Pope John Paul takes the vocation of the sick and disabled beyond their call to share God's life. As he explains in *Christifideles laici*, his encyclical on the mission and vocation of the lay faithful in the Church and in the world, in the earthly sphere:

> The Lord addresses his call to each and every one. *Even the sick are sent forth as labourers into the Lord's vineyard:* the weight that wearies the body's members and dissipates the soul's serenity is far from dispensing a person from working in the vineyard. Instead the sick are called to live their human and Christian vocation and to participate in the growth of the Kingdom of God in a *new and even more valuable manner.*[49]

He addresses this specifically to the marginalised and abandoned who the Church needs above all 'to teach the whole world what love is'. This teaching is not merely allowing others to show their love and their care even though John Paul does rightly associate it with the parable of the Good Samaritan and he celebrates the vocation of carers and healthcare workers, a call that 'becomes the living sign of Jesus Christ and his Church in showing love towards the sick and suffering'.[50] For Pope John Paul it is not enough to regard the sick or disabled person as simply 'an object of the Church's love and service'. What is more vital is to see that person as 'an *active and responsible participant in the work of evangelization and salvation*' (his italics).[51] Although Pope John Paul is keen to point out that every person possesses 'charisms and ministries, diverse yet complementary' and 'works in the one and the same vineyard of the Lord', he also ardently explains that 'simply in *being* Christians, even before actually *doing* the works of a Christian, all are branches of the one fruitful vine which is Christ' (his italics).[52] This unity of human beings with each other and with Christ becomes more deeply understood when it is seen that each person is called to participate in the 'salvific suffering of Christ' that is transformed in the joy of the resurrection and so each is called to 'become a force for the sanctification and building up of the Church'. And Pope John Paul is well aware that such a vocation may be easy to describe, yet it becomes an even more credible and enduring witness when it 'passes into a testimony of life'.[53]

Perhaps summing up his conviction that the disabled are indeed 'labourers in the vineyard' for Pope John Paul, people with disabilities can bring from within themselves exceptional energy and values of great use for the whole of humanity so that he or she is not only one to whom we give; he or she must also be helped to become one who gives to the best of his or her abilities.[54] Such help is involved in Pope John Paul's understanding of participation.

Participation and people with disabilities

Before he became Pope Karol Wojtyła wrote extensively on the importance of participation in his 1975 paper *Participation or Alienation?* As he explains participation has its foundation in the understanding each person has of the other as also 'an I', as neighbour.[55] It is, he says, 'the ability to exist and act together with others in such a way that in this existing and acting we remain ourselves and actualize ourselves, which means our own I's'.[56] In contrast to alienation where a person is closed in on himself or herself and so is neither fully open to others nor to his or her own self, 'participation arises from consciously becoming close to another, a process that starts from the lived experience of one's own I'.[57]

As Pope, John Paul is acutely aware of the isolation of the individual, particularly those who are often subject to marginalisation. In view of this Pope John Paul calls for the balanced but effective integration of disabled people, 'our brothers and sisters' so that they are 'fully members' of the community; furthermore that he or she must be helped to participate in the life of society in all its aspects and 'at all levels accessible to their capacities'.[58] Pope John Paul explains that integration opposes the tendency to isolation, segregation and marginalisation. However he adds that integration is not a mere attitude of tolerance; rather it involves the effort to uphold the disabled person as a fully human subject in his or her own right.[59] Pope John Paul is clear that every disabled person is a fully human subject with 'sacred and inviolable rights'.[60] Moreover, he questions those who seem to view disability in terms of deviation from the norm. Instead he thinks that disability places more emphasis on the mystery of being human with all its dignity and grandeur;[61] it is an aspect of our shared common humanity and by recognising and promoting the rights and dignity of the disabled we recognise and promote our own dignity and rights.[62] He further reminds us that 'the quality of a society and civilisation is measured by the respect it has for the weakest of its members'.[63] Notably, Pope John Paul believes that the disabled have their own aspirations and particular qualities, especially spiritual ones, and they are givers.[64]

Participation then involves affirming and confirming the other as an other and it involves a relationship of equals where each gives to each. For Pope John Paul relationships where each gives to each are naturally found in family relationships, particularly in the bond between parents and their children. Karol Wojtyła's own experience of family life was marked by tragedy: his sister died before Karol was born, his mother when Karol was nine and his beloved brother Edmund died when Karol was twelve. He had a strong and close relationship with his father who died in 1941 when Karol was twenty-one and surviving in war-torn Poland working in a chemical factory in order to avoid deportation to Germany. In his personal life and in the situation of war and oppression in which he found himself Karol was no stranger to suffering and he recognises that suffering is a part of the human condition.

However, perhaps it is the suffering he himself experienced later on in his life that enables him to follow more closely the text of *Gaudium et spes* 22, that 'in reality it is only in the mystery of the Word made flesh that the mystery of man truly becomes clear'. As the footnote to Tertullian explains, 'for in all the form which was moulded in the clay, Christ was in his thoughts as the man who was to be'. The principles of Catholic Social Teaching connect every human being to Christ as the 'way of man'. Pope John Paul profoundly explores this connection and in particular the notion of participation specifically of people with disabilities to Christ through his reflection on the sick and suffering.

Notes

1.   *2Co* 8–9.

2.   *Ac* 2:42–47.

3.   *1 Tm; 1 Pt.*

4.   Pope John XXIII, *Mater et Magistra*, 222.

5.   Vatican II, *Gaudium et spes*, 9; K. Wojtyła, *Sources of Renewal* (London: Fount, (1975) 1980), p. 70.

6.   Vatican II, *Gaudium et spes*, 10.

7.   *Ibid.*, 10.

8.   *Ibid.*, 11.

9.   For extensive writings on human dignity in bioethics see the *Essays Commissioned by the President's Council on Bioethics: Human Dignity and Bioethics* (USA: USA Government Printing Office, 2008).

10. Statistics from Dignity in Dying, http://www.dignityindying.org.uk/research/slippery-slope.html [accessed 14 November 2011].

11. Deborah Annetts, (January 2006), <http://www.dignityindying.org.uk/news/general/n4-voluntary-euthanasia-society-changes-name> [accessed 14 November 2011].

12. Dignity in Dying, <http://www.dignityindying.org.uk/research/slippery-slope.html> [accessed 14 November 2011].

13. See http://news.bbc.co.uk/1/hi/health/4638766.stm.

14. D. Sulmasy, 'Dignity in Bioethics: History, Theory and Selected Applications' in *Essays Commissioned by the President's Council on Bioethics: Human Dignity and Bioethics*.

15. See L. Kass, 'Defending Human Dignity' in *Essays Commissioned by the President's Council on Bioethics: Human Dignity and Bioethics*.

16. See *Vatican Conference on the Family and Integration of the Disabled: Conclusions* 1999.

17. *Ibid.*

18. D. Wasserman, 'Disability, capability and thresholds for distributive justice', in A. Kaufman (ed.), *Capabilities Equality: Basic Issues and Problems* (New York: Routledge, 2006), p. 215.

19. See, for instance, D. Wasserman's analysis in 'Disability, capability and thresholds for distributive justice' in *Capabilities Equality: Basic Issues and Problems* Ch10.

20. T. Beauchamp, J. Childress, *Principles of Biomedical Ethics* (Oxford: Oxford University Press, 2009), Ch.7.

21. See M. Stein, *Distributive Justice and Disability: Utilitarianism against Egalitarianism* (Yale: Yale University Press, 2006), p. 10.

22. P. Singer, *Practical Ethics* (Cambridge: Cambridge University Press, 1997), p. 24.

23. See J. Bickenbach's discussion in 'Disability, Non-talent and Distributive Justice', in K. Kristiansen et al (eds.), *Arguing About Disability: Philosophical Perspectives* (New York: Routledge, 2009), Ch7.

24. Pope John Paul II, *On the Occasion of the International Symposium on the Dignity and Rights of the Mentally Disabled Person* (5 January 2004), 3.

25. Pontifical Council for Justice and Peace, *Compendium of the Social Doctrine of the Church*, 201.

26. Pope John Paul II, Angelus *Jubilee of the Disabled* (3 December 2000), 1.

27. Pope John Paul II, *On the Occasion of the International Symposium on the Dignity and Rights of the Mentally Disabled Person* (5 January 2004), 3.

28. *Ibid.*, 4.

29. Pope John Paul II, *Laborem Exercens*, 22.

30. Pope John Paul II, *On the Occasion of the International Symposium on the Dignity and Rights of the Mentally Disabled Person* (5 January 2004), 5.

31. *Ibid.*, 4.

32. Pope John Paul II, *Sollicitudo Rei Socialis*, 40.

33. *Ibid.*, 39.

34. *Ibid.*

35. *Ibid.*

36. Pope John Paul II, *Novo Millennio Ineunte*, 42.

37. *Ibid.*, 43.

38. *Ibid.*

39. Pope John Paul II, *Novo Millennio Ineunte*, 50–51.

40. Pope John Paul II, Speech *To the participants in the International Games for disabled persons* (3 April 1981), 3.

41. *Ibid.*, 4–5.

42. *Ibid.*, 5.

43. *Ibid.*, 6.

44. *Ibid.*, 7.

45. St Augustine, *On the Merits and Remission of Sins*, I,32.

46. *Vatican Conference on the Family and Integration of the Disabled: Conclusions* II.a.

47. See Pope John Paul II, *Christifideles laici*, 38.

48. *Ibid.*

49. *Ibid.*, 53. His italics.

50. *Ibid.*

51. *Ibid.*,54.

52. *Ibid.*, 55.

53. *Ibid.*

54. Pope John Paul II, *Document of the Holy See for the International Year of Disabled Persons* (4 March 1981), II.12.

55. K. Wojtyła, 'Participation or Alienation?' (1975) in *Catholic Thought from Lublin Vol.IV Person and Community* (New York: Peter Lang, 1993), p. 200.

56. *Ibid.*, p. 200.

57. *Ibid.*, p. 201.

58. Pope John Paul II, *Document of the Holy See for the International Year of Disabled Persons* (4 March 1981), I.1; *Laborem Exercens* 22.

59. Pope John Paul II, *Document of the Holy See for the International Year of Disabled Persons* (4 March 1981), I.4.

60. *Ibid.*, I.1; Idem, *Laborem Exercens* 22.

61. Pope John Paul II, *Document of the Holy See for the International Year of Disabled Persons* (4 March 1981), I.1.

62. *Ibid.*, I.3.

63. *Ibid.*

64. *Ibid.*, II.7.

7

POPE JOHN PAUL II: REFLECTIONS FOR

THE DISABLED, THE SICK AND SUFFERING

In his encyclical *Evangelium vitae, The Gospel of Life* Pope John Paul writes that one of the greatest maladies of the modern world is the emergence of a 'culture of death' and he says that paradoxically this culture is 'an even larger reality' than the widespread moral uncertainty that characterises the modern world.[1] Among other things this culture seems to deny the concrete reality of the human being as an integrated unity of body and soul in relationship with others and with God. It does so by adhering to an excessive materialism that either elevates physical beauty to the neglect of the person's spiritual dimension or reduces the body to a 'complex of organs' so that 'the body is no longer perceived as a properly personal reality'.[2] He notes that in this materialism the first to be harmed are the weak and vulnerable because the culture of death is fuelled by the criteria of 'efficiency, functionality and usefulness': it is 'supremacy of the strong over the weak'.[3] Indeed, he observes that in this culture 'a person who, because of illness, handicap or, more simply, just by existing, compromises the well-being or life-style of those who are more favored tends to be looked upon as an enemy to be resisted or eliminated'.[4]

Pope John Paul is well aware that a challenge to the culture of death cannot simply be a deeper or more innovative reflection on human life nor can it be merely a call for a raised consciousness for the need for changes in society. Even if attitudes are altered more is needed. Instead the challenge has to be rooted in the person of Jesus since it is in Jesus that the complete truth about human beings can be found and this truth embraces not just earthly existence but also eternal life.[5] After all, the culture of death is not merely a contemporary permissive attitude towards abortion or euthanasia. It is more the denial of the fullness of life that goes beyond earthly life; a culture that sets store by things that cannot last.[6] However, Pope John Paul also realises that it is the problem of suffering that presents the greatest stumbling block in the challenge to this prevailing culture.[7] So, whilst he accepts that suffering is a mystery that defies thorough understanding, Pope John Paul sets about deepening a reflection of suffering addressed specifically to those who suffer. For, according to Pope John Paul it is precisely the disabled, the sick and the suffering who witness to the transformative power of Jesus and the culture of life.

World Day for the Sick

Pope John Paul instituted the Pontifical Commission for the Pastoral Assistance to Health Care Workers on the feast day of Our Lady of Lourdes, 11 February 1985. The title of his Motu Proprio setting up this Commission was *Dolentium Hominum,* on the suffering of man. With the Apostolic Constitution *Pastor Bonus* in 1988 the commission became the Pontifical Council for the Pastoral Assistance to Health Care Workers, its aim being to coordinate different areas of the Roman Curia that related to healthcare, to explain Church teaching on health issues and to follow the health care policies of individual countries. To ground this initiative Pope John Paul established by a pontifical letter the World Day for the Sick in 1992 to be celebrated on 11 February, each year having a particular link to a different Marian shrine, the first being the shrine to Our Lady of Lourdes, and the others included the pilgrimage sites of Our Lady of Czestochowa, Yamoussouko, Guadalupe, Fatima, Loreto, Harissa Beirut, Rome, Vailankanny South India. As Pope John Paul explains, this connection to Mary expresses her theological place as a 'living icon of the Gospel of suffering'.[8] Perhaps it also reinforces Pope John Paul's view that human suffering is not a subject of easy explanations rather it is a subject of witness and discipleship.

Whilst he directs *Dolentium Hominum* principally to healthcare workers and the fostering of the service of the Church to the sick, Pope John Paul uses his letters on the annual world days of the sick to speak also to those who are suffering themselves, for, he says, the sick are 'the main actors of this World Day'.[9] The rationale of these world days is that they should be 'a special time of prayer and sharing, of offering one's suffering for the good of the Church and of reminding everyone to see in his sick brother or sister the face of Christ who, by suffering, dying, and rising, achieved the salvation of mankind'.[10] The focus then seems to be on people who are disabled and sick themselves. However, this is not to cast them in a 'sick' or disabled role that points to vulnerability as an occasion for pity. Instead Pope John Paul considers their role in the Church, he explores the challenge of how they can offer their suffering for the good of the Church and he reflects on the fact that they represent the image of Christ, a fact that is there to be discerned by those who come to their assistance.

Of course Nancy Eiesland draws attention to the problem of seeing suffering as virtuous[11] as if suffering is in itself in some way good and it is important at the outset to note that Pope John Paul does not extol suffering in this way at all. Sharon Betcher's complaint against the 'normative culture' is that it uses disabled people by, for instance, celebrating those who overcome tragedy.[12] Pope John Paul's world days of the sick do not fall into this category either. However, in contrast perhaps to liberation theologies of disability where stress is placed on refocusing traditional theology and reinterpreting it through the experience of people with disabilities, Pope John Paul explores theology with a view to enriching and deepening, and perhaps refocusing the personal experience of disability and suffering.

To be sure the possibilities for people with disabilities to model themselves on and identify with Nancy Eiesland's disabled God may allow their experience of disability to gain in depth. But Nancy Eiesland's disabled God is there to challenge perceptions of what is 'normal': as the disabled writer Deborah Creamer explains the 'lens of disability' is 'a promising way to challenge both the ideal body and the normal body'; it suggests that the 'normal' only exists in our imagination and points out that limits on human beings are unsurprising and embrace us all.[13] Deborah Creamer further claims that disability theology is moving towards 'queering', that is to questioning, complicating and pushing towards a complexity that is beyond the assertion that 'we are all disabled'.[14]

Pope John Paul's approach is different. Certainly he sees that 'it is society which is sick and is creating profound distortions in man' and he acknowledges that people with disabilities challenge the perceived norm but this goes further than addressing physical perfection or structural barriers. Pope John Paul refers instead to 'raging egoism', 'individualistic utilitarianism' and 'indifference' to the true destiny of human beings.[15] The problem of the sickness of the world does not relate so much to the reality of human suffering, a reality that is a fact, albeit inexplicable one, of every human life. Rather the problem lies in attitudes and sickness of the heart. Although he draws attention to inequalities in resources and care[16] and he notes in particular injustices and inequalities across the world when it comes to the provision of basic medicine and care[17] Pope John Paul does not concentrate on barriers and exclusion. Although he sees that 'suffering and illness belong to the condition of man, a fragile, limited creature' he does not simply level out everyone so that, even in its complex form, everyone is disabled and therefore somehow equal. Nor does he restrict the limits of human beings to the physical for, he says, the human being is a 'limited creature, marked by original sin from birth'.[18] Moreover, Christians, he says, honour God 'in the human body, both under the captivating aspects of strength, vitality and beauty and under those of fragility and decline'.[19] Although he recognises that people with disabilities are 'among the least' in the world, are often alone and marginalised and that one of the main goals of the world days of the sick is 'to make public opinion sensitive' to people who are suffering[20] Pope John Paul looks more to what people with disabilities do for the world. Although he sees that the Church's 'preferential option for the poor and those suffering in body and soul' is a 'journey of authentic conversion to the Gospel' and part of the quest towards the building up of a 'civilisation of love', Pope John Paul also sees this solidarity with the marginalised as not only of 'sacred and religious value' but as having a value for all since it highlights the significance of life as a gift from God that 'continues to be a gift from him in every circumstance'.[21] Although he urges the creation of concrete projects in Church communities and points to the demand to make the preferential option for the poor, marginalised and disabled 'concrete and visible' the 'special place' reserved for them in the Church is not merely physical, rather it is as signs of hope to the world.[22] Pope John Paul's approach is different because he returns to the theology of mission and it is in mission that all people with disabilities come into their own. People who are sick and have disabilities are, after all, 'also sent out as labourers in the vineyard'.[23]

'Difficult witness' to the new evangelisation

As 'a living part of the Church' Pope John Paul calls attention to the 'difficult witness' and 'special mission' entrusted to people with disabilities and people who suffer. In a reversal of what the 'world' views as the work of the strong supporting the weak Pope John Paul asks disabled persons to 'become a source of strength for the Church and humanity'. Insofar as people who suffer are called to embrace the Cross, they 'give the world the reason for its Gospel hope'.[24] These 'main actors' are challenged to see illness and disability in the light of Christ's death and resurrection so that illness no longer appears an 'exclusively negative event' rather it is 'an opportunity to release love'.[25] In the case of the profoundly intellectually disabled they are witnesses to this. No doubt some would take exception at the apparent description of disability as a 'negative event' but the point Pope John Paul is making is that there is a temptation to see illness and disability as grounds for doubting the goodness of God.[26] On the contrary, according to Pope John Paul the suffering and tribulations that often accompany disability can 'become signs and foundations of future glory'.[27] However, finding meaning in suffering is, he reminds us, a 'difficult path' and it can only take place through the grace offered by the suffering Christ.[28]

The negative aspect of disability perhaps becomes more acute in societies marked by advances in technology and science. Pope John Paul's pontificate spanned a time of great possibilities, opportunities and breakthroughs in the field of medicine. However, as Pope John Paul notes, advances do not necessarily indicate 'real progress' especially where these advances no longer focus on the person and the inviolable dignity of every human being. Pope John Paul observes a 'cult of the body' and a 'hedonistic quest for physical fitness' that brings with it a reductive consideration of 'life as a mere consumer good, setting a new scale of marginalisation for the disabled, the elderly and the terminally ill'.[29] In contrast to contemporary society which seeks to 'build its future on well-being and consumerism and measures everything in terms of efficiency and profit' where the disabled are often seen as redundant or inconvenient Pope John Paul reminds us that people with disabilities, the sick and suffering are witnesses to 'the transcendent value of the human person whose dignity remains intact even in the experience of pain, illness and aging'.[30] And Pope John Paul is in no doubt that those who suffer 'occupy the first place among those whom God loves'.[31]

At the turn of the new millennium, in the year leading up to the days when he watched the pilgrims enter the Holy Door at the end of the Great Jubilee Year of 2000, Pope John Paul, who had suffered from Parkinson's disease since 1992, acknowledged that through his own recent experiences of illness he had come to 'understand more and more clearly' the value of a personal experience of illness for his ministry,[32] testifying perhaps to the importance of reflecting on actual experience. Despite more and more new and effective ways to alleviate suffering Pope John Paul frequently reminds us that suffering remains 'a fundamental fact of human life' that cannot be wholly explained nor overcome by research and treatment.[33] To be sure we should seek new ways to address suffering but illness and suffering will always be a part of human existence: even if cures are found for all devastating illnesses there will always be accidents, natural disasters, human-made tragedies. Moreover, illness and disability seem to be almost moments of *kairos* that prompt, Pope John Paul says, 'even the most heedless person.... to wonder about his own life and its meaning, about the reason for evil, suffering and death'.[34]

Pope John Paul is particularly concerned about a contemporary 'secular mentality' where the powerful predominate and where some societies try to 'remove or ignore urgent questions of suffering' by setting aside and even eliminating the 'powerless'.[35] Not only is this demonstrated in the apparent progress of bioethics where instead of recognising the limits of life, life is prolonged by excessive aggressive medical treatment,[36] where some are not allowed to come to birth or where death is hastened, but it is also evident in the field of genetics, a field 'fundamental in healthcare' that is used as 'an opportunity for inadmissible choices and callous manipulation'.[37] Pope John Paul may be thinking here of genetic engineering, an advance that carries much promise but also many threats to human dignity. On the one hand the promise in genetic engineering is that it can be used to provide therapies to cure a person suffering from a specific illness and when it is directed to the person's well being, when it is not unduly harmful and when proper consent has been given it may be permissible. Pope John Paul encourages this form of genetic engineering 'as long as it respects the rights and dignity of the person from conception'.[38] On the other hand genetic engineering that claims to 'cure' certain genetic conditions by genetic testing so that only healthy embryos are implanted is in fact an example of a eugenic mentality since it reinforces the notion that the youngest of human beings is merely disposable tissue and the undesirable condition is 'cured' by the elimination of the disabled embryo.

In the face of this denial that suffering is an inevitable part of human existence, the refusal to see any meaning in suffering and therefore the modern tendency to deny or remove the experience of suffering by ultimately designating as redundant or inconvenient those who do suffer and even by eliminating them, Pope John Paul believes that sick and disabled people can make an effective contribution. He calls attention to two duties in particular:[39] the first is the defence of life. Pope John Paul explains that at the root of what he calls the 'culture of death' lies a 'Promethean attitude', an attitude of the strong and powerful that seeks to control life and death yet in the process 'crushes hope'. Such an attitude prefers death to living in any form of dependence. Instead he calls for solidarity among all human beings in the defence of life so that even when a person is frail and vulnerable he or she remains a witness to the dignity of every human being. The second duty is the promotion of 'a health worthy of the human being'. Understanding health as 'worthy of human beings' involves being aware of the risks of making health 'an idol to which every other value is subservient'. The problem as Pope John Paul sees it is that some limit health to 'biological perfection' and reduce it to 'pure exuberant vitality and satisfaction with one's own physical fitness'. In this reduction the spiritual and social aspects of the person are ignored and inevitably those who do not match up lose out.

Addressed specifically to those who are ill or suffering Pope John Paul's letters on the world days of the sick offer interesting reflection on the experiences of people with disabilities who suffer as a result of their condition. However perhaps as an impetus to those annual reflections and written a year before *Dolentium hominum* Pope John Paul explored more deeply the experience of suffering in his apostolic letter on the Christian meaning of human suffering, *Salvifici Doloris* written on the liturgical Memorial of Our Lady of Lourdes, February 11 1984. It is necessary to point out that this letter is not specifically addressing people with permanent disabilities, after all some do not think that their condition is one of suffering, rather they view disability as part of their identity. However, many other people do regard their disabilities as a form of suffering and even if a disability in itself is not seen as something 'suffered', suffering often accompanies impairment.

Pope John Paul's reflections on suffering seem to complement the extensive discussion on disability demonstrated by critiques of the various models of disability. Those who criticise the medical model of disability do so on the grounds that it places the 'problem' of disability in the person with disabilities and it seeks to normalise people who it regards as abnormal. Moreover, it does not take account of the structures and attitudes that constitute disability as social exclusion. Those who criticise the social model of disability do so on the grounds that by claiming disability is to do with social barriers it does not take account of the actual experience of impairment suffered by people with disabilities and, in some cases, it is precisely this impairment not social barriers that cannot be overcome. The relatively new 'biopsychosocial model' takes account of both health conditions and contextual factors such as environmental and personal factors and looks at the level of the individual's functioning in terms of the whole of his or her daily life, thus intending to incorporate the best of both the medical and social models of disability. However, this model also can be criticised for attempting to normalise the person though in terms of dysfunction as opposed to function rather than abnormal as opposed to normal. The emphasis on dysfunction as opposed to function and how to assist or manage this 'problem' suggests that what is central is a thinking about ability rather than disability, about how to assist in functioning instead of helping people with disabilities to deal with their lives on their own terms. Certainly each of these models has plus and minus points and it is worthwhile deliberating over them. Nevertheless, it also seems necessary to move beyond descriptive accounts of people's experience of disability or attitudes towards disability and to reflect on the meaning of suffering itself as suffering is often part of the disabled experience. Such suffering is not limited to that which may accompany physical or intellectual impairment. It also includes the experience of isolation, alienation, vulnerability and discrimination.

Salvifici Doloris *On the Christian meaning of human suffering*

Pope John Paul explores suffering in his apostolic letter *Salvifici Doloris* and the perspective he takes is 'the Gospel of Suffering'.[40] In general 'Gospel' refers to the 'good news' of Christ's salvific work as well as the actual telling of the story of Jesus, his life, mission, death and resurrection. To identify suffering with 'good news' is not an oversight on Pope John Paul's part nor is it extolling of suffering for suffering's sake. According to Pope John Paul suffering is an inevitable aspect in the life of every human being and, unlike the actual gospel accounts in the New Testament, Christ himself wrote the Gospel of Suffering: through the suffering of Christ human suffering has been transformed so that every human being can see meaning and hope in his or her suffering and so can come to bear it.

So at the outset Pope John Paul is going to disappoint those who hold to a strong version of the social model of disability that sees disability solely in terms of social barriers and those who urge a liberation theology of disability where liberation is freedom from oppressive structures and attitudes. This is because Pope John Paul does believe that suffering is an experience of evil[41] and that evil is 'a certain lack, limitation or distortion of good'; a human being, he says, particularly suffers when he or she 'ought—in the normal order of things—to have a share in this good and does not have it'.[42] Moreover, he says that salvation is closely bound up with the problem of suffering because 'salvation means liberation from evil'.[43] Pope John Paul adds that this liberation from evil is achieved by Christ through his own suffering, an expression of God's salvific love.[44] So, unlike some liberation theologies that may see liberation in the hands of the suffering and oppressed themselves, for Pope John Paul it does not appear to be a liberation by suffering people themselves without reference to God. Pope John Paul explains that through suffering and disability the body and also the soul is hurting in some way; it is 'a question of pain' not only of a physical nature but also of a spiritual nature. Moreover this suffering is not confined to pain associated with disability. Just as the 'option for the poor' is not exclusive, concerning only the poor, so too is suffering not experienced exclusively by people with disabilities or illness. Suffering, according to Pope John Paul, is 'much wider, more varied, and multidimensional'. And, to disappoint those who hold to a strictly medical model that sees disability in terms of a medical problem to be solved, Pope John Paul continues 'man suffers in different ways, ways not always considered by medicine' and in ways that cannot always be reached by therapy.[45]

To address this pain at least in a partial way Pope John Paul reflects on the salvific meaning of suffering. Speaking more precisely, it is not suffering itself that is the end point so Pope John Paul is not talking of the virtuous suffering critiqued by Nancy Eiesland. Rather the end point is redemption that is accomplished through suffering and more specifically through the Cross of Christ.[46] Pope John Paul can speak with St Paul of rejoicing in suffering as long as it is understood that they refer to rejoicing in the discovery of the salvific meaning of suffering.[47] Here it is important to note that Pope John Paul considers not simply temporal suffering but more significantly 'definitive suffering: the loss of eternal life'; and the Son was given to the world 'primarily to protect man against this definitive evil and against definitive suffering'.[48] This is perhaps why the Church tradition has focused more on the disabling effects of spiritual sins like pride and malice, sins which persuade the sufferer that they are not sick and which distance the sufferer from God as opposed to physical and intellectual impairments which are part of the

human condition and which may lead the sufferer to an awareness of dependence and so closeness to God and others.

Whilst acknowledging its eternal dimension Pope John Paul
also recognises that suffering is 'inseparable from man's earthly
existence' yet it 'remains an intangible mystery': on the one hand it
can be spoken of in its 'objective reality' as an 'explicit problem'; on
the other hand in its 'subjective dimension', found in the 'concrete
and unrepeatable interior' of the person, suffering seems 'almost
inexpressible and not transferable'.[49] Furthermore, Pope John
Paul notes the link between soul pain, or 'moral sufferings' and
physical sufferings since the human person is 'a psychological and
physical whole'.[50] Still, despite the very personal and individual
nature of each person's suffering Pope John Paul identifies a 'social
dimension', a dimension that seems to have resonance with theories in liberation theologies: the world of suffering possesses 'its
own solidarity', 'people who suffer become similar to one another
through the analogy of their situation, the trial of their destiny, or
through their need for understanding and care, and perhaps above
all through the persistent question of the meaning of suffering'.[51]

The main question of suffering is, says Pope John Paul, the
question why. He sees that this question, though difficult, is a
particularly human question and one, moreover, frequently addressed to God or one that causes a denial of God.[52] Referring
to the story of Job, Pope John Paul reminds his readers that not
all suffering is a consequence of a fault nor is it a punishment
though significantly an important aspect of suffering is that it
can serve for conversion.[53] However, Pope John Paul does note
that even though it is not permissible to apply 'the narrow criterion of direct dependence', there can be said to be a 'complex
involvement' of suffering with sin: the 'sin of the beginnings' and
'the sinful background of the personal actions and social processes in human history'.[54] This perhaps stands in contrast to writers
like Sharon Betcher who argue that 'we who are disabled refuse
to live as if broken and therefore refuse to discard the world as
broken'.[55] Sharon Betcher seems to see traditional theology as
problematic. As Pope John Paul explains human beings live in a
fallen world and as a result of that fall originally occasioned by
the disobedience of human beings sin, suffering and death have
entered the world. However, this is not to 'discard the world as

broken', rather it is to see the world as good in God's eyes and of such worth that God sends his only Son to redeem it. So, more significantly for Pope John Paul the 'true answer to the "why" of suffering' lies in this revelation of divine love, 'the richest source' of that meaning even though it 'always remains a mystery'.[56]

By his work of salvation the Son liberates humanity from sin, death and suffering and according to Pope John Paul this means 'for the saved, that in the eschatological perspective suffering is totally blotted out'.[57] It is here perhaps that it is necessary to make the distinction between suffering and disability explicit rather than allow it to remain implicit. To be sure disability often carries with it suffering and disabled persons are assumed to be 'bodies in pain'.[58] Certainly it can be agreed that the actual suffering that often follows in the wake of disability is 'a trial—at times a very hard one'.[59] However, for many people with disabilities their impairment itself is a part of their identity and not a defect to be made good whether here or in the afterlife.[60] Although Pope John Paul does not discuss the disabled condition as opposed to suffering that may accompany it the kind of suffering that he addresses is suffering as 'the undergoing of evil before which man shudders. He says: "let it pass from me", just as Christ says in Gethsemane'.[61] If that is taken to be the case then it would not appear to be contradictory to say that at the resurrection of the body all suffering that goes with disability, what makes the disabled person 'shudder', will indeed be eliminated but what a person perceives to be a necessary part of who they are may remain.

In contrast to writers like Nancy Eiesland who prefer a description of Jesus as survivor to the suffering servant, Pope John Paul uses the Song of the Suffering Servant from the Book of Isaiah as the most expressive description of the intensity of the passion of Christ. Perhaps the significant point of dissimilarity between Nancy Eiesland and Pope John Paul is that they are focusing on the suffering and wounds of Christ for different reasons. On the one hand Nancy Eiesland looks to Jesus as a new model of wholeness for people with disability: just as the Resurrected Christ shows his wounds and is the disabled God so too in the next life can impairment be a normal and necessary part of people with disabilities. On the other hand Pope John Paul seeks to express both that there is a similarity in the suffering of Jesus and of every human being and yet there is also a radical dissimilarity that can only be understood partially: the suffering of Jesus is unique and of incomparable depth and intensity precisely because it is the suffering of the 'God-man'; it is suffering which is estrangement from God.[62] Pope John Paul finds it necessary to dwell on this suffering since, he says, 'with the Passion of Christ all human suffering has found itself in a new situation': not only is redemption accomplished but also human suffering is redeemed.[63] This is why Pope John Paul can then go on to say that just as every human being shares in the redemption every human being is also called to share in the redemptive suffering of Christ through his or her own suffering.[64] This idea that Christ has 'raised human suffering to the level of the redemption' may seem to come perilously close to glorifying suffering or to implying that suffering is somehow good in itself. Nevertheless it is necessary to realise that for Pope John Paul suffering is an inevitable part of human life, it is 'always a trial—at times a very hard one'.[65] As he quotes from St Paul, 'we are afflicted in every way' but the message is that we are 'not driven to despair' we are 'not forsaken', we have hope and can witness to that hope in the meaning we give to our suffering that with the Cross comes the Resurrection.[66] The apparent glory then of suffering is not found in suffering for its own sake but is found in sharing the sufferings of Christ and so sharing in his resurrected glory.[67] This is a profound message of hope.

Pope John Paul makes especial appeal to the 'gospel paradox' of weakness and strength: that 'Christ's emptying of himself on the Cross is at the same time his being lifted up; that in weakness he manifests his power'.[68] This is in particular an antidote to those tempted to despair and to prefer death to dependence or loss of control. Instead it is through their suffering and evident human weakness that those who suffer can become open to the salvific power of God for God's power is 'known precisely in this weakness and emptying of self'.[69] Pope John Paul again uses St Paul to show that suffering contains 'a special call' to virtue, to persevere in bearing suffering so that this perseverance can produce hope, a hope that does not disappoint since it is linked to God's love. The hope that is 'unleashed' leads to the conviction that suffering does not deprive the sufferer of his or her dignity as a human being.[70]

St Paul's influence on Pope John Paul's understanding of the place of suffering is clearly manifest in *Salvifici doloris* and Pope John Paul further explores the Apostle's thought in an area that some find particularly perplexing. Pope John Paul reminds his readers that in St Paul's letter to the Colossians St Paul says that he rejoices in his sufferings and in his flesh he completes 'what is lacking in Christ's afflictions for the sake of his body, that is, the Church'.[71] Pope John Paul explains that this text does not mean that the redemption achieved by Christ is somehow incomplete; after all, 'no man can add anything to it' since the good achieved is 'inexhaustible and infinite'.[72] Instead, Pope John Paul suggests St Paul's remarks point to the 'creative character of suffering': certainly in Christ's redemptive suffering the redemption of the world was accomplished. However, Christ also 'opened himself from the beginning to every human suffering and constantly does so' thus his redemptive suffering is 'unceasingly completed'. Since redemption 'lives and develops as the body of Christ, the Church' the Church indicates the 'context in which human sufferings complete the sufferings of Christ'.[73] Pope John Paul adds that suffering has 'a special value' in the eyes of the Church because suffering seems to share in the characteristics of the divine and human nature of the Church. Suffering then is 'something good' but only in the sense that it points towards the hope of redemption and glory.[74]

The idea that suffering might be 'good' is certainly one that is open to misinterpretation and so to avoid any distortion it seems worthwhile dwelling on what Pope John Paul is saying. In *Salvifici doloris* Pope John Paul brings in the theme of the persecution of the early Christians under the Roman emperors.[75] He does this in order to focus on the call to courage and fortitude experienced by the early Christians who suffered for the sake of Christ. However, early accounts of martyrdom itself and the rationale behind this witness to Christ may shed a brighter light on the 'good' of suffering. The Church Fathers certainly show admiration and praise of martyrdom yet clearly they do not approve of Christians voluntarily offering themselves up to death 'we do not commend those who surrender themselves, for not such is the teaching of the gospel'.[76] Genuine martyrs did not court death. Rather as witnesses to the good news of Christ they saw meaning in their suffering and death.

Although Pope John Paul speaks of the persecution of the martyrs he does not make a clear connection between the early martyrs and people who are suffering but who also unite their sufferings with Christ's. However, it would seem that the conversion of a pagan to Christianity in the early centuries that led him or her to be able to witness to Christ by finding the salvific aspect to his or her martyrdom is in a sense played out by those who suffer today. As Pope John Paul explains through the grace of a profound conversion to Christ a person may discover the salvific meaning of suffering and 'above all' may become 'a completely new person'. This is because he or she discovers 'a new dimension' of his entire life and vocation. This new dimension is not simply a new perspective on life that results from a change in priorities and altered possibilities or options. Certainly such a dimension is found in social models of disability where disability is seen as enriching or as definitive in a positive way of a person; indeed some studies show enrichment within the whole family circle.[77] Rather, Pope John Paul sees in this new dimension the discovery of 'spiritual greatness' which 'surpasses the body'.[78]

At first glance Pope John Paul appears to be addressing the 'acting' person, the person whose intellectual abilities enable him or her to make decisions and choices because this notion of 'spiritual greatness' and 'inner maturity' seems to belong to those who through the 'interior encounter with the Master' ask about the meaning of suffering and begin to perceive the answer interiorly. The answer is not abstract reasons for suffering. Instead it is above all a vocation, a call to take part through suffering in the work of saving the world, a call to take up the cross. So, greatness and maturity are the result of conversion and cooperation with the grace of the 'Crucified Redeemer'.[79] An acceptance of this vocation can lead to 'spiritual joy', the joy that St Paul experiences in his letter to the Colossians and the source of this joy is 'found in the overcoming of the sense of the uselessness of suffering' that is, the feeling of being a burden, condemned to receive help from others, and the 'depressing feeling' of being useless to oneself.[80]

But whilst Pope John Paul certainly does stress the 'active' dimension, the conversion and cooperation of the person who is suffering, he does not seem to rule out the 'non-acting' person that is the person who to all intents and purposes does not seem to be able to cooperate. This appears to be more the case if it is remembered that for Pope John Paul every human being who is still alive is an acting person. As Pope John Paul explains, 'when this body is gravely ill, totally incapacitated, and the person is almost incapable of living and acting, all the more do interior maturity and spiritual greatness become evident, constituting a touching lesson to those who are healthy and normal'.[81] This may have bearing on, for instance the vocation of the person in persistent vegetative state, the human being sometimes classified as the ultimate non-acting patient. It is possible to discern a call even to an individual with such a catastrophic disability because whilst that patient remains alive he or she is still suffering notwithstanding the scientific belief that sensory and conscious capacities no longer operate. The patient in persistent vegetative state suffers because he or she is not yet united with God. And he or she may still have a vocation because it is not so much the response of human beings that is paramount. Rather it is that the 'Crucified Redeemer... acts at the heart of human sufferings through his Spirit of truth', Christ 'transforms, in a certain sense, the very substance of the spiritual life, indicating for the person who suffers a place close to himself'.[82]

Summary

According to Pope John Paul a denial of suffering is linked to the denial of bodily life since he thinks that suffering as an objective reality is 'almost inseparable from man's earthly existence'.[83] Moreover he also thinks that human beings suffer on account of evil.[84] Nevertheless this does not mean we can fully explain suffering. It is of course vital to remember that Pope John Paul does not embrace suffering for suffering's sake. Furthermore he acknowledges that care and sensitivity are required in dealing with the challenging question of suffering and its meaning[85] where what suffices is not so much ready answers. Instead what is demanded is prayerful reflection on what is at times an intractable problem. He also recognises the complexity of suffering and that human beings suffer in many different ways. This sometimes involves ways that are not considered by medicine but encompass in addition to or sometimes instead of physical suffering moral suffering and 'pain of the soul'.[86] Pope John Paul notes that for some death is seen as 'liberation from suffering' but he explains that death is also the 'summing up' of its destructive work since 'the evil which the human being experiences in death has a definitive and total character'.[87] However, in the Christian tradition Christ's salvific work takes away the dominion of death because Christ's resurrection begins the process of our own future resurrection of the body and human beings can now exist on earth 'with the hope of eternal life and holiness'.[88]

Certainly Pope John Paul acknowledges that temporal suffering has not been abolished but nevertheless he demonstrates that the 'new light' of salvation has been thrown on it.[89] Pope John Paul explains love expressed through the Cross of Jesus, is 'the richest source' of the meaning of suffering that nonetheless remains a mystery.[90] Suffering thus finds itself in 'a new situation', it has been 'linked to love' by the voluntary suffering of Jesus which, even though it witnesses to the depth and intensity of all suffering, differs from every possible human suffering because it is the suffering of the God-man.[91] Just as Christ shares in the suffering of humanity so too does every human being share in the redemption if they so choose.[92] Yet each person is also called to share in Christ's redemptive suffering and although suffering is 'always a trial' it is also a 'special call to virtue', of perseverance and therefore hope that suffering will not get the upper hand and cannot deprive the person suffering of his dignity as a human being.[93] The 'special value' of suffering then is not based on suffering as an experience of evil. Rather suffering is transformed by grace and it makes present the 'powers of the Redemption'.[94]

According to Pope John Paul this is why the sick have a vocation, a call to take up the cross and follow Christ. Pope John Paul recognises that the acceptance of this vocation may take time and may begin with questioning. However he is convinced that the 'depressing feeling' of the uselessness of suffering that leads the sufferer to see him or her self as a burden to others can be transformed by grace into the discovery of its salvific meaning.[95]

The suffering person then is carrying out 'an irreplaceable service' because he or she is being asked in his or her weakness and vulnerability to become a source of strength[96] and a witness to the inalienable dignity of every human being whatever his or her condition since that dignity is based on the raising up of weak human beings to the glory of friendship with God.[97]

It can come as no surprise that Pope John Paul's reflection on suffering is founded on hope though some may claim it is unrealistic or too glib. However, it may be worthwhile to note that hope is the virtue that stands midway between the vices of despair and presumption. It is a constantly reflective point and it is this gift that the 'non acting' person brings that moves Pope John Paul to urge us to 'keep the sick and the handicapped at the centre of our lives. Let us treasure them and recognize with gratitude the debt we owe them'.[98] As Pope John Paul perhaps astutely points out, 'we begin by imagining that we are giving to them; we end by realising that they have enriched us'.[99]

Notes

1. Pope John Paul II, *Evangelium vitae*, 12.
2. *Ibid.*, 23.
3. *Ibid.*
4. *Ibid.*, 12.
5. *Ibid.*, 29.
6. *Ibid.*, 2.
7. *Ibid.*, 31.
8. Pope John Paul II, *World Day of the Sick*, II, 6.
9. *Ibid. I*, 5.
10. Pope John Paul II, *Letter Instituting the World Day of the Sick* (13 May 1992), 3.
11. N. Eiesland, *The Disabled God: Toward a Liberatory Theology of Disability* (Nashville: Abingdon Press, 1994), p. 73.
12. S. Betcher, 'Becoming Flesh of My Flesh: Feminist and Disability Theologies on the Edge of Posthumanist Discourse' in *Journal of Feminist Studies in Religion* 26/2 (2010), pp. 107–139 at p. 109.
13. D. Creamer, 'Embracing Limits, Queering Embodiment: Creating/ Creative Possibilities for Disability Theology' in *Journal of Feminist Studies in Religion* 26/2 (2010), pp. 123–127 at p. 124–125.

14. *Ibid.*, p. 126.
15. Pope John Paul II, *World Day of the Sick*, III, 1.
16. *Ibid.*, II, 8.
17. *Ibid.*, VIII, 4.
18. *Ibid.*, V, 4.
19. *Ibid.*, VI, 9.
20. *Ibid.*, V, 5.
21. *Ibid.*, VII, 2–6.
22. *Ibid.*, VI, 6–7.
23. *Ibid.*, VIII, 7.
24. *Ibid.*, IV, 2–6.
25. *Ibid.*, I, 5.
26. *Ibid.*, V, 4.
27. *Ibid.*, II, 5.
28. *Ibid.*, VIII, 7.
29. *Ibid.*, VIII, 5.
30. *Ibid.*, VI, 9.
31. *Ibid.*, V, 4.
32. *Ibid.*, IX, 1.
33. *Ibid.*, X, 2.
34. *Ibid.*, IX, 3.
35. *Ibid.*, XI, 1–2.
36. *Ibid.*, IX, 5.
37. *Ibid.*, VIII, 5.
38. *Ibid.*, XII, 6.
39. *Ibid.*, VIII, 11–13.
40. Pope John Paul II, *Salvifici Doloris*, 25.
41. *Ibid.*, 7.
42. *Ibid.*
43. *Ibid.*, 14.
44. *Ibid.*, 14.
45. *Ibid.*, 5.
46. *Ibid.*, 3.
47. *Ibid.*, 1.
48. *Ibid.*, 14.
49. *Ibid.*, 3–5.

50. *Ibid.*, 6.

51. *Ibid.*, 8.

52. *Ibid.*, 9.

53. *Ibid.*, 11–12.

54. *Ibid.*, 15.

55. S. Betcher, *Spirit and the Politics of Disablement* (Minneapolis: Fortress Press, 2007), p. 5.

56. Pope John Paul II, *Salvifici Doloris*, 13.

57. *Ibid.*, 15.

58. S. Betcher, 'Becoming Flesh of My Flesh: Feminist and Disability Theologies on the Edge of Posthumanist Discourse' in *Journal of Feminist Studies in Religion* p. 13.

59. Pope John Paul II, *Salvifici Doloris*, 23.

60. S. Betcher, *Spirit and the Politics of Disablement*, p. ix; H. Lewis *Deaf Liberation Theology* (Aldershot: Ashgate, 2007); J. W. Block *Copious Hosting: a theology of access for people with disabilities* (New York: Continuum International, 2002), pp. 17–18; N. Eiesland *The Disabled God: Toward a Liberatory Theology of Disability*.

61. Pope John Paul II, *Salvifici Doloris*, 18.

62. *Ibid.*, 18.

63. *Ibid.*, 19.

64. *Ibid.*, 19.

65. *Ibid.*, 23.

66. *Ibid.*, 20.

67. *Ibid.*, 21.

68. *Ibid.*, 23.

69. *Ibid.*

70. *Ibid.*

71. *Col* 1:24.

72. Pope John Paul II, *Salvifici Doloris*, 24.

73. *Ibid.*

74. *Ibid.*

75. *Ibid.*, 25.

76. *Martyrdom of Polycarp* 4; H. Chadwick, *The Early Church* (Middlesex: Penguin Books, 1974), pp. 30–31.

77. See for instance I. Brown and R. Brown, 'Family Quality of Life as an Area of Study', in A. Turnbull et al (eds.), *Families and Persons with Mental Retardation and Quality of Life: International Perspectives* (Washington: American Association on Mental Retardation, 2004), pp. 5–6.

78. Pope John Paul II, *Salvifici Doloris*, 26.
79. *Ibid.*, 26.
80. *Ibid.*, 27.
81. *Ibid.*, 26.
82. *Ibid.*
83. *Ibid.*, 3.
84. *Ibid.*, 7.
85. *Ibid.*, 9.
86. *Ibid.*, 5.
87. *Ibid.*, 15.
88. *Ibid.*
89. *Ibid.*
90. *Ibid.*, 13.
91. *Ibid.*, 18.
92. *Ibid.*, 19–20.
93. *Ibid.*, 23.
94. *Ibid.*, 26–27.
95. *Ibid.*, 26.
96. *Ibid.*, 31.
97. *Ibid.*, 23.
98. Pope John Paul II, *Southwark Cathedral: Anointing the Sick* (28 May 1982).
99. *Ibid.*

8

WHO IS THE GOOD SAMARITAN?

CARE-GIVERS AND RECEIVERS

If we take at face value the Latin expression *operari sequitur esse,* that acts disclose the person, then it seems to refer most obviously to those who care for the profoundly disabled. It has long been recognised that working with and caring for people who live in radical dependence can be particularly challenging and at times emotionally draining. Indeed such care is often termed a vocation that requires particular skills and virtues. Hence it could be said that the act of working with and caring for certain people demonstrates that the worker or carer is a certain kind of person, one who is caring, creative, patient, a good communicator and sensitive to his or her 'client's' needs: a 'good Samaritan'. On the one hand undoubtedly the signs of the times include the joy and hope found in those who minister to and care for the disabled and the witness they give to the intrinsic dignity that all human beings have no matter what their situation. On the other hand this attention to the virtuous practitioner to whom a person has been entrusted perhaps explains in part the outrage caused when trust is abused and the vulnerable person is treated with neglect or indifference.

Certainly outward actions do disclose the person and this is perhaps why as professor of ethics Karol Wojtyła is particularly interested in moral action and its links to freedom, the will and the roles played by the sense of obligation, conscience and the practice of virtue. However it seems that Karol Wojtyła understands *operari,* acts, in a more profound way than simply referring to outward actions. We grasp the subjectivity of the human being not only through what that person does but also through what happens in him or her: *operari* includes the whole human dynamism.[1] This is why for Karol Wojtyła a live human being cannot be described as a 'non-acting person'. Moreover, it also demonstrates that every human being is a person and the apparently 'non-acting' human being (in modern terms) is simply a person who is unable to express the person he or she is or even more likely it is we who are unable to grasp the subjectivity of that person because we have not fathomed how to engage successfully with him or her.

Pope John Paul makes a unique contribution to the field of disability particularly in the areas of human dignity, vocation, participation and solidarity, principles that are both empowering and championing of the disabled person. He also offers a rich theology of suffering and of finding meaning in disability. He speaks personally to each disabled human being. However, perhaps more significant given the threat to the very person of the disabled is his view expressed during his academic career and carried through in his pontificate that the person is waiting, as it were, to be discovered or to express himself or herself. Certainly he is thinking of all human beings including the very youngest, the unborn, though not specifically intellectually disabled people. It is interesting that this also seems to be the premise behind recent research into communication and learning disability, notably intensive interactive therapy, a relatively new therapy designed with autistic children in mind but that has application throughout a whole range of disabled people of whatever age. This is not to suggest that Pope John Paul endorses any one therapy. Rather it suggests that Pope John Paul's own insights can be understood and have relevance in many other fields outside theology. These insights make connections to actual practice even if Pope John Paul's thinking also goes beyond that practice.

Pope John Paul speaks clearly in one distinct area that is often neglected in disability studies even by those who offer liberation theologies of disability. This area concerns the contribution that the disabled person makes to the call to holiness of him or her self and of others, a call made to every human being. In terms of the enrichment that people with disabilities provide, the call that every human being is given to be friends with God is one that focuses on the uniqueness of each person. This perhaps is in contrast with some modern views of disability that critique the Christian tradition for holding a view of the disabled person as somehow deficient and that sees the non-disabled person as the one who gives and the disabled person as the one who only passively receives. Pope John Paul's understanding of the vocation of every sick, suffering and disabled person dispels this modern view and demonstrates that it is part of the rich Christian tradition that disabled people have a special and unique part to play in building up the kingdom of God.

The foundation of Pope John Paul's thinking in *Gaudium et spes* 24 where a person most fully finds him or her self in the gift of self shines perhaps unexpectedly in the caring situation. Unexpectedly that is for those who do not usually take on a caring role. In discovering the person who does not perhaps easily express him or her self outwardly the one who engages with that person also discovers him or her own self more profoundly. Both the apparently acting person and the apparently non-acting person are mutually involved in this process of discovery and so any reflection on the different aspects of Pope John Paul's thought has both persons intertwined. People with disabilities are also 'good Samaritans'.

We begin by imagining that we are giving to them

There are many reasons why people work and care for people who are disabled and no doubt the vocation that they follow does often demand a gift of time, energy, and also self, beyond the demands of many other careers. However, Pope John Paul sees the care of people with disabilities as a matter for the whole community and this is not so much based on the obligation or duty to act out of charity, though that is of course a biblical injunction directed at all human beings. Rather, the Decalogue is framed in terms of both a covenant and Yahweh's initiative of love that requires a response: as the redactors of *Exodus* and *Deuteronomy* remind the Israelites, 'I am Yahweh your God who brought you out of Egypt, where you lived as slaves'.[2] Moreover, Matthew's Gospel reminds us that what we do for the least we do for Christ[3] since all are one in Christ. It is a matter of solidarity, *agape* and the call to be holy as God is holy.

In addition Pope John Paul draws on what he sees as a vital and important truth:

The sick, the elderly, the handicapped and the dying teach us that weakness is a creative part of human living and that suffering can be embraced with no loss of dignity. Without the presence of these people in your midst you might be tempted to think of health, strength and power as the only important values to be pursued in life. But the wisdom of Christ and the power of Christ are to be seen in the weakness of those who share his sufferings.[4]

In his speech in Southwark Cathedral Pope John Paul speaks of the 'debt' we owe to people who are sick or have disabilities. This reverses the apparently common discriminatory attitude that is at least implicit in contemporary life or indeed the attitude of indifference that allows for neglectful treatment of people with certain disabilities. Moreover it challenges those who place certain categories of human beings on the margins of life or personhood on the grounds of their apparent lack of capacities. Pope John Paul's focus on the 'irreplaceable service' carried out by people who are suffering also counters those who judge that people with disabilities have lives of less worth than 'normal' people. However, Pope John Paul is still mindful of the difficulties that beset people with disabilities and these go beyond issues of access or barriers to living a 'normal' life. It is to do with countering alienation, isolation and loneliness; it is to do with belonging in community and participation. The vital starting point for community and participation is to engage those who are somehow cut off from the world. And for Pope John Paul the first cell of the community is the Christian family whose essence it is 'to guard, reveal and communicate love.'[5]

Much has been made of Pope John Paul's personal tragedies in shaping his views. Arguably these experiences may have led to an overly idealistic view of familial relationships. However it is more than possible that any tendency to idealism was countered by the very pastoral concerns that faced Karol Wojtyła as a priest. Nevertheless, it is the family and what Pope John Paul calls the 'genius' of women that can put into effect participation. His explanation of this 'genius' seems to have resonance with the theory of intensive interaction therapy in its positive aspect of engaging with the person with profound disability even if Pope John Paul's reflections also exceed what intensive interaction has to offer.

Intensive Interaction: 'Finding You Finding Me'

Intensive interaction was developed by the educationalists Dave Hewett and Melanie Nind in the UK at Harperbury Hospital School Hertfordshire in the 1980s in order to teach the basics of pre-speech communication. It came out of Dave Hewett's experience of dealing with people, most of whom were on the autistic spectrum, who did not seem to understand speech and who were socially isolated since they appeared to live in their own worlds.

Certainly like all methods it has its drawbacks. However it appears that these shortcomings are usually seen from a practical point of view as, for instance, whether the therapy respects age appropriateness, whether the actions it encourages fit the situation, whether it reinforces stereotypical behaviour, whether it is a source of embarrassment.[6] What is often neglected is the much more serious problem: the therapy encourages one of the partners precisely not to be him or herself. By asking the partner to copy the actions of the other in order to break into the other's world the partner's acts no longer reflect who he or she is. Moreover, it risks being intrusive instead of a way of 'being with' another in companionship. Therefore any therapy must be approached care-fully to ensure that the dignity of each person is maintained and that they are fully respected.

Having noted that there are problems with intensive interaction therapy it still seems that the theory does offer some deep understandings of the experience of the person with profound disability even if some of its therapeutic interventions are open to criticism. One of its most experienced practitioners, Phoebe Caldwell, explains the premises of intensive interaction in her book *Finding You Finding Me* published in 2006.

According to Phoebe Caldwell participants are called 'partners'[7] rather than patients and therapists or teachers and learners. This is because, as Phoebe Caldwell puts it, communication is a 'two-way thing': it is not just that they cannot communicate with me; I cannot communicate with them.[8] One of the greatest difficulties in creating engagement between partners seems to be the initial capturing of the attention of the partner who is withdrawn. Intensive interaction therapy is based on the relationship of mother and child where the natural interaction is one of copying, mimicking and imitation.[9] Through observation of this relationship it was noticed that the brain recognises its own sounds and movements and so if a person hears his or her own sounds or feels or sees his or her own movements even if done by another person then that person will start to attend. By copying the sounds and movements of the person a partner/therapist can focus on what has meaning for their partner and so the partner/therapist can work through their language. In a sense this is precisely what a mother instinctively does when she mimics her child's noises or expressions and in return the child watches and copies her. Although intensive interaction came out of the mother-child experience Phoebe Caldwell notes that its application is not gender specific. Moreover Phoebe Caldwell recognises that there are issues surrounding the fittingness of mimicking, of age appropriate behaviour and of respect for the person so she prefers to speak about 'learning the basic elements of a person's language and using these to respond'.[10]

Phoebe Caldwell explains that the reality for some people is a world where nothing quite makes sense or is confusing and painful. Indeed, outside events may seem hostile. This reality, she says, needs to be respected as 'valid for them' and so the partner/therapist is required to let go of his or her own sensory reality in order to avoid any sensory overload on the part of the other partner.[11] Sensory overload or times when the world seems to fall apart might simply be too painful for a person. This pain may lead to the kinds of coping strategies or fight/flight responses that close the person in on him or her self as a form of protection[12] and it is at such times when the person holds onto a sensation that is meaningful for him or her,[13] usually some form of apparently repetitive obsessive action. Phoebe Caldwell adds that safety is then sought in the inner world and in the internal 'conversation' with the self where through fixations and self-stimulation a person can become conscious of their inner world even if in turn the self becomes painful and the person can no longer get out.[14] This is an internal 'conversation' since repetitive behaviour appears to be part of a communication system used to communicate with the self rather than with the other.[15] Phoebe Caldwell explains that in some cases a person's brain is 'cluttered' with unprocessed images, sounds and information; notably in people with autism the sensory intake is scrambled.[16] She explains that the person who fears fragmentation, when his or her world falls apart, will pay attention to limited objects as a protection.[17]

In order to break through to a person living 'on the inside' his or her partner/therapist must 'learn their language'. By that Phoebe Caldwell means both the language the person uses to talk to him or herself and what is meaningful for that person. In learning this language the partners can focus on this rather than on things that may disturb one of them.[18] This does mean making a distinction between repetitive behaviour that is part of a person's inner conversation and behaviour that is a coping strategy used to respond to anxiety. However, whilst repetitive behaviour may help to cut out overwhelming senses so that the 'brain feels safe',[19] by responding in the same way, by copying the behaviour, the partner is drawn by curiosity to someone making the same sound or doing the same movement: they may come to see that someone understands their rules and values them.[20]

Of course to achieve this level of copying the partner/therapist needs to attach significance to everything the other does and therefore needs to pay attention to what the person is actually doing.[21] Such attention can move towards the 'surprise factor', shifting attention from the self to the other by becoming 'complicit' in what has meaning for the partner. Phoebe Caldwell gives the example of a person turning a dial and the partner/therapist drawing clockwise then anticlockwise on the person's hand: this, she says, is 'sharing the joke', it is finding pleasure in each other's company, it is friendship.[22]

What is significant here is that the 'helper' partner/therapist starts from bewilderment then moves to empty him or herself of his or her own agenda in order to see the other's meaning.[23] This interaction is intensely personal for both partners. For the 'helper' it involves apprehending behaviour that has intimate meaning for the other. This meaning is deeply private since it refers to the person's internal conversation. As the 'helper' copies this behaviour the other partner begins to recognise that what is being offered relates to his or her familiar patterns and this makes him or her pause in his or her self-stimulation. As Phoebe Caldwell puts it, 'if you copy me I know it is me you are copying'.[24] This begins the shift in attention away from the self in a way that is not threatening even if at this stage, as Phoebe Caldwell notes, the 'helper' seems to remain an object since the person is only interested in the activity.[25] Significantly, though, Phoebe Caldwell reminds the 'helper' that he or she needs to 'be with' his or her partner, the 'helper' needs to make him or herself present and be open. Notably Phoebe Caldwell adds, 'curiously we find that as we empty ourselves, we find our self more deeply'.[26]

According to Phoebe Caldwell the partnership develops as the person begins to realise that there is a meaningful response to what he or she initiates and so in turn he or she starts to look for another response; there is expectation of a response to the response. This develops into engagement which, Phoebe Caldwell says, is a shared feeling of excitement and sharing. The person makes the shift from noticing what the 'helper' is doing, where the 'helper' remains an object, towards the desire to engage with the 'helper' as a person. More often than not this seems to be the result of a surprise at the difference: the other is 'not me'.[27] This engagement is, then, not so much 'task-orientated' as 'person-orientated'[28] and crucial to this engagement is, naturally, a sense of humour.[29]

Phoebe Caldwell's use of 'partnership' language and the shared experience is a reminder that each of the participants is learning about the other. Moreover, she argues that each learns more about themselves as well. The significance on the part of the 'helper' is that he or she comes to recognise the reality of the other person, a reality that is often obscured by indifference or inability to see through the disability. As Phoebe Caldwell says it shows people that they are important to us.[30] Furthermore, since 'it is the sharing that is important,'[31] paradoxically, she believes the partners become more aware of self in the context that 'there is no longer "I" and "you"; the felt experience is of "we"'.[32] And the final outcome: 'joy'.[33]

Points of convergence and divergence

Phoebe Caldwell's title *Finding You Finding Me* encapsulates what she believes is going on in intensive interaction: through this 'being with' the other not only is each person discovered in turn by the other but also each person rediscovers something about him or her self. Phoebe Caldwell's discussion about the emptying of self that leads to the finding of self is in keeping with a number of philosophies and religions. Phoebe Caldwell herself notes that Buddhism has been of great influence for her. More specifically the idea of finding the self in a gift of self also comes from her own personal practical experience of the way things simply happen.[34] Nevertheless, there are clear parallels here to the text of *Gaudium et spes* 24.

There is a risk that some practitioners of intensive interaction implicitly believe that the person with disabilities is a person or mind trapped in a crippled body as if the body is a useless or indeed limiting extra, and that it is the job of the helper to reach out and free this person. However the approach taken by Phoebe Caldwell rejects this. Instead she avoids the Cartesian split between mind and body by explaining about embodiment, so 'when I see my mother, I not only see her but my brain receives another message saying that it is *my eyes* that are seeing her' (her italics).[35] This and the associated idea that the person does not 'have' a disability rather he or she 'is' disabled has resonance with Karol Wojtyła/Pope John Paul's adherence to a philosophy of being over a philosophy of consciousness.

Phoebe Caldwell says that in all human beings 'the brain and body are involved in numerous and continuous conversations', as in breathing, though we are often unaware of this.[36] However, she continues 'the vital question is *where* our attention is directed' (her italics): and in the case of many people with disabilities a fixation on some behaviour serves to control the environment and cut out what would otherwise be overwhelming sensory experiences.[37] By focusing on the bodily acts of the person the person is revealed to his or her partner as embodied and as expressing him or her self through the body even if at times the person is conveying that his or her internal messages are mixed or his or her world is beginning to fragment. This explanation that acts express the person seems to dovetail with Karol Wojtyła/Pope John Paul's extensive discussion of *operari sequitur esse*: action is the basis for disclosing and understanding the person.[38] Moreover, just as for Karol Wojtyła/Pope John Paul *operari* includes the whole human dynamism that is what merely happens in the human being and everything the human being does[39] so too for Phoebe Caldwell are acts that merely happen in human beings part of the internal conversation. Along with Karol Wojtyła/Pope John Paul it would seem that in the intensive interactive approach to people with disabilities action has 'the most basic and essential significance for grasping the subjectivity of the human being'[40] whether it be an ordered and coherent subjectivity or one affected by fragmentation and overwhelming sensations.

Phoebe Caldwell's assertion that the brain body dialogue is common to every human being and that intensive interaction is based on the paradigm of infant and mother interaction permits certain generalisations to be made in the application of intensive interaction. However, this still allows for the fact that each person has his or her own unique inner conversation and that each partnership is also unique. In a similar vein Karol Wojtyła/Pope John Paul notes that 'each human being, myself included, is an "eyewitness" of his or her own self – of his or her own humanity and person'.[41]

In spite of these points of convergence it has to be said that intensive interaction therapies are limited. These therapies rely on the skill of the practitioner and his or her own resources and resourcefulness in identifying communication and possible inroads into the world of his or her partner. It is about what one person does for another as well as being a way of each finding the other and a deeper meaning of self. Certainly it is a two way conversation but inevitably it is only as good as the practitioner and it is limited to the goals of the therapy even if the actual encounter is not, as Phoebe Caldwell puts it, 'task orientated'. Relationship and being open to the other seem to be present but only insofar as they serve the therapeutic aims, anything further seems incidental. Moreover becoming aware of how the partner expresses him or her self and makes sense of the world risks remaining on the level of the acquisition of knowledge: the practitioner learns how to read the signs of his or her partner in order to move onto the next stage of the therapy. Sometimes the disabled person lies open to the interpretation of the other and so vulnerable to the other; yet other disabled people remain isolated and unreadable. Nor does the practice of intensive interaction necessarily recognise and respect the dignity of each person if the relationship is said to begin when a response is elicited. At times it does not seem to be able to avoid one person becoming an object for the other.

Still, it does seem that exploration of intensive interaction therapies uncovers some partial truths about the human person who is waiting to be discovered and so chimes with many of Pope John Paul's insights into the human person. Nevertheless the understanding that Pope John Paul has of the family and the perspective he takes on the significance of women as mothers, whether it is physical or spiritual motherhood, in helping people to grow and flourish as persons gives a deeper grounding to reflection on the apparently non-acting person because it goes beyond simply persons in partnership.

The domestic Church: the Christian family

The family has great significance for Pope John Paul not least because it is 'the primary institution at the basis of our existence as human beings'; it is where every human being appears in his or her uniqueness and unrepeatability; and it is where 'the personality of the new human being is formed.'[42] Certainly in the tradition there have at times been difficulties in seeing marriage as grace-filled. Nevertheless the idea that married family life is an expression of 'the domestic Church' has its roots in the New Testament where whole households were baptised and where the Eucharist was often celebrated in Christian houses. It can be found in a homily of St John Chrysostom who sees that 'the household might become a church' by the way in which parents, fathers in particular, speak on spiritual matters.[43] In his letter to the widow Juliana St Augustine says that the family can be where a life of holiness is followed and so he asks her to 'set me also in your prayers with all your household church.'[44]

To a large extent the universal call to holiness is a central theme for the Fathers of the Second Vatican Council which is why perhaps the first Constitution of the Council is on the Sacred Liturgy. Notably the Council returns to the patristic idea of the family as domestic church by pointing out that married couples help each other and their children attain holiness and by highlighting the role of parents as 'the first heralds of the faith' for their children.[45] Pope John Paul picks up the theme of the family as the domestic Church and he situates it theologically in baptism and in its very identity as being a part of the plan of God and in its mission to manifest to all Christ's 'living presence in the world and the genuine nature of the Church.'[46] He focuses the family by orienting it towards Christ in its prophetic nature as a believing and evangelising community; in its priestly nature as a community in dialogue with God; and in its kingly nature as a community at the service of humanity.[47] These three missions perhaps show up most strongly in the families of the disabled.

To be sure Pope John Paul believes it is vital that society gives adequate support to families who care for the disabled[48] and in particular give care and assistance from the very beginning when parents first learn of their child's disability.[49] However he also points out the prophetic nature of the family in that the family, as a 'community of persons' is engaged in developing 'profound esteem' for the personal dignity of all children and, more urgently for the equal dignity of the disabled child.[50] The way in which families welcome all children as gifts of God's goodness is, he thinks, a 'convincing response' to those who see disabled children as a burden.[51] Perhaps it is also worth noting that the call to holiness involves living 'as is fitting among the saints', it is to be called to 'the fullness of Christian life and to the perfection of love'. This holiness is also directed towards fostering 'a more human manner of life' in earthly society. [52] There is a strong temptation for some to see disabled children as angels, as if they do not quite belong in the earthly realm. Undoubtedly this springs from an appreciation that the profoundly disabled child is pure and free from the guile and deceit that affects other human beings. However the profoundly disabled are human beings and they live human lives so, as Christians they also are to have the sacraments, take part in the liturgy and pray as far as they are able. An understanding of the disabled child as a human being with human needs brings out the priestly nature of the family. This nature is discovered in the way in which the family fosters the spiritual qualities that disabled people undoubtedly have.[53] The family's kingly nature is demonstrated by the way in which the family receive the new human life as 'a splendid gift of God's goodness'[54] with a view to understanding first of all, and conveying this to a world that values function over being, 'that the value of *life* transcends that of *efficiency*'.[55] Indeed, Pope John Paul sees the family as the place where the disabled child learns that he or she is not alone and that 'life is always worth living'.[56] The family as domestic church has a vital part then in addressing the culture of death especially since, as Pope John Paul puts it, 'people are marked by the culture whose very air they breathe through the family and social groups around them, through education and the most varied influences of their environment, through the very relationship which they have with the place in which they live'.[57] Moreover since cultural climates operate on the world stage in his 2001 message for the World Day of Peace Pope John Paul calls for a culture that builds up a civilisation of love and peace. According to Pope John Paul there can be no peace unless the basic good of human life is protected[58] and he believes that women play a pivotal role in testifying to the value of life.

The genius of women: making room for each other

In his letter to women, *Mulieris Dignitatem*[59] Pope John Paul returns to his model source, *Gaudium et spes* 24 when he explains that all human beings find themselves through the gift of self.[60] However he also sees that women in particular are almost natural witnesses to this by their very femininity. Referring to *Genesis* and the *Book of Revelation* he notes that in Scripture Eve and Mary represent the joy and suffering of all humanity in its struggle for salvation and the fundamental 'yes' or 'no' to God's plan for humanity. Mary's 'fiat' and the 'Annunciation dialogue' represent, he says, the personal dignity of the archetypal woman under the influence of grace.[61] Pope John Paul explains that the 'genius' of women lies in their 'sensitivity for human beings in every circumstances', and notably this is 'because they [human beings] are human!': Pope John Paul himself adds the exclamation mark[62] to indicate perhaps that this sensitivity has almost a pre-reflective sense. However Pope John Paul is especially concerned that people are beginning to lose sight of this sensitivity 'for what is essentially human' through apparent progress in material well-being and technological success.[63] Nevertheless as part of their 'genius' he also acknowledges that women can retain this sensitivity even where humanity is under threat and even in situations of their own social discrimination.[64]

Undoubtedly Pope John Paul does view actual motherhood as a paradigm of the relationship between persons where one person makes room for another. After all there is an element of a physical as well as spiritual making room. Moreover for Pope John Paul the relationship of mother and child is automatically always 'unique and unrepeatable' and is equally unrepeatable even if a mother goes on to have more children.[65] Nevertheless he does not limit the 'genius' of women to physical motherhood. Women's vocation to love is, he says, actualised and expressed in their many different vocations in the Church and the world. His focus on that vocation to love falls on the acceptance of a unique and unrepeatable relationship that is involved when a person is entrusted to another. According to Pope John Paul 'God entrusts the human being to her in a special way' and in turn a woman's 'moral and spiritual strength' grows from an awareness of that entrusting.[66] The meaning of this discovery can, he says, only be discovered through the Spirit of Christ: it is grace led.[67] Certainly he is concerned to show that God entrusts every human being to each other but he sees women as special witnesses to this entrusting by reason of their natural sensitivity to the other and this sensitivity is, he says, a kind of 'prophetism' as it is a witness to the truth that 'all are loved by God in Christ'.[68]

Of course some have viewed Pope John Paul's understanding of the genius of women with dismay. He has been charged with generalisations, with stereotyping women and romanticising the role of motherhood whilst neglecting the role of fathers in parenthood[69] and he has been criticised for his seemingly patronising appeal to the 'genius' of women.[70] Furthermore, references to 'special sensitivity' and being particularly entrusted with the care of others seems to play into the hands of those who argue that an ethics of care legitimises placing the burden of care on women often to the detriment of their own care and that it stresses emotional aspects with the implication that women are less rational.[71] However the practical application of Pope John Paul's view that mothers especially show a particular sensitivity to human beings and consequently affirm and confirm the human being entrusted to them as a person seems to be demonstrated by the initial theory based on practical experience underlying intensive interactive therapies. Moreover Pope John Paul is at pains to emphasise the equality and complimentarity of men and women.[72]

In his 1995 encyclical on the Gospel of Life *Evangelium vitae* Pope John Paul calls for a 'new feminism' just as in earlier encyclicals he has called for a new evangelization and a new theology of liberation. He writes:

> In transforming culture so that it supports life, *women* occupy a place in thought and action which is unique and decisive. It depends on them to promote a 'new feminism' which rejects the temptation of imitating models of 'male domination', in order to acknowledge and affirm the true genius of women in every aspect of the life of society, and overcome all discrimination, violence and exploitation.[73]

He adds, through motherhood women who are mothers

> first learn and then teach others that human relations are authentic if they are open to accepting the other person: a person who is recognized and loved because of the dignity which comes from being a person and not from other considerations, such as usefulness, strength, intelligence, beauty or health. This is the fundamental contribution which the Church and humanity expect from women. And it is the indispensable prerequisite for an authentic cultural change.[74]

Being with and a companion to a person with profound disabilities and the way in which that person is a companion too can develop from a renewed vision of seeing life as a gift and cultivating a 'contemplative outlook'[75] rather than putting store solely on activity, usefulness and functionality. However, such a vision does not rest merely on a foundation of persons in partnership engaged on a common enterprise. It requires a transcendental dimension whereby each of the persons is not constituted as a person simply by acceptance of another person. Rather each person is discerned as a person and an image of God and also entrusted by God to another.

And the Good Samaritan

At the end of *Salvifici Doloris*, his apostolic letter on suffering Pope John Paul offers a meditation on the parable of the Good Samaritan. Certainly for Pope John Paul a 'good Samaritan' is one who shows him or her self to be a 'real neighbour', one who carries out 'the commandment of love', and here he includes not only those who support the disabled but also those families that welcome the gift of disabled children. Pope John Paul is clear that we are not allowed to '"pass by on the other side" indifferently; we must "stop" beside him' and he emphasises that this is not out of curiosity but out of availability.[76] This is perhaps an important point to make in the professional field of disability therapies where practitioners seek not only to offer effective help but are also involved in researching new methods. Stopping and sympathising is the beginning of 'unselfish love'.[77] As Pope John Paul explains it is a 'universally human' truth that 'any activity on behalf of the suffering and needy is called "Good Samaritan" work', and this is especially the case in a professional capacity. [78]

However according to Pope John Paul the disabled also give to others. Part of this gift is that the profoundly disabled entrust themselves totally to others. Pope John Paul's understanding of how children complete and enrich their families perhaps fills this out. In his *Letter to Families* Pope John Paul explains that children are gifts to the whole family: parents and siblings. Moreover, he says that they contribute to the common good and the community of the family such that they cannot be seen merely as takers not givers. For Pope John Paul the common good of the whole of society dwells in each human being, in this particular human being with his or her new and unique 'adventure of human life'.[79] Adapting a saying from St Irenaeus Pope John Paul reminds us that 'the glory of God is man fully alive'.[80] Furthermore, he believes that disability is an effective 'challenge to individual and collective selfishness', it is 'an invitation to ever new forms of brotherhood'. It calls into question 'those conceptions of life that are solely concerned with satisfaction, appearances, speed and efficiency'.[81] As such the disabled are important witnesses to aspects of humanity that are frequently overlooked or ignored. More especially they help others on the path to holiness.

Pope John Paul also points to the biblical statement that whatsoever a person does he or she does it also to Christ: Christ is present in each suffering person so that Christ himself receives help and love.[82] Similarly, all those who suffer become 'sharers' in Christ's suffering.[83] This reflects a deeper solidarity than simply 'being with' another. Nor is the love of the Good Samaritan based merely on a care ethic or the Golden Rule do to others as you would have done to you. Rather it has its foundation in Christ's injunction to love as he has loved.

Summary

Pope John Paul appears to be optimistic that a way of being with the other, of seeing the other as another 'I' is achievable and he cites the work of the Christian family and the 'genius' of women as an indication of this. Moreover he draws attention to the role that each person plays in helping the other to flourish as a person. Each can be a Good Samaritan and make the gift of self to the other. Each can witness to the presence of Christ in the other. Nevertheless in the case of certain profoundly disabled people it seems more difficult for some to discern the image of God. How do we see life as a gift when others claim that such a life is not worth living? That a person would be 'better off dead' is frequently said of people with the profoundest of disabilities and in particular the patient in persistent vegetative state. In such a case many carers are overwhelmed and find it hard to be a Good Samaritan; that patient does not seem to be able to offer much response to be a Good Samaritan either. In terms of disability the case of the person in persistent vegetative state is especially perplexing. The following chapter demonstrates why Pope John Paul is particularly concerned with and speaks out for the patient in persistent vegetative state. However, the deeper issue, that of the spiritual dimension of people with the profoundest disabilities is reserved for the final chapter. And to anticipate, if we ask who is truly the Good Samaritan then the answer, as always in the parables, is that it is Christ who binds up our wounds when no one else can.

Notes

1. K. Wojtyła, 'The Person: Subject and Community' (1976) in *Catholic Thought from Lublin Vol.IV Person and Community* (New York: Peter Lang, 1993), p. 224.

2. *Ex* 20; *Dt* 5.

3. *Mt* 25:31–46.

4. Pope John Paul II, *Southwark Cathedral: Anointing the Sick* (28 May 1982).

5. Pope John Paul, *Familiaris Consortio,* 17.

6. For an instance of an analysis that focuses on practicalities see G. Firth, H. Elford, C. Leeming and M. Crabbe, 'Intensive Interaction as a Novel Approach in Social Care: Care Staff's Views on the Practice Change Process' in *Journal of Applied Research in Intellectual Disabilities* 21 (2008), pp. 58–69.

7. P. Caldwell, *Finding You Finding Me* (London: Jessica Kingsley Publishers, 2006), p. 15.

8. *Ibid.,* p. 64.

9. *Ibid.,* p. 14.

10. *Ibid.,* p. 14.

11. *Ibid.,* p. 18.

12. *Ibid.,* pp. 28–29.

13. *Ibid.,* p. 37.

14. *Ibid.,* p. 18.

15. *Ibid.,* p. 121.

16. *Ibid.,* p. 135.

17. *Ibid.,* p. 123.

18. *Ibid.,* p. 99.

19. *Ibid.,* p. 103.

20. *Ibid.,* p. 105.

21. *Ibid.,* p. 108.

22. *Ibid.,* pp. 109–111.

23. *Ibid.,* 2006 p. 117.

24. *Ibid.,* 2006 p. 119.

25. *Ibid.,* p. 122.

26. *Ibid.,* p. 123.

27. *Ibid.*, p. 124.

28. *Ibid.*, p. 152.

29. *Ibid.*, p. 125.

30. *Ibid.*, p. 143.

31. *Ibid.*, p. 146.

32. *Ibid.*, p. 148.

33. *Ibid.*, p. 153.

34. Phoebe Caldwell was kind enough to reply to my e-mail query seeking clarification of the influence here on her thinking.

35. P. Caldwell, *Finding You Finding Me*, p. 135.

36. *Ibid.*, p. 101.

37. *Ibid.*, p. 102.

38. K. Wojtyła, 'The Person: Subject and Community' (1976) in *Catholic Thought from Lublin Vol.IV Person and Community* p. 223.

39. *Ibid.*, p. 224.

40. *Ibid.*, p. 224.

41. K. Wojtyła, 'Subjectivity and the Irreducible in the Human Being' (1975) in *Catholic Thought from Lublin Vol.IV Person and Community* p. 214.

42. K. Wojtyła, *Love and Responsibility* (London: Fount (1979) 1982), p. 217, also footnote 57; p. 242.

43. St John Chrysostom, *Homily*, 2.13.

44. St Augustine *On the good of widowhood*, 29.

45. Vatican II, *Lumen Gentium* 11; see also *Apostolicam actuositatem* 11.

46. Pope John Paul II, *Familiaris Consortio*, 17, 50.

47. *Ibid.*, 50.

48. Pope John Paul II, Homily *Jubilee of the Disabled* (3 December 2000), 2; *Familiaris Consortio* 77.

49. Pope John Paul II, Documento de la Sancta Sede para el 'año internacional de los minusválidos' in *L'Osservatore Romano* (Spanish edition) (4 March 1981), II.6.

50. Pope John Paul II, *Familiaris Consortio*, 26.

51. Pope John Paul II, 'To the Congress on Integration of Disabled Children' in *L'Osservatore Romano* (English edition) (5 January 2000).

52. Vatican II, *Lumen Gentium*, 40 quoting *Eph* 5:3.

53. Pope John Paul II, Documento de la Sancta Sede para el 'año internacional de los minusválidos' II.7.

54. Pope John Paul II, *Familiaris Consortio*, 22.

55. Pope John Paul II, 'To the Congress on Integration of Disabled Children' 4. His italics.

56. Pope John Paul II, 'To the Congress on Integration of Disabled Children' 3.

57. Pope John Paul II, Message *For the Celebration of the World Day of Peace* (1 January 2001), 5.

58. Pope John Paul II, Message *For the Celebration of the World Day of Peace* (1 January 2001), 19.

59. Pope John Paul II, *Mulieris Dignitatem*, 30–31.

60. *Ibid.*

61. *Ibid.*, 5.

62. *Ibid.*, 30.

63. *Ibid.*

64. *Ibid.*, 30–31.

65. Pope John Paul II, *Redemptoris Mater*, 45.

66. *Ibid.*, 30.

67. *Ibid.*, 31.

68. *Ibid.*, 29.

69. See M. Segers, 'Feminism, liberalism and Catholicism', in R.B. Douglass and D. Hollenbach (eds.), *Catholicism and Liberalism* (Cambridge: Cambridge University Press, 1994), Chapter 10.

70. See J. Redmont, 'Letter to women bares John Paul's isolation' in *National Catholic Reporter* 31/35 (1995), p. 11.

71. On care ethics and feminism see H. Kuhse and P. Singer, *Bioethics: An Anthology* (Oxford: Blackwell, 2006), p. 5.

72. Pope John Paul II, *Mulieris Dignitatem*, 10.

73. Pope John Paul II, *Evangelium vitae*, 99.

74. *Ibid.*

75. Pope John Paul II, *Evangelium vitae*, 83.

76. Pope John Paul II, *Salvifici Doloris*, 28.

77. *Ibid.*, 29.

78. *Ibid.*

79. Pope John Paul II, *Letter to Families*, 11.

80. Pope John Paul II, Homily *Jubilee of the Disabled*, 7.

81. *Ibid.*, 5.

82. Pope John Paul II, *Salvifici Doloris*, 30.

83. *Ibid.*

9

POPE JOHN PAUL II, THE PATIENT IN

PERSISTENT VEGETATIVE STATE AND

THE 'BETTER OFF DEAD'

The situation of the patient in persistent vegetative state is both perplexing and perilous. It is perplexing because the patient is clearly alive yet it appears that there is no evidence of awareness either of self or of surroundings. It is perilous because this lack of evidence is not seen as the inability of science so far to detect awareness. Rather it is treated as a fact that there is no awareness. At the same time it is recommended practice to sedate the patient before painful treatment is given or food and fluids withdrawn. Moreover when new research finds evidence of awareness the patient is said not to be truly in persistent vegetative state or the notion of awareness is finessed so that only a certain type of awareness counts. The condition of persistent vegetative state seems to dovetail well with those who argue that there is a clear separation between biological and biographical life. The patient seems to be the archetypal non–acting person. So it comes as no surprise that Pope John Paul comes to the defence of this particularly vulnerable person.

The perilous situation of the patient in persistent state does not end at interpretations of the diagnosis. Research indicates that many people think that patients in persistent vegetative state are 'more dead than dead' and, ironically, that the minds of these patients are less valuable than those of the dead.[1] As Peter Singer puts it, they may be alive but 'their life's journey has come to an end'.[2] Suggestions have been made that patients in persistent vegetative state are more morally appropriate subjects than higher primates for research experiments into treatments that are of no benefit to them.[3] It is admitted that such research on the 'bodies' of persistent vegetative patients should require the consent of the patient before he or she enters the vegetative state and so becomes unable to consent. However it has been proposed that prior consent is in fact irrelevant on the grounds that the patient in persistent vegetative state no longer has any interests and so no longer has an interest in whether or not his or her wishes are respected.[4] Indeed in a notorious case in France in 1985 a certain Professor Alain Milhaud sent a request to the French National Consultative Ethics Committee to *continue* trials on *other* patients in vegetative state for treatments that he accepted would be of no benefit to those patients. The professor had already experimented on a patient in persistent vegetative state in a trial unconnected to treatment of his condition without any consent either in advance from the patient or from the patient's relatives, nor had he sought any authority from an ethics committee. The patient had been given a sedative before being experimented upon and he died shortly after the project. According to Professor Alain Milhaud patients in persistent vegetative state constituted 'an intermediate state between animal and human' and so were 'almost perfect human models'. The Ethics Committee refused to endorse any subsequent research.[5]

Proposals have been made that patients in persistent vegetative state could be useful candidates for organ donation.[6] Members of an international forum for transplant ethics have presented what they see is a clear case for organ transplantation. The forum explained that 'it is legal in the UK to accelerate the death' of patients in persistent vegetative state by the withdrawal of food and fluids. However organs are no longer suitable if the donor is allowed to die from dehydration and starvation. So the forum suggests that these patients be exempt from the normal legal prohibition against killing thus allowing for early organ retrieval, though it also accepts that patients may be sentient and so should have analgesics. Moreover the forum claims that there is no difference between allowing patients to die by withdrawal of treatment such as food and fluids and 'more actively ending life' since 'the outcome is the same': the patient dies. The forum therefore proposes that fatal drug injections could legitimately be used to bring about death.[7] To be sure the forum betrays thinking that is essentially utilitarian and consequentialist. However the whole issue is complicated by reductive thinking where euthanasia is defined only as taking active steps to end life. A more comprehensive definition is offered by the Sacred Congregation for the Doctrine of the Faith: 'by euthanasia is understood an action or an omission which of itself or by intention causes death, in order that all suffering may in this way be eliminated'. This understanding encompasses not just the act or omission but also the intention of the will and the methods used.[8]

Conclusions have also been drawn that the profoundly disabled patient is merely a human body that is better off dead and that the withdrawal of artificial nutrition and hydration is one method of achieving this. Moreover some argue that it is a moral duty to bring about the death of the patient in persistent vegetative state[9] or that the administration of an agent that causes cardiac arrest would be preferable to allowing an 'agonizing period of "dying" of starvation'.[10] Furthermore to 'resolve problems' there have been calls for a redefinition of death to include persistent vegetative state.[11] Such proposals and attitudes indicate that in some circles these patients are no longer seen as persons deserving of care. Rather the person has gone and only a live body is left. They are "problems, or merely bodies to be medically acted upon or, like patients on ventilators, yet unlike them since patients in persistent vegetative state can breathe on their own, they are 'respiring cadavers'".[12]

In a way the unfolding story of diagnosis and decision-making in the case of persistent vegetative state seems to bear out Pope John Paul's views about science and technology. In setting up the Pontifical Council for Pastoral Assistance to Healthcare Workers in 1985 and then the Pontifical Academy for Life in 1994 coupled with his active interest in the work of scientific and medical bodies Pope John Paul demonstrates a full appreciation that scientific and technological advances raise new moral questions. Moreover rather than seeking easy practical solutions these new questions demand profound reflection on the truth about human beings. Pope John Paul's interest in fostering dialogue with those involved in science shows that there need be no conflict between science and faith. However, whilst Pope John Paul certainly thinks that scientific investigations and reasoned conclusions are important he nevertheless recognises the dangers of seeing science merely as 'a technical fact', as a collection of knowledge that is 'purely functional' and removed from the truth. As he points out, technical knowledge can be used for good as well as evil: poisons can cure and kill, and he warns that science alone cannot give complete answers. Indeed he suggests that when science fails to give the expected ready response then 'ideologies' may break in under the guise of scientific answers[13] hence practical solutions to either using or disposing of what appear to be inconvenient people.

For the most part Catholic debate on the patient in persistent vegetative state has centred on the provision of artificial hydration and nutrition and whether this provision is optional and extraordinary or obligatory and ordinary. This debate intensified in 2004 after Pope John Paul's *Address to the Participants in the International Congress on "Life–Sustaining Treatments and Vegetative State: Scientific Advances and Ethical Dilemmas"* and its subsequent commentary from the Congregation for the Doctrine of the Faith in 2007. Some charge Pope John Paul with holding a 'revisionist' position that is, with departing significantly from Catholic tradition and they interpret the Pope's speech as saying that artificial feeding is absolutely obligatory 'in all cases'.[14] Apart from the fact that this accusation fails to appreciate the nuance of the Pope's view and it disregards the clarification made by the Congregation of the Faith in 2007, the charge is undermined by an exploration of the tradition itself.

However in the debate there is another charge levelled against Pope John Paul that places the person in persistent vegetative state in an even more perilous situation. It is more perilous because the argument has moved from a focus on treatment to a focus on the actual life of the patient. The charge is that Pope John Paul supports vitalism: since the only benefit offered by artificial nutrition and hydration is the prolongation of the patient's biological life this is keeping the patient alive no matter what.[15] It is claimed that Pope John Paul's position is 'contrary to Catholic teaching' on the grounds that the tradition denies that 'mere continued biological existence constitutes a benefit in itself'.[16] In contrast to the Pope's teaching it is argued that there is a 'theological basis for distinguishing between the death of the body with its residual movements and the death of the person', between biological and biographical life. In persistent vegetative state not only is there no person, there is also no communication with God[17] and no possibility to strive for the purpose of life, friendship with God.[18] Moreover it has been suggested that prolonging this 'state of existence' actually 'precludes spiritual activity'.[19]From these accounts it seems that not only is the patient in persistent vegetative state 'more dead than dead' the person is also out of touch with God.

On one level Pope John Paul's intervention in the care of patients in persistent vegetative state in 2004 seems to anticipate Pope Benedict's view that bioethics has become 'a particularly crucial battleground' for the cultural struggle between technology and human moral responsibility.[20] Pope John Paul enters this struggle in the defence of the human person who always has the dignity of being a person whatever his or her capacities, abilities or situation. To understand this battle requires an extensive exploration of both sides of this cultural divide and the person in persistent vegetative state appears to be at the centre of the battlefield. The person in persistent vegetative state is under consideration not only in academic circles but also in the practical spheres of law, clinical practice and social attitudes to the severely disabled. However much of the discussion follows the method of practical ethics that involves looking to find a ready solution on how to treat or not treat the patient. In contrast Pope John Paul calls attention to the neglected deeper issues by reminding that this discussion concerns reflection on the inherent dignity of the human person in an extreme situation. His critics may feel that he is interfering at too detailed a level into clinical practice but this may be because he has accurately read the signs of the times and is well aware of what is at stake.

On another level anthropology is also the battlefield. Certainly for Pope John Paul the issue is not about keeping people alive no matter what. On many occasions the Pope speaks of the need to recognise the limits of human life yet he also warns of the dangers of applying quality of life considerations that attack the principle that human life is 'a fundamental good'[21]. Indeed he reminds us that 'man is called to a fullness of life which far exceeds the dimensions of his earthly existence'. Nevertheless he points out that earthly life 'life in time' is 'the fundamental condition, the initial stage and an integral part of the entire unified process of human existence'. He adds 'after all, life on earth is not an "ultimate" but a "penultimate" reality; even so, it remains a *sacred reality* entrusted to us' (his italics). [22] By opposing approaches that separate biological life from biographical life and that devalue human life itself Pope John Paul's views on the person in persistent vegetative state reinforce that sacred reality.

Persistent vegetative state: the background

In the *Practical Handbook of Neurosurgery* one of Britain's leading practitioners, Graham Teasdale offers what has become the classic description of persistent vegetative state:

> the vegetative state was defined by Jennett and Plum in 1972 as being survival with no evidence of psychologically meaningful activity as judged behaviourally. Their criteria included cycles of spontaneous eye closure and opening but a strict absence of obeying simple commands, expression of any words or evidence of appropriate responsiveness to the environment. [23]

Even though a neurosurgeon, Bryan Jennett and a physician, Fred Plum have credit for describing this state the title of their paper, published in the *Lancet* in 1972, 'A syndrome in search of a name', reflects the fact that the condition was not new. Bryan Jennett points out that the condition had already been described by the German psychiatrist Ernst Kretschmer in 1940 who named it the 'apallic syndrome', apallic referring to 'without cortex' since Ernst Kretschmer assumed that all functions of the cerebral cortex were lacking. [24]

What is noteworthy is that as early as 1972 Bryan Jennett and Fred Plum realised that Ernst Kretschmer's assumptions might be incorrect; it could not be absolutely said that there was no functioning cortex. Bryan Jennett explains that he and Fred Plum preferred 'vegetative state' since that implies 'a mental state rather than types of motor dysfunction' that would indicate levels of cortex functioning. [25] The term 'persistent vegetative state' was then widely adopted by philosophers, lawyers and those outside medicine [26] to cater for patients who would otherwise have died but who had been kept alive by new technological medical advances. Indeed, Bryan Jennett's claim that although some people object to the demeaning term 'vegetative state' for postcomatose patients there seems little inclination to replace the term[27] appears to be backed up by those who demonstrate that 'persistent vegetative state' has taken a 'firm hold' in people's minds and 'resists revision' even if it has fallen out of use with neurologists[28] and despite attempts to replace 'vegetative state' with 'unresponsive wakefulness syndrome'.[29] In order to come to a better appreciation of what Bryan Jennett and Fred Plum were seeking to achieve and what they meant by persistent vegetative state it is necessary to return to the bioethical context of their 1972 paper.

Fred Plum and Bryan Jennett on the vegetative state

From an interview for the 1997 *International Journal of Trauma Nursing* it seems that in the 1960s and 1970s Bryan Jennett and Fred Plum were separately funded by the National Institutes of Health, Public Health Service, US department of Health and Human Services to collect data on comatose patients who had suffered severe head injuries and undoubtedly their research fed into their 1972 paper. It is interesting to note that just a few years before Fred Plum and Bryan Jennett's invention of the term persistent vegetative state the Harvard Medical School Committee was considering the possibility of a new definition of death, brain death. At much the same time there were discussions surrounding the developing new technology of organ transplants, though how closely the organ donation and redefinition of death debates were linked remains contentious. Certainly organs harvested from a beating–heart brain–dead donor are the most viable since the organs remain oxygenated. Still, what seemed to drive the Harvard Committee's discussion was finding a guide for discontinuing futile treatment, though ironically donors must be kept on some form of prolonged treatment to facilitate the removal of viable organs.

There is some ambiguity over the aims of the Harvard Medical School since its Report begins by stating that its 'primary purpose is to define irreversible coma as a new criterion for death'.[30] Nevertheless the outcome of the Report was to identify 'brain death' with death even though a comment in the Report that 'the burden is great on individuals who suffer permanent loss of intellect' suggests otherwise since, after all, dead patients do not carry burdens. Following this Report the US adopted the whole brain criterion for defining death and in the UK the permanent functional death of the brain stem constitutes death. Although the Report itself states that both the burden on patients, families, hospital resources of futile treatment and issues of obtaining transplant organs were behind their redefinition, Peter Singer's analysis of events leading up to the Report[31] and its chairman's enthusiasm for transplant surgery suggests that redefinition of death to facilitate organ transplants perhaps was foremost in the minds of members and at the very least 'stimulated' debate.[32] For Bryan Jennett and Fred Plum the more absorbing aspect may have been the Report's search for a guide for discontinuing futile treatment.

Returning to the early days of research into comatose patients Bryan Jennett and Fred Plum had to evaluate and modify the scores on a coma scale for a particular group of patients who had undergone new methods of treatment and so survived what in the past would have been fatal injury but were left with severe and permanent brain damage. As part of his research into comatose patients Bryan Jennett soon realised that a tool was needed to measure function in comatose patients objectively and so he and Graham Teasdale developed the Coma Index. Initially just a research tool, the Coma Index was simple to use and originally, it seems, even an inanimate object could receive a score at the minimum level of three.[33] Bryan Jennett explains that what later came to be known as the Glasgow Coma Scale referred to fourteen previously published descriptions of altered consciousness, involved three to seventeen different levels and it depended on the skilled observations by healthcare professionals of responses of patients 'at the bedside'.[34] However early research using the Glasgow Coma Scale also pointed to a severe and permanent state of altered consciousness and although there were a number of pathways that led to this level of brain damage Bryan Jennett and Fred Plum decided that a new term would be useful to describe the state and so aid communication between doctors, the patient's relatives and others.[35]

The idea that such a description would in fact help in practical decision–making seems to have been uppermost in the minds of the authors. As they explained,

> there is a group of patients who never show evidence of a working mind. This concept may be criticised on the grounds that observation of behaviour is insufficient evidence on which to base a judgement of mental activity; it is our view that there is no reliable alternative available to the doctor at the bedside, which is where decisions have to be made.[36]

To clarify the types of decisions they expected, 'it may well become a matter for discussion how worth while life is for patients whose capacity for meaningful response is very limited'.[37] Perhaps as an indication of what lay implicitly behind their comments, Bryan Jennett took an interest in high technology medicine in the context of limited medical resources and, according to Tony Smith, the 1984 editor of the BMJ, Bryan Jennett believed that patients who are 'too ill to benefit' should not be in intensive care.[38] In his paper *Letting Vegetative Patients Die* published in the BMJ in 1992 Bryan Jennett argues that treatment is only justified 'if there is a reasonable probability of meaningful recovery and of regaining life as a social person' and that the decision to stop feeding vegetative patients is 'an extension' of the 'good practice' of avoiding treatment that will not benefit. Moreover, he says that 'the recovery of a limited degree of awareness may indeed be worse than non–sentience'. Bryan Jennett's notion that what matters is life as a social person seems reflected in his rejection of a life of 'incapacitating mental impairment and total dependency'.[39] Fred Plum himself was an advocate of the right to die and according to his obituary in the *Lancet* he 'often said that the practice of medicine is about preserving the brain. "We are our minds"', he told the *Los Angeles Times* in 1994'.[40]

Whilst the Glasgow Coma Scale was recognised to be an invaluable tool and as Bryan Jennett says, it has become everyday practice in many countries and is part of nursing training[41] it was also accepted that an outcome scale was needed. As Graham Teasdale explains the outcome of acute brain injury is 'foremost in the minds of patients and their families' and a pointer on a scale can give them a 'realistic and understandable account of the range of possibilities' and inform them of the patient's prospects.[42] In the initial Glasgow Outcome Scale five categories were identified with the aim of summarising 'the social capacity of the patient rather than listing specific disabilities';[43] these disabilities were after all expressed in the Glasgow Coma Scale. The questions on the Outcome Scale reflect its emphasis on social disability, life–style, work status and leisure, quality of relationships.[44] The five categories were firstly, good recovery; secondly, moderate disability; thirdly severe disability; fourthly persistent vegetative state; fifthly, death; though Bryan Jennett accepts that 'persistent' has now been dropped.[45] The five categories were broadened into eight in 1981 in order to take account of gradations in disability in the first three conscious survival categories. Given new research another category may have to be introduced between vegetative state and severe disability, that of the 'minimally responsive state'. However, it is noteworthy that vegetative state is not categorised as 'severe disability' but rather has a status one up from death. As Daniel Wikler reports vegetative state can be considered either as 'the lowest–functioning phase of life' or 'the highest–functioning phase of death'[46]

The Harvard Report's reference to irreversible coma was sometimes interpreted as permanent loss of consciousness so that death would be defined not by loss of all brain functions but loss of the higher functions that separate human beings from higher primates, the higher–brain death criterion.[47] However this was clarified in the US President's Commission Report *Defining Death: Medical, Legal and Ethical Issues in the Definition of Death* 1981 which rejected the higher–brain death criterion of the loss of cerebral functions on the grounds that it would 'depart radically' from traditional standards and would place certain categories of patients, the severely retarded, senile, in persistent vegetative state, outside personhood and even dead.[48]

Certainly in 1972 Bryan Jennett and Fred Plum did not consider the patient in persistent vegetative state to be dead albeit they also thought that any further treatment was futile and could not benefit the patient. However, Bryan Jennett also says that this lack of a 'working mind' is 'widely perceived to be an outcome of medical intervention that is worse than death'.[49]

As far as Bryan Jennett is concerned when he and Fred Plum first invented the term 'persistent vegetative state' the designation 'vegetative' seemed entirely appropriate and indeed he thinks it remains so.[50] The term 'vegetative' itself indicates that the patient is alive though as Bryan Jennett explains, 'vegetative' is not obscure; it refers to patients who live merely a physical life, who have limited and primitive responsiveness to external stimuli.[51] The contentious aspect of the term lies, he thinks, not with the implications of 'vegetative' but rather with 'persistent' since this has been mistakenly, in his opinion, taken to refer to 'irreversibility' and irreversibility was not, he argues implied by the 1972 paper.[52] Notwithstanding the problem of the ambiguity of 'persistent' and Bryan Jennett's dismissal of concerns over 'vegetative', the term he and Fred Plum chose to replace apallic syndrome, 'vegetative state', seems to have reinforced the now rather persistent myth that there is a total lack of functioning in the cortex. It also seems significant that on some accounts of the Glasgow Outcome Scale the 'comment' added to 'vegetative state' declares 'absence of function in the cerebral cortex, although cortex may be structurally intact'.[53] It seems that this shorthand explanation of persistent vegetative state is pervasive with many commentators conflating the fact that it is difficult to detect functioning in the cortex with the declaration that therefore there is no functioning.

Still, when Bryan Jennett looks back from 2002 to his and Fred Plum's understanding in 1972 he reflects that the designation of 'persistent vegetative state' was a 'broad descriptive term, indicating only absence of observed cognitive function' and that this therefore 'invited further clinical and pathological investigations rather than giving the impression of a problem already fully understood'.[54] Indeed, rather than simply an absence of observed cognitive function Bryan Jennett accepts that there are 'some islands of cortical activity'.[55] Often the assertion that 'patients in a vegetative state have no cortical function' is made at the outset even if the discussion goes on to be more nuanced.[56] This leads to ambiguous statements like the one offered by NHS Choices, 'a reliable source of health and social care information' that 'while a person who is in a vegetative state may be technically conscious, they are really unconscious' and this leads to the recommendation that if the state persists over twelve months an application can be made to the courts to withdraw nutritional support and 'the person will be sedated, allowing them to die peacefully in their sleep.'[57] Of course one might ask why the patient is sedated if he or she is 'really unconscious' and whether an unconscious patient can die 'peacefully'.

A similar move seems to be made when it comes to feeding the patient in vegetative state. The patient appears to retain the ability to chew and swallow though this lacks coordination[58] and it seems that nutritional and hydration needs could be met orally even though this has risks and requires great care.[59]However it is often reported that 'the capacity to chew and swallow in a normal manner is lost because these functions are voluntary, requiring intact cerebral hemispheres'.[60] Certainly there are serious problems with the possibility of aspiration and this is often the reason why patients in persistent vegetative state are fed and hydrated artificially.[61] Moreover oral feeding is often seen as too time consuming.[62] Nevertheless simply because artificial feeding is established for safety or efficiency reasons it does not mean that the capacity to chew and swallow is lost.[63] Perhaps the telling phrase is 'in a normal manner', a phrase that suggests that reflexes are not normal or that only voluntary behaviour counts. Whilst the ability to chew and swallow is of no relevance to those who see persistent vegetative state in terms of right to die cases,[64] it does seem to become relevant where it is claimed that once artifical nutrition and hydration are withdrawn the patient dies from a 'fatal pathology', that is the inability to chew and swallow.[65] So it is argued that removal of artificial nutrition and hydration 'merely allows the pathology in question to take its natural course' and the pathology which directly causes death is 'the dysfunction of the cerebral cortex. Because of this pathology, the patient is unable to eat and drink on his own'.[66]

Certainly Bryan Jennett accepts that patients in vegetative state are left 'without any *normal* function in the cerebral cortex, and therefore [are] bereft of thought or perception'; there is 'no evidence' of the patients being aware of their surroundings (my italics)[67] and he further agrees that there is 'some residual cortical function' in many vegetative patients.[68] Bryan Jennett and Fred Plum perhaps recognised this when they placed the point of focus in persistent vegetative state on a mental state rather than a particular anatomical abnormality. This is brought out in what Bryan Jennett and Fred Plum refer to as 'the essential component of this syndrome' which is 'the absence of any adaptive response to the external environment, the absence of any evidence of a functioning mind which is either receiving or projecting information, in a patient who has long periods of wakefulness'.[69] Bryan Jennett and Fred Plum noted that unlike patients in comas, patients in vegetative state had wake sleep cycles though they also appeared to be unaware of their surroundings. Later observations and research have led Bryan Jennett to go beyond the initial 1972 description and add that some patients in vegetative state may indeed 'smile, frown and occasionally laugh or weep' but 'these emotional behaviours show no consistent relation to an appropriate stimulus'. Even though carers and relatives report certain behaviours that appear to demonstrate anxiety, discomfort or relaxation he says the 'most skilled observers accept them as part of the extensive repertoire of reflex responses shown by some vegetative patients'.[70] Moreover, Bryan Jennett argues, this unawareness of the surroundings and of the self implies 'loss of the capacity to experience pain or suffering' and he adds that patients in vegetative state show no behavioural responses that might indicate pain of suffering and the depression of the cerebral metabolic rate for glucose is at levels equivalent to deep surgical anaesthesia.[71]

New Evidence

Bryan Jennett's acceptance that all along he and Fred Plum were aware that the designation 'apallic', meaning no functioning cortex was mistaken and their satisfaction with vegetative state as the alternative even though it carries pejorative connotations seems to contribute to the view that they downplayed the difficulties of definitively establishing lack of awareness and were not overly concerned about the possibility of misdiagnosis.[72] The latest research has now shown that some patients classified as in a vegetative state have demonstrated some reactivity and also mental responses to tests. Some argue that such patients are not in fact in vegetative state and that what is required is the creation of a new category of clinical state up from vegetative state, one suggestion being 'the Cartesian stage or state of consciousness', the 'I think therefore I am', to express the 'very essence of Homo sapiens' as expressed by the possibility of these mental responses.[73] Others caution against making 'strong claims about awareness'.[74] Still others, on the basis of extensive research, have questioned whether consciousness is mediated by the cerebral cortex alone.[75] Moreover some have come to doubt the formerly stated certainty that patients in vegetative state are incapable of any conscious experience including pain and suffering.[76] However, all of these positions seem to forget that the issue may not be presence or absence of activity but rather a disconnection between different regions of the brain such that there can be no reliable evidence. Perhaps more telling, and something that Bryan Jennett and Fred Plum originally recognised when they moved away from a description relying on motor dysfunction to an interpretation of a mental state, the kinds of responses or apparent lack of response are 'first–person' events, events of the patient, and as such cannot be proved or indeed disproved by third person observation.[77]

Old Attitudes

What may be of more significance is the attitude taken towards patients in vegetative state, an attitude already implicit in the term vegetative itself. Notably, whilst the notion of a life not worth living first seems to have appeared with the eugenic movement of the 1930s, the claim that a person may be better off dead appears with the rise of bioethics in the 1970s. Bryan Jennett's view that it would be better to let patients in vegetative state die seems to be a common attitude to patients in this condition even if the reasons behind it vary. On the one hand and arguing from the patient perspective, for Bryan Jennett simply the possibility that a patient might recover limited awareness which, he says, might be worse than non–sentience is reason enough.[78] On the other hand and arguing from the patient and relative relationship, according to James Bernat most patients do not wish to be a burden on their loved ones 'particularly without the benefit of conscious experience' and since 'continued vegetative state represents an emotional and financial burden' on families this is reason enough to discontinue treatment and allow the patient to die.[79] Bryan Jennett also appeals to the more generalised claim that the vegetative state is 'widely perceived to be an outcome of medical intervention that is worse than death'.[80] Similarly Bernard Lo refers to the view that 'many persons would be horrified to be kept alive if there were virtually no likelihood of regaining consciousness. To them life as a "vegetable" is a fate worse than death'.[81]

Certainly most people if asked would not wish to be in persistent vegetative state and it seems that these attitudes rather than science are precisely what carry weight in determining how to treat patients in vegetative state. After all there are continuing new discoveries about consciousness and neurologists and scientists are discovering more pathways to identify its possible activity even though the task of re–establishing connections, arguably the real issue in the condition, remains elusive. When Ernst Kretschmer first identified what he called apallic syndrome the apparent lack of consciousness was decisive. By the apparent scientific nature of their 1972 paper Bryan Jennett and Fred Plum shifted the debate so that a diagnosis of persistent vegetative state offered a clear course of action: any treatment was futile so could be discontinued. Indeed there appear to be good reasons to stop treatment sooner rather than later since any recovery however unlikely or slight might leave the patient worse off in the sense that he or she might gain some awareness of his or her condition.

Given that science cannot be certain about levels of consciousness and despite this elusiveness there is now another shift towards finessing the notion of consciousness. As the ethicists Julian Savulescu and Guy Kahane state just because a brain damaged patient is 'conscious in *one sense*' does not mean that this makes any moral difference if he or she is 'not conscious in the *relevant sense*' (their italics).[82] The authors ground the moral significance of consciousness in 'the moral significance of interests' and, they say 'it is doubtful that a mental life consisting only of a bare stream of consciousness – a sequence of random and hedonically neutral sensations – could be said to involve interests of any kind'.[83] They argue that since there are no experiential interests, there is no 'genuine' suffering even if there is a pain or pleasure response to stimuli.[84] Moreover, for Julian Savulescu and Guy Kahane as for Bryan Jennett the very possibility of some level of consciousness provides 'positive reasons' not to sustain life, and this applies particularly if the patient is in a minimal conscious state: being 'painfully aware' of his or her condition with little hope of communication, inability to pursue desires or projects. As the authors say with reference to the experience of a person with less than completely locked in syndrome 'no agency or meaningful social relations' is 'an extremely horrific experience' that would not be wished upon even one's worst enemy.[85] The authors conclude, 'even if using fMRI we can establish that brain–damaged patients still enjoy phenomenal consciousness and a significant measure of sapience, terminating these patients' lives might be morally required, not merely permissible'.[86]

The idea that there is a distinction between bodily pain and 'genuine' pain, that is pain experienced in the mind of someone with 'a sufficient degree of cognitive capacity'[87] seems to be a return to a Cartesian outlook and the belief in the person as rather immaterial and insubstantial. Perhaps more seriously, Julian Savulescu and Guy Kahane seem to be adopting precisely the discriminatory attitudes towards people with disability that have been identified by proponents of the social model of disability. Even if others may be horrified by the thought of 'existence' in vegetative state, however much they may dismiss bodily suffering, the able–bodied person cannot 'speak for' the profoundly disabled person in terms of the 'normal' person's own preference: the 'I would not want to be like that' so therefore he or she should not be allowed to exist like that. This is not to deny that this condition of profound disability is challenging, deeply problematic and perplexing. But it does indicate that despite scientific breakthroughs and the resultant clear signs of learning using eye blinking responses and microswitch–based technology[88] such discriminatory attitudes with their focus on the futility or indeed harm of treatment or therapies end up closing off any pathway into the condition through communication.[89]

Arguably it is still the case that the patient, like all persons, is incommunicable. By this it is not meant that the patient cannot communicate. Rather it is to assert that, as with every other person, no one else can think or understand or feel as he or she does; the patient in vegetative state is a unique person, as unique as any other person. No one can grasp fully the being of the patient in vegetative state.

Not dead yet: the non–acting person and the patient in vegetative state

Any description of the patient in vegetative state taken from the perspective of those who argue his or her existence is worthless, futile or even worse than death seems to hinge not only on the patient's insentience but also on his or her lack of agency and total dependency.[90] It seems that the patient in vegetative state, following the Glasgow Outcome Scale exists in the state one up from death and so is the archetypal non–acting human being. As was said of Tony Bland, one of the UK's most well known patient in persistent vegetative state, well known that is because his was a high profile case brought specifically to allow doctors to bring about his death, Tony Bland existed in a 'living death'.[91]

Looking at Pope John Paul's definition of death in his *Address to the International Congress on Organ Transplants*[92] it would seem that Tony Bland was somewhat further from living death than Lord Justice Goff would have it. According to Pope John Paul in seeking 'complete certainty' on when a person can be considered dead 'it is helpful to recall that the death of the person is a single event.' This 'single event' consists in 'the total disintegration of that unitary and integrated whole that is the personal self. It results from the separation of the life–principle (or soul) from the corporeal reality of the person' and this event cannot be identified directly by scientific techniques or empirical methods. It may be that Pope John Paul has in mind here those who say that the death of the person is not the same as the death of the human being: the person can cease to exist before his or her body dies. Pope John Paul continues even if the 'exact moment' of death cannot be ascertained, certain identifiable biological signs indicate that the person has indeed died. One such sign 'if rigorously applied' seems to be 'the complete and irreversible cessation of all brain activity', a sign that can provide the 'moral certainty' for ascertaining death.

The significance of Pope John Paul's definition of death can be grasped more fully if his understanding of the acting person is called to mind. Remembering that both *actus humani*, that is an act involving the will, and *actus hominis*, whatever happens in a human being, properly belong to the human person as his or her acts, then as long as there is some brain activity the human being is still alive since this is still evidence of an *actus hominis*, what 'happens' in the person. This is presumably one reason why Pope John Paul finds the designation 'vegetative state' so lamentable. However, Pope John Paul is also aware of the complexities of defining death. In his letter to the Pontifical Academy of Sciences in 2005, some five years after he said that brain death could be regarded as a 'sign' of death, Pope John Paul declares that there is still a need to explore the 'signs of death' in order to continue a 'constant dialogue' that can 'guarantee respect for life'. Total and complete brain death, 'rigorously applied' may indicate that death has occurred but Pope John Paul remains clear that the death of a person is an event that cannot be directly identified either by techinique or by empirical methods. This is because it involves the 'definitive loss of the constitutive unity of body and spirit'[93] and this loss of unity, the separation of body and soul is not the subject of observation.

The patient in persistent vegetative state may not yet be dead. However extensive debates on the provision or withdrawal of treatment and a series of highly publicised cases, in particular the high profile and contentious case of Terri Schiavo, led Pope John Paul to comment on the 'very significant issue' of the vegetative state in his *Address to the participants in the International Congress on "life–sustaining treatments and vegetative state: scientific advances and ethical dilemmas".*[94] However the discussion on whether or not to treat does not appear to be the main motivating force behind the Pope's strong remarks. What seems to drive Pope John Paul's intervention are specific presumptions about the status of these most profoundly disabled human beings, presumptions that threaten their personal dignity. It is therefore a mistake to view his comments simply as if they are unwarranted interference in clinical decision–making or the result of inadequate medical knowledge.[95] Certainly he objects to the term 'vegetative state' since it demeans the 'value and personal dignity' of patients in this clinical condition.[96] Nevertheless his primary concern seems to be that the term 'vegetative' whose use is, he admits, 'solidly established' seems to lend support to those people who 'cast doubt on the persistence of the "human quality" itself' in the case of these patients with such profound disability. And a decision to remove food and fluids on the grounds that the patient will not recover an acceptable mental life is a clear attack on human dignity.

Care and treatment of the patient and support of the family

There can be no doubt that Pope John Paul recognises the tragedy for the patient who has been 'struck down by this terrible clinical condition'[97] and he acknowledges the enormity of caring for these most profoundly disabled patients. He urges practical support for families, prevention of any social isolation and, notably, that the medical team help the family 'understand that they are there as allies who are in this struggle with them'.[98] This last point may perhaps cause reflection for those like Bryan Jennett who seem somewhat dismissive of the possibly over–optimistic views of some relatives in contrast to his support of the possibly over–pessimistic views of some healthcare professionals.[99] As an illustration that no one falls outside the boundaries of his profound reflection on the meaning of suffering Pope John Paul asks for spiritual and pastoral care as a way into 'recovering the deepest meaning of an apparently desperate condition'.[100]

In contrast perhaps to those like Bryan Jennett, Julian Savulescu and Guy Kahane who consider that treatment may in fact do more harm than good since it may result in some level of awareness Pope John Paul calls for 'appropriate, concrete initiatives'. His suggestions here seem particularly forward thinking, including as they do 'intensive rehabilitation programmes' and 'a network of awakening centres with specialized treatment'.[101] However, it seems that it was his stated view on the provision of nutrition and hydration that caused the most significant controversy. It is perhaps useful to situate Pope John Paul's concern over the withdrawal of artificial hydration and nutrition for patients in persistent vegetative state in the context of discussions in the US and UK around three high profile cases, those of Nancy Cruzan, Tony Bland and Terri Schiavo: signs of the times in action.

Not feeding the 'vegetative' patient

One implicit rationale behind the cessation of food and fluids for the vegetative patient is offered by Daniel Callahan, one of the co–founders of the Hastings Center and a prominent bioethicist in the USA. In his article 'On Feeding the Dying', published in 1983, Daniel Callahan ominously predicted that 'a denial of nutrition may in the long run become the only effective way to make certain that a large number of biologically tenacious patients actually die'.[102] Notably the patient in persistent vegetative state can remain in this condition for some time if given proper care so he or she is arguably not dying. Nevertheless, as Bryan Jennett and Clare Dyer put it, the patient's 'prolonged survival' presents a 'dilemma' for family, carers and society[103] and so this particularly 'tenacious patient' has become the focus for much bioethical discussion.

According to Bryan Jennett and Clare Dyer there is a consensus in the US that life sustaining treatment, including the cessation of artificial hydration and nutrition, should be discontinued and this is related, they argue, to the issue of informed consent and advance directives. The implication is that no one would wish to exist in persistent vegetative state and that death is preferable. They explain this link in their discussion of arguably the first 'right to die' case in the US, that of Nancy Cruzan, a woman brain–damaged after a car accident in 1983 and left in vegetative state. Realising that their daughter would not recover even though she was not terminally ill, the parents of Ms Cruzan had asked for the removal of her gastronomy tube. The Missouri Supreme Court ruled that there was insufficient evidence of her wishes and that her parents could not make a substituted judgment on her behalf. However, in 1990 'new evidence' that the court considered was 'clear and convincing' was provided by three friends to demonstrate that Ms Cruzan did not wish to remain in persistent vegetative state and the court authorised removal of the feeding tube. Ms Cruzan died after twenty–four hours.

In contrast in the UK case of Tony Bland, left in persistent vegetative state after being crushed in the Hillsborough disaster in 1989, the matter of the teenager's wishes were not as important. In the Court of Appeal it was accepted that Tony Bland had not made his wishes known, indeed it was recognised that most adolescents would not have addressed the issue. Nevertheless, Tony's parents argued that their son would not have wanted to remain in a vegetative state and it seems that this helped the judges in their decision. The judges looked at what they considered to be the best interests of the patient and they decided that mere continuation of biological life would be of no benefit to him. Lord Keith of Kinkel accepted that it was difficult to make a value judgment on human life. However he continued 'to an individual with no cognitive capacity whatever, and no prospect of ever recovering any such capacity in this world, it must be a matter of complete indifference whether he lives or dies'.[104] Even if the *Bland* case was arguably not so much about whether it was in the patient's best interests to die but rather whether it was in his best interests that life be prolonged, still it was admitted that the sole purpose of stopping his feeding was in order to bring about Tony Bland's death.[105]

The *Bland* case defined the administration of food and fluids as medical treatment in the UK, so if Tony Bland had been competent or had made a valid and applicable advance directive refusing such treatment then the decision to withdraw artificial hydration and nutrition would have been clear cut. Certainly cases like *Cruzan* and *Bland* have led to significant promotion of advance directives in the US and in the UK. However, Bryan Jennett and Clare Dyer point out that not everyone makes their wishes so clearly known and so they suggest that the removal of artificial hydration and nutrition might be considered the appropriate and normative way of dealing with patients in persistent vegetative state.[106]

However the case that seems to have provoked the biggest outcry over the removal of artificial hydration and nutrition from a patient in persistent vegetative state and not only in the US was the case of Terri Schiavo. Mrs Schiavo collapsed with what appeared to be a cardiac arrest in 1990. Although there was some speculation that her collapse had been caused by possible bulimia or diet related issues there was insufficient evidence for this though her blood component levels, particularly her potassium levels were abnormal.[107] Mr Schiavo petitioned to have her feeding tube removed but Terri's parents contested the petition. At the first hearing and relying on evidence presented by Terri's husband, Michael, Judge Greer ruled that Mrs Schiavo would have chosen to have her feeding tube removed. However, Terri's parents began a series of appeals and whilst these were being considered the tube was alternately reinserted under a special statue, called 'Terri's Law', issued by the Governor of Florida, and then removed. After this series of well publicised hearings that polarised the public and press the Florida federal court decided that there was no likelihood that Terri's parents would succeed in their appeals and there was no reason why Judge Greer should not have relied on Michael Schiavo's evidence about Terri's wishes so the court authorised Terri's feeding tube to be disconnected. Terri died thirteen days later in 2005.

According to the autopsy the cause of death was put as 'complications of anoxic encephalopathy', an all–encompassing term for degenerative brain damage caused by lack of oxygen. There had been significant disagreement about whether or not Terri Schiavo was actually in a persistent vegetative state and this was perhaps exacerbated by the mistaken belief on the part of some that persistent vegetative state involves total lack of cortical function rather than the possibility of islands of consciousness. In his autopsy report Stephen Nelson, the Chief Medical Examiner, explained that a post–mortem examination of the patient's brain, or indeed any brain, 'cannot prove or disprove a diagnosis of persistent vegetative state or minimally conscious state'.[108] This is because the state is a clinical diagnosis not a pathological one. He also noted that an MRI scan had not been done when Terri was alive since there was a risk of further injury given that she had an implanted thalamic stimulator. Although patients in persistent vegetative state are still able to chew and swallow it seems that Terri was not a candidate for oral nutrition and hydration because of a significant risk of aspiration. According to the autopsy report whilst the 'cause and manner' of her death was 'severe anoxic brain injury' whose initial cause was 'undetermined', the 'mechanism' by which Terri died was 'of marked dehydration but not starvation'.[109]

Daniel Callahan's 1983 prediction seems to have been realised even if in the cases of Nancy Cruzan, Tony Bland and Terri Schiavo the provision of hydration and nutrition was considered medical treatment that could be withdrawn on the grounds that it was assumed that the patients would not have wanted to be kept alive that way or, as in the *Bland* case, such an existence was not in his best interests. However the clear implication is that there is little or no value or meaning in living a life of total dependence or profound disability. Certainly in the *Bland* case the judges felt that it was more appropriate for parliament to legislate on the issue of withdrawing or withholding treatment and the status of artificial hydration and nutrition. Indeed they also went out of their way to state that their ruling did not create a precedent. Nevertheless, in the UK the decision in the *Bland* case has become highly influential and was soon followed in two other cases.[110]

Parliament did in fact legislate and under the *Mental Capacity Act 2005 Code of Practice* the provision of hydration and nutrition is considered to be medical treatment. Notably, in the 2010 GMC guidelines *Treatment and care towards the end of life: good practice in decision making* the GMC refers to the *Bland* decision as having established the medical status of hydration and nutrition.[111] Under this guidance the physician is advised to listen to the patient and to those close to him or her and although a competent patient's wishes are usually the 'deciding factor', the physician does not have to provide the competent patient with artificial hydration and nutrition even if the patient requests it if it is judged not to be clinically appropriate.[112] This judgment is made by weighing up the benefits, burdens and risks of the treatment. As for a patient who does not have sufficient capacity to express his or her wishes and who cannot eat or drink efficaciously but where 'death is not expected' then the guidelines state that artificial nutrition and hydration is 'usually' of overall benefit. However it may be withdrawn or withheld if the physician, after consulting a senior clinician or seeking further opinion from colleagues, believes provision would not be in the patient's best interests.[113] Where a patient without capacity is expected to die the provision of artificial hydration and nutrition is 'not usually appropriate'.[114] Whilst in the case of incompetent patients the decision to discontinue this treatment is simply made by the physicians in consultation with the family if appropriate, curiously in the case of a patient in vegetative state or 'a condition closely resembling pvs', presumably also an incompetent patient, in England, Wales and Northern Ireland the physician has to go to court for a ruling.[115]

A not insignificant ramification of designating the provision of food and fluids as treatment so that they can legally be withdrawn or withheld is that many argue the patient dies from starvation or dehydration, though in fact it is dehydration rather than malnutrition.[116] This argument is presented on both sides of the case, both by those who say that food and fluids are basic care and so should in principle always be offered and, more vociferously it seems by those who argue for the legalisation of euthanasia and assisted suicide on the grounds that these forms of actively ending life are 'more humane' than allowing a patient to starve to death. Indeed the growing evidence that patients in persistent vegetative state have some affective experiences even if there are no cognitive experiences lead some to urge that discontinuation of treatment should be supplemented with some form of active euthanasia in order to avoid slow euthanasia.[117] Notably Pope John Paul sees that death by starvation or dehydration is 'the only possible outcome' once nutrition and hydration are withdrawn and so he says that if this is done 'knowingly and willingly', and, quoting *Evangelium vitae* 65 which in turn refers to the Sacred Congregation for the Doctrine of the Faith (SCDF) *Declaration on Euthanasia*, 'with intention to bring about death', then this is 'true and proper euthanasia by omission'.[118]

Pope John Paul and the patient in 'vegetative' state

Of course for Pope John Paul when it comes to accepting or refusing overzealous treatment the wishes of the patient have considerable weight because, as he explains in connection with human rights, the person 'cannot be subjected to domination by others'.[119] However, at the same time he is equally clear that true freedom is not a question of the absolute exaltation of the individual so that choices become merely the result of subjective and changeable opinion. Freedom, he says, is distorted and destroyed 'when it no longer recognises and respects *its essential link with the truth*' (his italics).[120]

For Pope John Paul the two particular truths that are relevant to accepting or refusing overzealous treatment are firstly the truth of the '*greatness* and the *inestimable value* of human life' since 'life in time' is the 'initial stage' of human existence and secondly the truth that earthly life is not the ultimate reality, rather it is the penultimate reality for life reaches its 'full realisation' in eternity (his italics).[121] Thus life remains 'a sacred reality' entrusted to each one and to be preserved with 'a sense of responsibility'. This means that whilst the pursuit of overzealous treatment may in fact indicate a failure to recognise the limits of earthly life, a choice to forgo basic care, the level of care warranted by good stewardship, may be a failure to cherish life. From this comes the requirement on the person to apply practical wisdom in discerning the nature of the treatment or care offered and to cherish life both by exercising good stewardship of it and also by recognising the limits of the human condition in the face of death.

However assuming that he or she has not made an advance directive, the case of the patient in vegetative state appears different: here the patient cannot express his or her wishes. Yet for Pope John Paul this difference does not alter the application of these two truths nor the fact that human beings cannot be subjected to domination by others and he draws attention in particular to the oppressive mentality which 'tends to *equate personal dignity with the capacity for verbal and explicit,* or at least perceptible, *communication*'. This he contrasts with the communication of the radically dependent person and the 'silent language of a profound sharing of affection'.[122] So for Pope John Paul the other truths of human existence are joined by another truth, that 'every man is his "brother's keeper", because God entrusts us to one another'.[123] Although this truth applies in all circumstances it perhaps comes more to the fore in the case of the patient in vegetative state. What is notable, especially given the focus on the non–acting person, is the attention Pope John Paul gives to the person who cannot act and communicate as expected yet who remains an acting person.

Pope John Paul and feeding people

In March 2004 Pope John Paul made a speech that apparently surprised much of the medical world, caused consternation among some theologians and provoked vigorous responses. One response includes the charge that the Pope's speech and various Church statements from the 1980s mark a significant shift from traditional Catholic teaching.[124] It therefore seems necessary to place the Pope's speech in context.

The Pope's speech was addressed to participants attending an international congress on life sustaining treatments and the vegetative state organised by the Pontifical Academy for Life. The series of lectures, debates and presentations of scientific, bioethical and religious views reflected the secular and theological controversies happening at the time. In academic, legal and clinical practice questions were being raised about the status of the patient in persistent vegetative state, whether he or she could be considered properly alive never mind whether or not a person. In the legal sphere there were moves to classify the provision of food and fluids as treatment rather than ordinary care so that patients could refuse them. The cases of Nancy Cruzan and Tony Bland gave scope for those campaigning for assisted suicide, euthanasia and the 'right to die' to argue that the removal of nutrition and hydration had as its goal death and that it was more humane to achieve this by lethal overdoses.

Certainly there had been previous discussions on the withholding or withdrawal of artificial nutrition and hydration in other medical situations. However in the case of the patient in persistent vegetative state the issue seems to turn not so much on the benefits and burdens of treatment. Rather it turns on thinking about the person: on whether this person is dying, exists in merely biological life or is profoundly disabled.

The topics of withholding or withdrawing treatment and of a person's obligations to conserve his or her life had been addressed in 1957 by Pope Pius XII though in the context of artificial ventilation. The line taken by Pope Pius is regarded as key for all subsequent discussion. According to Pope Pius

> normally one is held to use only ordinary means—according to circumstances of persons, places, times, and culture—that is to say, means that do not involve any grave burden for oneself or another. A more strict obligation would be too burdensome for most men and would render the attainment of the higher, more important good too difficult. Life, health, all temporal activities, are in fact subordinated to spiritual ends.[125]

With the increasing use of technology it seemed that Pope Pius's understanding of 'ordinary means' required clarification. In the tradition 'ordinary' corresponded to 'obligatory' and 'extraordinary' referred to 'optional'. However some healthcare professionals like Bryan Jennett understood 'ordinary' to refer to treatment that was 'generally available and widely used' and 'extraordinary' to include 'advanced technological methods that were scarce and expensive'.[126] This kind of confusion led the SCDF in its 1980 *Declaration on Euthanasia* to suggest the terms 'proportionate' and 'disproportionate' as preferable. The SCDF then explained the distinction between proportionate and disproportionate means, therapeutic treatment and normal care in the context of life sustaining treatments so that attention did not focus on the treatment as being common or highly technical, rather it looked to the condition of the patient. The SCDF reiterated the tradition that everyone has a duty to care for his or her own health or to seek such care from others but there is no duty to have recourse to all possible remedies. A patient can refuse treatment 'that would only secure a precarious and burdensome prolongation of life' 'when inevitable death is imminent' as long as the normal care owed to a patient who is immiently dying is not interrupted.[127]

Whilst it was accepted that basic care should be provided whatever the condition of the patient the provision of artificial nutrition and hydration seemed more problematic since it could be classed as both basic care and medical treatment. The debate continued and two non–authoritative reports, one from the Pontifical Council Cor Unum issued in 1981 and one from the Pontifical Academy of Sciences issued in 1985 suggested that artificial nutrition and hydration should be considered ordinary and proportionate means of prolonging life.[128] In its *Charter for Health Care Workers* the Pontifical Council for Pastoral Assistance to Health Care Workers affirmed that 'the administration of food and liquids, even artificially, is part of the normal treatment always due to the patient when this is not burdensome for him or her; their undue interruption can have the meaning of real and true euthanasia'.[129]

Meanwhile in the US throughout the 1980s and 1990s there was an ongoing debate on the subject of persistent vegetative state between the Catholic bishops of Texas and Pennsylvania. The majority though not all the Texas bishops argued that persistent vegetative state was a lethal pathology leading to death, that vegetative patients had come to the end of their pilgrimage and 'should not be impeded from taking the final step' and that where there was no reasonable hope of recovery preservation of life was not worthwhile.[130] The Pennsylvania bishops argued that the condition was not imminently terminal and that preserving life was a benefit.

In the media and in the political arena the case of Terri Schiavo was causing an international outcry. 'In defence of life' Pope John Paul identified that 'a great teaching effort is needed to clarify the substantive moral difference between discontinuing medical procedures that may be burdensome, dangerous or disproportionate to the expected outcome… and taking away the ordinary means of preserving life, such as feeding, hydration and normal medical care'.[131]

The Pope's speech

In his Address to the congress regarding the care and treatment of patients in vegetative state Pope John Paul's starting point is that the patient is a 'sick person…..awaiting recovery or a natural end' and so he or she 'still has the right to basic health care'. He begins from an option for life and from the perspective that in life when we can we feed people who cannot feed themselves. According to Pope John Paul a list of basic care includes cleanliness and warmth as well as nutrition and hydration. Moreover, the patient has the right to be protected from complications associated with confinement to bed, to appropriate rehabilitation and monitoring.[132] Pope John Paul continues in stronger tone and it is worthwhile quoting the paragraphs in full given the reaction in some quarters,

> I should like particularly to underline how the administration of water and food even when provided by artificial means, always represents a *natural means* of preserving life, not a *medical act*. Its use, furthermore, should be considered, in principle, *ordinary* and *proportionate*, and as such morally obligatory, insofar as and until it is seen to have attained its proper finality, which in the present case consists in providing nourishment to the patient and alleviation of his suffering.

> The obligation to provide the "normal care due to the sick in such cases" (Congregation for the Doctrine of the Faith, *Iura et Bona* p.IV) includes, in fact, the use of nutrition and hydration (c.f. Pontifical Council Cor Unum, *Dans le Cadre,* 2, 4, 4; Pontifical Council for pastoral Assistance to Health Care Workers, *Charter of Health Care Workers,* n.120). The evaluation of probabilities, founded on waning hopes for recovery when the vegetative state is prolonged beyond a year, cannot ethically justify the cessation or interruption of *minimal care* for the patient, including nutrition and hydration. Death by starvation or dehydration is, in fact, the only possible outcome as a result of their withdrawal. In this sense it ends up becoming, if done knowingly and willingly, true and proper euthanasia by omission.[133]

Although many welcomed the Pope's intervention some Catholic ethicists did not and a vigorous debate on what the Pope meant by his speech ensued. Given the controversy the United States Conference of Catholic Bishops formulated some questions and in 2005 asked the CDF for comment and clarification. In 2007 the CDF gave a detailed response affirming Pope John Paul's speech and the United States Conference of Catholic Bishops brought their directives into line with the Pope's teaching in their 2009 guidelines for healthcare institutions.[134]

Nevertheless some influential theologians remain unpersuaded by both the Pope's teaching and its affirmation by the CDF[135] and their thinking continues to fuel the debate. It is useful perhaps to identify two principal areas of disagreement in what some see as a shift in the Catholic tradition. The first centres on the Pope's views that food is basic care and that life itself though finite is always a good in that it is the pre–condition for other goods. The second is more pertinent to the apparently non–acting person since disagreement centres on differing anthropological views of that person.

A challenge to the tradition

The Jesuit ethicist, Father Peter Clark states that the Pope's speech has caused a 'profound crisis' for 'individuals, medical professionals and Catholic healthcare in general'.[136] Father Clark thinks that Pope John Paul's declaration that artificial hydration and nutrition is ordinary care that is beneficial is a 'distinct shift in methodology' and that the Pope's position brings about 'a complete revision of the Catholic tradition dating to the sixteenth century'.[137] According to a leading American bioethicist and Dominican, Father Kevin O'Rourke Pope John Paul's statement was received 'with dismay' by many.[138] Father O'Rourke and Father Clark argue that if the patient is 'unable to strive for the purpose of life' then continued life is of no benefit and so there is no moral obligation to prolong life.[139] James Walter and Thomas Shannon, two American professors who write extensively on the Catholic moral tradition, claim that the Pope's speech 'seems to represent a significant departure from the Roman Catholic biethical tradition' from the mid–1600s since 'historically, the method for making a determination about the use of a medical intervention was the proportion between the benefits of the intervention and its harms or burdens to the individual, family, and community'. They argue that the tradition begins from an analysis of burdens and benefits whereas what they term 'the revisionist position' of Pope John Paul 'begins with a presumption and then moves to disprove the presumption'.[140]

The provision of food and fluids in Church tradition

Certainly Catholic tradition in this area exists before the sixteenth century even if the language of ordinary and extraordinary measures is not used. However any exploration of this tradition is bound to encounter difficulty given the vast difference between ancient medicinal practice and current medicine. In the ancient world anyone could set himself up as a physician so those who sought out a doctor could just as easily submit themselves to superstitious practice, quackery and experimentation as possible healing. As such a decision to forgo apparent medical treatment seems to have been a non–issue in the first centuries of Christianity. In early Christianity the focus was primarily on God's action in people's lives and whilst the early Fathers seem to think that recourse to the art of the physician is not incompatible with Christianity many of the Fathers also believe that healing could sometimes come from satanic forces and indeed be used for sinful ends.[141] So if someone decides to consult a physician it must be with the correct perspective: healing lies within the power of God who works through the skill of the physician and through treatment. Yet God is not limited by human beings so in his wisdom and care God can also withhold healing or indeed heal without the medium of the physician.[142]

What is of concern for the early Fathers is that reliance on the physician's art may persuade people to think they are self–sufficient or put their trust solely in other human beings and in doing so they may forget that they are really dependant on God. After all, sickness was seen as an aspect of the human condition that called for an attitude of patient endurance in the face of Satan's temptation towards discouragement and the sin of despair. This attitude of patient endurance is important since for the Fathers the context of care in earthly life is seen in the perspective of eternal life, a life that might be jeopardised if faith and trust in God is lost. For the Fathers, as St Augustine explains, there are two deaths. the first death is temporal and 'ready and waiting for all'; the second is everlasting. St Augustine admonishes his congregation who, he says are eager to live for a few extra days and so will promise great rewards to doctors who claim to be able to save them yet seem to do little on the same scale for eternal life. He adds, a person may be able to take steps to put off the first death nevertheless it will eventually come. However, we do not want to suffer both deaths.[143] St Augustine is not criticising people for wanting to extend their lives. Rather he is pointing out how little thought the same people put into preparing for eternal life.

Notwithstanding the problems in interpreting the practice of medicine in early Christianity according to the Dominican Anthony Fisher, bishop of Parramatta, New South Wales, food and drink has traditionally been seen as basic nursing care not medical treatment. Indeed, as Bishop Fisher indicates Aristotle and Hippocrates accept that certain foods have medicinal properties however they also recognise that the primary purpose of such food and drinks is nourishment and hydration.[144]

In the Christian tradition discussion on the provision of food and fluids to patients prior to the sixteenth century takes place mostly in the context of monastic life. St Pachomius is regarded as the founder of the cenobitic or community form of monasticism. In the *Precepts* for his community Pachomius says that the sick are to receive whatever is necessary and whatever food they need.[145] Moreover, it seems that any extra food brought by relatives or back from visits to relatives should be handed over to the infirmary.[146] For St Pachomius it is the hallmark of the *koinonia* that, just as relatives look after a loved one, the community should comfort the sick with pillows, take care of them and ensure that they are not 'short of bread'.[147] Indeed this natural care of the sick, supplemented if necessary by extra rations is continued by Horsiesios, one of the successors to Pachomius in his regulations.[148] This commitment to the sick leads St Jerome to note with approval that in Pachomian communities 'the sick are sustained with wonderful care and a great abundance of food'.[149]

St Pachomius's rule for his *koinonia* became influential for other monastic rules, notably the one written by St Basil the Great. Although perhaps best known for his contribution to Trinitarian theology St Basil was also an active diocesan bishop. He not only founded a monastic community but, as part of the Christian duty to take care of the sick and marginalised and from his pastoral initiative as bishop he set up an extensive building project that included a church centre, a hostelry for travellers and a hospital and hospice for the poor. Apparently he was no stranger to dealing with the qualms of officials over the expenses involved in this project[150] hence, perhaps, his designation as the patron saint of hospital administrators. St Basil's hospital–hospice complex appears to have provided the services of medics and physicians for the poor in general. However St Basil makes his comments on the provision of food and fluids to patients in his instructions to the monks. According to St Basil,

> whatever requires an undue amount of thought or trouble or involves a large expenditure of effort and causes our whole life to revolve, as it were, around solicitude for the flesh must be avoided by Christians....Therefore, whether we follow the precepts of the medical art or decline to have recourse to them...we should hold to our objective of pleasing God and see to it that the soul's benefit is assured, fulfilling thus the Apostle's precept: 'Whether you eat or drink or whatsoever else you do, do all to the glory of God' (1Corinthians 10:31).[151]

Whilst some conclude that St Basil is here equating food and fluids with medical treatment or extraordinary means this does not seem to be St Basil's intention. The point St Basil is making is that for Christians all things, even the most basic, should find their reference in God.

Similar healthcare systems to the one St Basil's community provided emerge during the 370s as the monastic movement became more socially organised. In the cenobitic monastic arrangements made under the influence of St Pachomius monastic community living seems to have included doctors and nurses who looked after the bodily needs of the occupants. Here it appears that the diet of the sick was of central importance and special food was provided as part of basic care.[152] Moreover, it was generally recognised that health was more important than asceticism so the sick were allowed to eat when others were fasting. As St Augustine writes in the rule for his community 'the sick may have something to eat at any time of the day' and the infirmarian may bring to the sick person whatever food he thinks is necessary.[153] As St Augustine makes clear 'the sick should obviously receive suitable food; otherwise their illness would only get worse'.[154]

On the whole in discussion on feeding patients the early tradition is neglected and so the significance of feeding patients is lost. Moreover given this early tradition it seems difficult to state, as do James Walter and Thomas Shannon, that there is no initial presumption about feeding people and that instead the tradition begins from an analysis of burdens and benefits. In addition they argue that in his encyclical *Evangelium vitae* Pope John Paul initiates a shift away from discussing the issue in the context of general illness towards the context of imminent dying.[155]

It seems that the 'tradition' often begins, as Father Clark does, with a brief mention of St Thomas Aquinas, followed by references to the sixteenth century Dominican moralists Francisco de Vitoria, Domingo Soto and Domingo Bañez. Certainly the sixteenth century marks a significant period. The Renaissance ushered in medical advances, the study of anatomy and the circulation of the blood as well as the study of diseases. Vitoria, Soto, Bañez and others were engaging in extensive commentaries on the work of St Thomas Aquinas and these three moralists 'articulated the foundation of the ordinary–extraordinary means distinction.'[156]

Father Clark points out that according to Francisco de Vitoria if a very sick person can take food 'with a certain hope of life' he is required to do so just as he is required to give food to one who is sick. However if he suffers from severe depression or there is 'grave consternation in the appetitive power so that only with the greatest effort and as though through torture' can he take food then 'this is to be reckoned as an impossibility': if eating is a grave burden then, says Father Clark, he is not morally obliged.[157] Father Clark then looks at the other two moralists. Considering amputation at a time when there were no anaesthetics Domingo Soto says that the excessive pain could make such a procedure optional. Of course in this situation the patient would have died without this drastic surgery and so was imminently dying. Domingo Bañez determines that if preserving life was reasonable then it was obligatory but no one is bound to extraordinary means.[158] Father Clark rightly sees this tradition in the perspective that life is a good but not the ultimate good and he adds that treatment was determined to be ordinary or extraordinary 'according to whether it was proportionate to one's condition or state in life.'[159] He then goes on to accept the Jesuit moralist Father Gerald Kelly's interpretation of the tradition that 'no person is morally obligated to use any means, and this would include natural or artificial means, that does not offer a reasonable hope of ameliorating the patient's condition'.[160] Father Clark believes that by declaring artificial nutrition and hydration ordinary care that is beneficial Pope John Paul does not give sufficient attention to the medical condition of the patient.[161] According to Father Clark artificial nutrition and hydration merely sustain life they do not give any meaningful benefit.[162]

Of these three moralists Francisco de Vitoria offers the more extensive commentary on feeding patients and some of the points he raises can be added to Father Clark's account of the tradition. Vitoria's approach is found in his relections, lectures open to the whole university community of Salamanca where professors were obliged to present a reprise of one of their courses; failure to do so resulted in a fine. His relections were printed from the notes of his students. Vitoria says that 'someone is not obliged to use every means to preserve his life, but it is enough to use those means which are of themselves ordered and fitting for this'.[163] As he explains a person is not obliged to sail to India where he believes the air is more beneficial or to spend what he has on expensive drugs or delicacies that would prolong his life for a few days; it is enough to use common remedies and eat common foods.[164] In response to Thomas Shannon and James Walter what is noticeable here is that Vitoria seems to be speaking of the patient as being 'without any hope of life' or with only a few days of life. Vitoria follows St Thomas Aquinas on the necessity of taking food since it expresses the natural inclination to preserve life, it is an act of charity to the self and to refuse food might violate the prohibition on suicide[165] that is unless food causes such torment that it would be considered an impossibility especially if there is little hope for life. Vitoria also points out that medicine and nourishment are not the same and since medicine is not part of the ordered means for natural life then there is no obligation to use it.

Certainly Pope John Paul resists the notion that feeding and hydrating patients is medical treatment and this seems to reflect Vitoria's position. Some commentators assume that the designation of food and fluids as normal ordinary care is purely in order to make it obligatory and, this is, they argue a shift in the tradition.[166] However, equally on this reasoning to designate artificial nutrition and hydration as medical treatment is to make it extraordinary and so optional. Moreover according to the UK Mental Capacity Act s.5 patients can refuse treatment such as artificial hydration and nutrition in an advance decision whether or not treatment is burdensome or futile but they cannot refuse basic care. The point Pope John Paul seems to be making is that the terms ordinary and extraordinary do not primarily refer to the means used: it is not a question of whether feeding tubes are commonly used or not. Pope John Paul's understanding that 'the administration of water and food, even when provided by artificial means, always represents a natural means of preserving life' is in step with the tradition of the early Church fathers with their focus on the person and his or her obligation to care for his or her health and on the Christian practice of feeding the sick even if the fathers did not have the expertise of artificial hydration and nutrition. His injunction that the use of artificial hydration and nutrition should be considered 'in principle ordinary and proportionate, and as such morally obligatory insofar as and until it is seen to have attained its proper finality' is a strong statement supporting the position that where possible human beings feed those who cannot feed themselves. Pope John Paul's statement points to the fact that in the case of patients in persistent vegetative state the issue has been skewed because some are asking whether these profoundly disabled people who are not imminently dying should be given nutrition and hydration. His statement stresses that ordinarily we feed people. In a way it is similar to identifying where the burden of proof lies: it is not for clinicians to decide reasons in favour of feeding, rather they are to feed their patients unless there are serious contraindications.

Understanding the serious nature of any contraindications is also specified in the tradition, principally by St Thomas Aquinas and developed by the sixteenth century moralists. Albeit in the context of fraternal correction St Thomas makes the distinction between negative and positive precepts. According to St Thomas it is always possible not to do negative precepts such as 'do not murder': 'negative precepts bind always and for all time'.[167] In contrast it is sometimes impossible to fulfil positive precepts. As a positive precept a person has a duty to conserve his or her life. However this duty can be excused in the case of physical impossibility or in the case of moral impossibility where observance of the duty is extremely difficult. The CDF identifies such contraindications in its clarification to the United States Conference of Catholic Bishops on hydration and nutrition and the patient in persistent vegetative state: the provision of artificial food and water may be physically impossible for instance in very remote places or situations of extreme poverty, and no one is bound to do what is impossible. Nor is the patient bound where he or she cannot assimilate food and fluids so their provision becomes useless. In addition the patient is not bound where 'in some rare cases' artificial nutrition and hydration may be 'excessively burdensome for the patient or may cause significant physical discomfort'.[168]

The case of physical impossibility makes it relatively easy to determine that a person be excused the duty to conserve life. However moral impossibility appears to be relative to the actual concrete situation of the patient.[169] Nevertheless, based on the work of the sixteenth century moralists the gravity of moral impossibility is underlined by its possible causes.[170] The first cause identifies great effort, *summus labor*, such as Vitoria's example of moving to the healthiest country or eating only the healthiest food; the second cause is enormous pain, *igens dolor*, which is an unreasonable amount of pain such as Soto's example of an amputation where there is no pain relief; the third cause is exquisite means and extraordinary expense, *media exquisite et sumptus extraordinarius*, such as Vitoria's expensive drugs and delicacies; the fourth cause is severe dread, *vehemens horror*, as identified by the nineteenth century moral theologian St Alphonsus Liguori that amounts to an ardent repulsion. Certainly the Church's teaching invites reflection on how to apply moral impossibility in the context of treatment that is excessively burdensome and the category of *vehemens horror* may have particular application for patients in persistent vegetative state.[171] Moreover it is significant that Church teaching stresses the gravity of moral impossibility in the concrete situation of the patient. This stand is especially important given some current assumptions that the removal of food and fluids should be the usual default position when dealing with patients in persistent vegetative state and that the burden of justification should fall not on those who seek to dehydrate patients but on those who would continue hydration and nutrition.[172]

Although Father Clark thinks that Pope John Paul does not pay sufficient attention to the medical condition of the patient in persistent vegetative state Pope John Paul's reference within paragraph 4 of his 2004 Address demonstrates that he does have both the concrete situation of the patient and the practical wisdom of healthcare professionals in mind. He calls attention to the *Charter of Health Care Workers*[173] which states

> aware that he is 'neither the lord of life nor the conqueror of death' the health care worker, in evaluating means, should make appropriate choices, that is, relate to the patient and be guided by his real condition... for the doctor and their assistants it is not a question of deciding the life or death of an individual. It is simply a question of being a doctor, that is, of posing the question and then deciding according to one's expertise and one's conscience regarding a respectful care of the living and the dying of the patient entrusted to him.[174]

Perhaps what is of more significance is that according to Pope John Paul the practical wisdom utilised by healthcare professionals is to be guided by the truth about the real condition of the person entrusted to them. Father O'Rourke and Father Clark differ from Pope John Paul in what they see as the real condition of the patient.

The apparently non–acting person

Both Father O'Rourke and Father Clark argue that it is a mistake to think that artificial hydration and nutrition can benefit the patient in vegetative state. They say that the death of such a patient after artificial hydration and nutrition is withdrawn is a 'result of underlying pathology not starvation or dehydration'.[175] They categorically state this based on the understanding that patients in vegetative state do not feel pain so any suffering associated with the withdrawal of artificial hydration and nutrition is a 'non issue'.[176] The previous analysis of persistent vegetative state has demonstrated that it cannot be said categorically that patients do not suffer. The views of Father O'Rourke, his colleague Father Patrick Norris and Father Clark rely on the belief that the patient dies from the 'underlying pathology' of 'dysfunction of the cerebral cortex' because of which 'the patient is unable to eat and drink on his own'.[177] However it is not at all clear that these patients are dying: causes of death are reported to be from infection, generalised systemic failure, respiratory failure, recurrent stroke and in some cases sudden inexplained death. It does not appear to be the case that patients in persistent vegetative state are trying to die yet are unable to do so. Arguably a patient does not die from being in a 'state' just as infants do not die from being in the state of infants. However infants (and patients in persistent vegetative state) do die if no one feeds them. Moreover the autopsy report on Terri Schiavo notes that the 'mechanism' that brought about her death was dehydration. Similarly the US Multi–Society Task Force on Persistent Vegetative State reports that the 'immediate cause of death is dehydration and electrolyte imbalance rather than malnutrition'.[178]

Nevertheless since the stance of Father O'Rourke and Father Clark continues to fuel the debate it is worth exploring their challenges to the Pope's statement in depth. This becomes particularly relevant as it soon becomes clear that the reason for their dissent hinges on their belief that food and fluids do not benefit the patient in persistent vegetative state chiefly because they think that the patient is no longer an acting person. Indeed Father O'Rourke demonstrates unwavering dissent and goes out of his way to give reasons justifying this including an excursus into the status of the Pope's speech[179] and, with his colleague the bioethicist John Hardt, a challenge to the CDF clarification[180] thus perhaps indicating just how serious the issue is for thinking about the human person.

From the thinking of Father O'Rourke and Father Clark the implication is that in the case of the patient in persistent vegetative state personal life or biographical life has been lost and simply biological life remains. As far back as 1986 Father O'Rourke took the position that the obligation to prolong life ceases if it 'no longer enables one to strive for the purpose of life' and 'to pursue the purposes of life one needs some degree of cognitive–affective function'.[181] He further argued that some life support systems may prolong 'a state of existence' that both involves great burdens for the patient and that 'precludes spiritual activity' and so the ethically responsible course of action is to cease their use.[182] To be sure Father O'Rourke and Father Norris think that 'the soul of the person still maintains the radical power to perform human acts of cognitive–affective function' but they say 'the actual performance of these acts is impossible'.[183] Father O'Rourke and Father Clark seem to think that in the concrete situation of the patient in persistent vegetative state life is of no benefit. Father Clark says that 'in the Catholic moral tradition, a medical treatment was beneficial if it restored a patient to a relative state of health' and artificial nutrition and hydration will never improve the condition of the patient in persistent vegetative state to the point where he or she 'can again pursue the spiritual goods of life'. Mere preservation of life is not sufficient in itself to oblige using certain means.[184]

Father O'Rourke is more specific and he appeals to Thomistic anthropology to justify his position.[185] According to Father O'Rourke the goal of human life is friendship with God and, he says, 'to strive for this goal we must perform human acts'. He uses the distinction St Thomas makes between human acts, *actus humanus,* and what Father O'Rourke calls 'acts of man', *actus hominis.* By Father O'Rourke's account 'acts of man' are bodily acts and 'if a person does not have the ability nor the potency to perform human acts now or in the future, then that person can no longer strive for the purpose of human life so it does not benefit the person in this condition to have life prolonged'. Certainly Father O'Rourke denounces the killing of patients even if it alleviates suffering and he believes that he is affirming the principle of the sanctity of life.[186] However Father O'Rourke is suggesting that life is only of benefit for the person who acts and he designates the patient in persistent vegetative state as a non–acting person.

Both Father Clark and Father O'Rourke appear to be endorsing the separation of biological life from biographical life. In part Father Clark and Father O'Rourke rely on the address made by Pope Pius XII to anesthesiologists in 1957 for their interpretation of the life of the patient in persistent vegetative state. In his Address Pope Pius XII says that 'life, health and all temporal activities are in fact subordinated to spiritual ends'.[187] Certainly Pope Pius XII speaks clearly in the tradition of St Basil, St Augustine, St Thomas and the sixteenth century moralists to affirm that everything, even life, is understood in reference to God and that life though good is not the ultimate good. However this tradition also affirms the dignity of the life of every human being until natural death. Pope John Paul follows this tradition when he recognises that the real condition of patients in persistent vegetative state is of people who 'remain prisoners of their condition' yet who 'retain their human dignity in all its fullness' and upon whom 'the loving gaze of God the Father continues to fall'.[188] Nevertheless the clash of anthropologies is such that Father O'Rourke replies that Pope John Paul's reference to the loving gaze of the Father 'does not imply that persons in this condition are able to fulfill their part in the reciprocal relationship of friendship'.[189] Ultimately it must be said that Father Clark and Father O'Rourke seem to use Pope Pius to move beyond what he intended and they shift the emphasis onto the acting person: if the person can no longer pursue the spiritual goods of life his or her life is of no benefit. In short Father Clark and Father O'Rourke appear to overlook the primacy of God's action in a person's life. They seem to forget that, as Pope John Paul explains 'when God turns his gaze on man, the first thing he sees and loves in him is not the deeds he succeeds in doing, but his own image'.[190] And even if the image of God in human beings is obscured or defaced it always remains.[191]

However the issue does not end at whether or not life is in itself a benefit. It is a short step from claiming that life is no longer a benefit to saying that the patient is better off dead. Indeed Father O'Rourke's belief that prolonging the 'state of existence' of certain patients 'precludes spiritual activity'[192] seems to suggest precisely this. Certainly the view that life is a good is not to assert that it is a good to be pursued no matter what. Rather it seems that an affirmation of the good of life is especially necessary given that death is preferred to mere biological existence for patients like Tony Bland and Terri Schiavo and then is actively sought. Moreover the assertion that death is preferable seems to be becoming more commonplace for many other categories of human beings. In particular the claim is made that the person would make the same appraisal of his or her life if he or she were competent enough to do so.

Can death come too late?

There appears to be a significant difference between those who argue that certain patients would be better off dead and those who argue that their own lives are not worth living. In both cases death seems to be coming too late for them but where someone personally decides that his or her life is worthless this seems somehow more acceptably distant from situations where others decide that the patient is better off dead. This seems to be proved by the thinking of those who appeal to the belief that the patients themselves would assess their condition as 'better off dead' if they were competent. So, as in the cases of Cruzon, Bland and Schiavo the apparently objective assessment appears to be placed on surer ground: if Nancy, Tony and Terri had been aware of their situation they would have said that they did not want to exist in persistent vegetative state. Moreover, rather than dwelling on 'worth' of life the phrase 'better off dead' suggests that the patient's best interests remain the motivation behind such a declaration unlike the determination that the patient has a life that is not worth living. The doctor is somehow benefiting the patient by terminating his or her life.

The reluctance to declare someone 'better off dead' from an apparently objective perspective, the keenness to use 'better off' language associated with the patient's best interests and the attempt to bring the situation closer to that of the exercise of autonomy, albeit fictional, may be attempts to mark a distance from the idea that there are some lives that are 'not worth living'. This notion emerged in the eugenic movements of the 1920s and 1930s and culminated in the atrocities of Nazism. Particularly influential was a book written in Germany by the jurist Karl Binding and the psychiatrist Alfred Hoche in 1920. The authors claimed that 'worthless people', that is, those with 'a life not entitled to be lived', *lebensunwerten*, should be killed to spare society the burden of their care. Programmes were introduced to eliminate certain categories of patients and the same reasoning was used by the Nazis to justify genocide. Notably, the idea of a 'life not worth living' was not restricted to Germany: it seems that its roots lie in the legacy of Charles Darwin and his notion of the 'survival of the fittest' that was applied to human beings by Darwin's cousin, Francis Galton; in the 1930s the US also had in place arrangements to starve disabled babies and programmes of involuntary sterilization.[193]

The horrors of Nazism and eugenic movements that eliminate people on the discriminatory grounds of worthwhileness of life have, for the most part, been recognised as inhuman and as crimes against humanity. Indeed, many have distanced themselves from such movements. Still, what is at issue is the extent to which a patient's subjective determination that his or her life is not worth living influences attitudes such that people begin to assume that others would in some circumstances be better off dead. So the distance between 'better off dead' and a judgment on the worthwhileness of life may not be as great as first thought. However, it remains necessary to explore the arguments that view them as worlds apart.

As an expert in euthanasia law and in favour of voluntary euthanasia Margaret Otlowski draws attention to those who say that voluntary euthanasia necessarily involves acceptance of a policy that objectively states that certain lives are not worth living. She argues that this is to be 'flatly rejected as being both misleading and inaccurate'.[194] She explains 'respect for a patient's right of self–determination does not involve an objective assessment about the value or worth of that life.[195] Furthermore, she believes that legislation for euthanasia based on an autonomy principle can safeguard against extensions into involuntary or non–voluntary forms of killing that do lead on from policies based on utilitarianism.[196] So it seems that for Margaret Otlowski the conclusion that one's own life is not worth living as a subjective assessment and as an action of self–determination can be a sound basis for euthanasia and it will not lead to a slippery slope.

Following Margaret Otlowski's line may not be as straightforward as she suggests and arguably the kinds of factors involved, particularly fear of an apparently bleak future may compromise the exercise of pure autonomy. However in their book that is comfortingly entitled *Easeful Death* the influential peer Mary Warnock and the cancer specialist Elisabeth Macdonald attempt just that. Viewed as a subjective assessment the causes that lead a person to decide that he or she would be better off dead are many and varied. It seems that unrelieved pain, whilst being a serious issue, can, by and large, be factored out of the equation given the advances in palliative care. However, for the self–aware person pain notably soul pain comes in many other guises: the fear of dehumanisation or being considered not a person, loss of independence and control, a sense of meaninglessness, of being a burden on others, the fear of deterioration especially increasing mental confusion. According to Mary Warnock and Elisabeth Macdonald death seems to be a relief in the face of an ever bleaker future. Terminal illness appears to offer a graspable end point and so may provide some relief. However the authors explain that for those who are not terminally ill yet who can only see that darkest of futures soul pain seems to be much worse. In the case of those who are not terminally ill and still have capacity to make health decisions Mary Warnock and Elisabeth Macdonald see that the refusal of treatment may offer the relief, death that these sufferers seek. However, even then, the refusal of treatment may not result in a peaceful death and for that reference is often made to the refusal of hydration and nutrition.[197] Hence the calls for something more active: for assisted suicide and euthanasia.

These calls seem particularly strong for those who are concerned that they are becoming a burden both emotionally and financially on their loved ones and on society. Mary Warnock articulated this theme in an interview when in the UK the House of Commons was preparing to debate the Mental Capacity Bill.[198] Mary Warnock believes that the frail and elderly should consider suicide to avoid burdening their families with their care and also that the parents of a premature baby should pay for life support care if doctors write off the infant's chances of having a healthy life. She is a strong campaigner for changes in UK legislation to permit assisted suicide for competent people and euthanasia for neonates and incompetent adults particularly for those with dementia 'who do not have the luck to need artificial nutrition and hydration' refusal of which is, she says, currently the only way to bring about death.[199] The idea of a 'duty to die' based on being 'a burden' moves the discussion away from the usual appeal to autonomy, my right to choose. In order to avoid a charge of excessive individualism some proponents of the 'duty to die' bring into play the recognition that in a way every person is involved in relationships and that sometimes the demands of relationships are so great that a person does become a burden. Margaret Otlowski says that 'the objective of active voluntary euthanasia is the promotion of individual autonomy and self–determination'.[200] She argues that the '*mere* possibility' that legislation permitting voluntary euthanasia may be broadened in future is not sufficient justification for refusing to allow its enactment (her italics).[201] Nevertheless she seems to underestimate the influence that certain attitudes may have.

Once the discussion has moved from autonomy to an existence that is burdensome then it seems easier to make a further shift towards seeing the continuing lives of certain patients as, in Bryan Jennett and Clare Dyer's words, 'prolonged survival' that presents a 'dilemma' for family, carers and society. Then the life of a human being who cannot express a preference can be categorised as 'not worth living' leading to the determination that a person can be better off dead.[202] Mary Warnock and Elisabeth Macdonald make precisely this move and their book *Easeful Death* is subtitled *Is there a case for assisted dying?* Ostensibly the intention of the authors is to respond with support to UK calls in parliament for the legalisation of assisted suicide and voluntary euthanasia. However, 'looking further ahead' as the authors put it, certain patients, most obviously those in persistent vegetative state, have lives 'like that of a vegetable', merely biological life such that the 'pointlessness of keeping them alive is now generally recognised'.[203]

A similar judgment is made in the Netherlands under the Groningen Protocol which sets a standard of practice whereby doctors can 'responsibly' end the lives of certain categories of newborn babies. 'Responsibly' seems to equal without fear of prosecution. As the feminist writers Hilde Lindemann and Marian Verkerk clarify in the face of criticism of the protocol, where as in the case of the Netherlands there is a 'socially shared understanding that death is not the worst thing that can befall a human being' then actively ending a life can sometimes be 'more humane'.[204] This applies not only to newborns who may not survive without intensive treatment and who are suffering unbearably but also to those who could survive into adulthood but with 'complete lifelong dependency' or 'permanent inability to communicate in any way',[205] and the 'unbearable suffering' requirement includes cases where suffering may take place in the future.[206] As the authors explain 'the baby is judged to be better off dead than forced to endure the only kind of life it can ever have'.[207]

Of course this idea that certain patients are better off dead may more correctly be translated as we would be better off if the patient were dead. Two bioethicists have unapologetically made this move in the case of what they call 'after–birth abortion'. Writing in the *Journal of Medical Ethics* Alberto Giubilini and Francesca Minerva argue that since abortion is accepted for reasons that have nothing to do with the health of the foetus and since infants and foetuses do not have the same moral status as actual persons because they cannot attribute value to their own existence then after–birth abortion (killing a new born) should be permissible in all cases where abortion is permissible. This includes, they say, cases where the newborn is not disabled. They claim that the term 'after–birth abortion' is more appropriate than infanticide since they say the moral status of the infant is more like a foetus than a child; the term is more precise than euthanasia since the best interests of the one who dies is not necessarily the primary criterion for the choice of death as it is, they argue, in euthanasia.[208] In the face of strong criticism the editors felt they had to justify their decision to publish the article. Julian Savulescu, one of the editors points out that the novelty of the article lies not in the argument about infanticide as after all these arguments had already been made by Michael Tooley and Peter Singer. Rather it is in the emphasis the authors place on the interests of the mother and family.[209]

Those who claim that another human being is 'better off dead' seem to be suggesting that life in itself is not in some cases a good. However it appears that from antiquity, as illustrated by Aristotle 'life is by nature a good'.[210] To be sure Socrates famously comments that for a human being 'the unexamined life is not worth living' (as presented by Plato[211]). Still this seems to refer to the idea that a person who is not reflective is a slave to another's opinions rather than the person is better off dead and certainly contemporary philosophical debate takes many differing positions on whether or not death can be better than life.[212]

From a Christian theological perspective life is always a good. Nevertheless it seems that the mistake frequently made about the Catholic theological position is to regard this perspective as an 'absolutist life ethic', a charge made by some of those who criticise Pope John Paul's position on the provision of food and fluids as the demand to 'extend life indefinitely'.[213] This charge seems to be made on both the grounds that the Church holds a vitalist position, that as a good life is to be preserved no matter what, and that positive action, providing food and fluids, must be done no matter what.

Indeed the Church is 'absolutist' in its belief that no one should deliberately and directly kill an innocent human being: traditionally negative precepts such as 'do not kill' bind absolutely. Thus, the Groningen Protocol and Mary Warnock's proposals for euthanasia and assisted suicide come directly in conflict with Church teaching. Still, in Church tradition positive precepts such as 'provide normal care to the sick' are seen as limited either by physical impossibility or moral impossibility. This is precisely the basis on which the CDF does not exclude the possibility that there are certain situations where artificial nutrition and hydration may be impossible though it still maintains that in principle the administration of food and fluids is morally obligatory. So, for instance in extraordinary disaster situations where there are too many patients and not enough doctors the normal care of the sick may fall short. This is not to say that failure to provide care means that care has lost its value. Rather it is to accept that sometimes there are things, even otherwise obligatory things, that cannot reasonably be expected of a person and that failure is not a part of his or her intention. As for the charge that implies vitalism, in the theological tradition earthly life is indeed always a good but it is not the ultimate good.

For the earliest Christians life in itself is good on the basis that creation is good. Not only was this belief rooted in the *Genesis* story but also the very fact of the Incarnation demonstrated God's love for the world and in particular for human beings. The

Genesis stories counteract some ancient pagan thought that saw the material world as essentially evil or at least the work of an evil deity. This belief resurfaced with the thinking of Marcion[214] who believed that the God of the Old Testament was an incompetent and vengeful demigod so was not the same as the God of the New. The *Genesis* stories also call human beings to stewardship over the world and this includes the proper care each person is to have for his or her own life and health. However this attitude towards the proper care of the self is set in the perspective of eternal life for God's salvific action also indicates that the destiny of human beings lies beyond this world in becoming 'friends with God'.[215] A person may be 'better off dead' only in the sense that he or she has now reached his or her eternal destiny and is a friend of God, sharing in the life of the Trinity. However this is only achieved through the gracious action of God who reaches out and plucks us from the jaws of death. Simply being dead is not better than being alive because without the action of God the state of death is a closed point, a place without hope. For death to be in any sense 'good' requires the redemptive action of God.

If, as Pope John Paul explains, earthly life is the penultimate reality[216] then the issue is not about prolonging life as a basic good no matter what. Rather it is about good stewardship of earthly life so that it serves its ultimate reality, eternal life and part of good stewardship is to consider whether a person has done all that could be reasonably expected to cherish the gift of life whilst accepting that earthly life is limited.

This point is clearly reflected in Pope John Paul's explanation of the struggle between the 'culture of life' and the 'culture of death'.[217] According to Pope John Paul, the 'culture of death' does not simply advocate acts such as abortion and euthanasia whilst the 'culture of life' promotes earthly life. Rather, for Pope John Paul the 'culture of death' exists where God has been forgotten and this leads to a profound distortion in the meaning of things. Most notably in such a culture the result is a 'practical materialism' in which human beings see themselves merely as other living beings, as purely material beings and in turn life becomes 'a mere "thing", which man claims as his exclusive property, completely subject to his control and manipulation'. In this culture the acting person as agent, as the one in control, becomes definitive: the person 'is concerned only with "doing", and, using all kinds of technology, he busies himself with programming, controlling and dominating birth and death'. Pope John Paul continues, 'birth and death, instead of being primary experiences demanding to be "lived", become things to be merely "possessed" or "rejected"'. The modern opposition of the acting person and the non–acting human being can perhaps be found in this culture where 'being' has been replaced by 'having', where 'the body is no longer perceived as a properly personal reality' but is reduced to its material aspects and where 'the first to be harmed are women, children, the sick or suffering and the elderly'. As Pope John Paul explains, 'the criterion of personal dignity—which demands respect, generosity and service—is replaced by the criterion of efficiency, functionality and usefulness: others are considered not for what they "are", but for what they "have, do and produce". This is the supremacy of the strong over the weak.'[218]

Summary

In a way the situation of the patient in persistent vegetative state captures much of what Pope John Paul thinks about disability though it is disability at its profoundest. Persistent vegetative state seems to offer the clearest illustration of what some see as the separation of biographical from biological life where biological life is of no benefit and indeed may be burdensome. Perhaps looking at how Father O'Rourke and Father Norris regard the term 'vegetative' compared with how Pope John Paul sees the term can illuminate the situation. Father O'Rourke and Father Norris see the term as essentially accurate since it 'refers to the person's ability to function only at the biological level'.[219] In contrast Pope John Paul fundamentally objects to its use. As he explains

> the intrinsic value and personal dignity of every human being do not change, no matter what the concrete circumstances of his or her life. *A man, even if seriously ill or disabled in the exercise of his highest functions, is and always will be a man,* and he will never become a "vegetable" (his italics).[220]

As a matter of solidarity and justice Pope John Paul emphasises that proper, adequate and appropriate therapies and healthcare are due to these patients in the same way as they are due to all human beings. As a matter of ordinary care in principle people in persistent vegetative state should be fed and hydrated unless there are clear contraindications. Pope John Paul recognises the difficulties involved and calls for suitable support for the patient's carers and family However he is principally concerned with challenging those who deny full personal dignity to these people with the profoundest of disabilities. Since the focus of this denial appears to have settled on the issue of feeding patients it is on this issue that he is more forthright. Above all he stresses that the patient in this apparently unresponsive state remains a person. Indeed he recognises that what is at stake is human dignity.

Nevertheless in the case of patients in persistent vegetative state it is not simply physical and mental capacities that have been questioned. Analysis of the thinking of those who are particularly against Pope John Paul's approach to the person in persistent vegetative state demonstrates that some also question whether such patients, even though still living human beings, have any spiritual life if they appear no longer to be able to respond to their God given vocation. To consider this the final chapter looks at one of Karol Wojtyła's earliest work: on faith and St John of the Cross.

Notes

1. K. Gray, T. A. Knickman, D. Wegner, 'More dead than dead: Perceptions of persons in the persistent vegetative state' in *Cognition* 121/2 (2011), pp. 275–280.

2. P. Singer, *Practical Ethics* (Cambridge: Cambridge University Press, 1997), p. 192.

3. S. Curry, 'Living patients in a permanent vegetative state as legitimate research subjects' in *Journal of Medical Ethics* 32/10 (2006), 606–607; H. Draper, 'Research and patients in permanent vegetative state' in *Journal of Medical Ethics* 32/10 (2006), p. 607, though this is with prior patient consent.

4. A. Ravelingien, F. Mortier, E. Mortier, I. Kerremans, J. Braeckman, 'Proceeding with clinical trials of animal to human organ transplantation: a way out of the dilemma' in *Journal of Medical Ethics* 30/1 (2004), pp. 92–98.

5. French National Consultative Ethics Committee, *Opinion on experimentation on patients in a chronic vegetative state, report.* No.7 (24 February 1986) <http://www.ccne–ethique–fr/docs/en/avis007.pdf>[accessed 2 March 2012].

6. R. Veatch, *Transplantation Ethics* (Washington: Georgetown University Press, 2000), p. 185.

7. R. Hoffenberg, M. Lock, N. Tilney, C. Casabona, A.S. Daar, R.D. Guttmann, I. Kennedy, S. Nundy, J. Radcliffe–Richards, R.A. Sells, (International Forum for Transplant Ethics) 'Should organs from patients in permanent vegetative state be used for transplantation?' in *Lancet* 350/9087 (1997), pp. 1320–1321.

8. Sacred Congregation for the Doctrine of the Faith, *Declaration on Euthanasia,* (30 May 1980), II.

9. G. Kahane, J. Savulescu, 'Brain Damage and the Moral Significance of Consciousness' in *Journal of Medicine and Philosophy* 34/1 (2009) 6–26 at p. 21.

10. D. Wikler, 'Not Dead, Not Dying? Ethical Categories and Persistent Vegetative State' in *The Hastings Center Report* 18/1 (1988), 41–47 at p. 46.

11. *Ibid.,* pp. 41–47.

12. R. Veatch, *Transplantation Ethics* (Washington: Georgetown University Press, 2000), p. 185.

13. Pope John Paul II, Speech *To Teachers and University Students in Cologne Cathedral: Science and Faith in the Search for Truth* (15 November 1980), 3–4.

14. J. Blandford, 'An Examination of the Revisionist Challenge to the Catholic Tradition on Providing Artificial Nutrition and Hydration to Patients in a Persistent Vegetative State' in *Christian Bioethics* 17/2 (2011), pp. 153–164 at p. 153.

15. *Ibid.,* pp. 157–158.

16. *Ibid.,* p. 153 and pp. 157–158.

17. R. Rakestraw, 'The Persistent Vegetative State and the Withdrawal of Nutrition and Hydration', in D. Clark and R. Rakestraw (eds.), *Readings in Christian Ethics Vol.2 Issues and Applications* (Grand Rapids: Baker Publishing, 1996), p. 129 and p. 127.

18. K. O'Rourke, 'Reflections on the Papal Allocution Concerning Care for Persistent Vegetative Patients' in *Christian Bioethics* 12/1 (2006), pp. 83–97 at p. 93.

19. K. O'Rourke, 'Development of church teaching on prolonging life' in *Health Progress* 8 (1988), pp. 29–35.

20. Pope Benedict XVI, *Caritas in veritate,* 74.

21. Pope John Paul II, Speech *To the participants in the International Congress on 'life sustaining treatments and vegetative state: scientific advances and ethical dilemmas'* 5.

22. Pope John Paul II, *Evangelium vitae*, 2.

23. G. M. Teasdale, 'The Glasgow Coma and Outcome Scales: Practical Questions and Answers', in M. Sindou (ed.), *Practical Handbook of Neurosurgery Vol 3* (Wien: Springer, 2009), p. 404.

24. B. Jennett, *The Vegetative State: Medical Facts, Ethical and Legal Dilemmas* (Cambridge: Cambridge University Press, 2002), p. 1.

25. *Ibid.,*p. 2.

26. *Ibid.,*p. 3.

27. *Ibid.,*p. 5.

28. C. J. Borthwick and R. Crossley, 'Permanent vegetative state: usefulness and limits of a prognostic definition' in *NeuroRehabilitation* 19 (2004), 381–389 at p. 383.

29. See European Task Force on Disorders of Consciousness 'Unresponsive wakefulness syndrome: a new name for the vegetative state or apallic syndrome' in *BMC Medicine* 8/68 (2010) <http://www.biomedcentral. com/1741–7015/8/68> [accessed 7 March 2011].

30. Harvard Medical School Report, *Journal of the American Medical Association* 205/6 (1968), 337–340.

31. P. Singer, *Writings on an Ethical Life* (London: Fourth Estate, 2001), pp. 170–172; see also P. Ramsey, *The Patient as Person* (Yale: Yale University Press, 2002), pp. 106–107.

32. R. Veatch, 'The Ethics of Death and Dying: Changing Attitudes towards Death and Medicine', in A. Jonsen et al (eds.), *Source Book in Bioethics: A Documentary History* (Washington: Georgetown University Press, 1998), p. 114.

33. Three not zero was the minimum according to C. Rush, 'The history of the Glasgow Coma Scale: an interview with Professor Bryan Jennett' in *International Journal of Trauma Nursing* 3 /4 Oct–Dec (1997), 114–118 at p. 115.

34. B. Jennett, 'Development of Glasgow Coma and Outcome Scales' in *Nepal Journal of Neuroscience* 2 (2005), 24–28 at p. 25.

35. B. Jennett, F. Plum, 'Persistent vegetative state after brain damage. A syndrome in search of a name' in *Lancet* 1 (1972), 734–737 at p. 734.

36. *Ibid.,* p. 737.

37. *Ibid.*

38. T. Smith, 'Taming High Technology' in *BMJ* 289/6442 (1984), 393–394 at p. 393.

39. B. Jennett, 'Letting vegetative patients die' in *BMJ* 305 (1992), 1305–1306.

40. C. Richmond, 'Obituary Fred Plum' in *Lancet* 376 /9739 (2010), p. 412.

41. B. Jennett, 'Development of Glasgow Coma and Outcome Scales' in *Nepal Journal of Neuroscience*, p. 26.

42. G. M. Teasdale, 'The Glasgow Coma and Outcome Scales: Practical Questions and Answers' in *Practical Handbook of Neurosurgery* Vol 3, p. 402.

43. B. Jennett, 'Development of Glasgow Coma and Outcome Scales' in *Nepal Journal of Neuroscience*, p. 27.

44. G. M. Teasdale, 'The Glasgow Coma and Outcome Scales: Practical Questions and Answers' in *Practical Handbook of Neurosurgery* Vol 3, p. 404.

45. B. Jennett, 'Development of Glasgow Coma and Outcome Scales' in *Nepal Journal of Neuroscience*, p. 27.

46. D. Wikler, 'Not dead, not dying? Ethical categories and persistent vegetative state' in *Hastings Center Report*, pp. 41–47.

47. See J. B. Brierley, J. A. H. Adams, D. I. Graham, and J. A. Simpson 'Neocortical death after cardiac arrest' in *Lancet* (1971), pp. 560–565.

48. US President's Commission Report, *Defining Death: Medical, Legal and Ethical Issues in the Definition of Death* (1981), Ch.3, p. 127. <http://bioethics.georgetown.edu/pcbe/reports/past_commissions/defining_death.pdf> [accessed 31 January 2010].

49. B. Jennett, *The Vegetative State: Medical Facts, Ethical and Legal Dilemmas*, p. ix.

50. *Ibid.*

51. *Ibid.*

52. *Ibid.*

53. See table in C. Rush, 'The history of the Glasgow Coma Scale: an interview with Professor Bryan Jennett' in *International Journal of Trauma Nursing.* 3 /4 (1997), 114–118 at p. 118.

54. B. Jennett, *The Vegetative State: Medical Facts, Ethical and Legal Dilemmas* p. 4.

55. *Ibid.*, p. 16.

56. See for instance B. Lo's *Resolving ethical dilemmas: a guide for clinicians* (Philadelphia: Lippencort Williams and Wilkins, 2009), p. 162.

57. <http://www.nhs.uk/conditions/vegetative–state/Pages/Introduction.aspx> [accessed 4 July 2011].

58. 'Multi–Society Task Force on PVS: medical aspects of the persistent vegetative state' (First part of two parts) in *New England Journal of Medicine* 330/21 (1994), pp. 1499–1508 at p. 1503.

59. R. Cranford, 'Commentary Facts, Lies and Videotapes: The Permanent Vegetative State and the Sad Case of Terri Schiavo' in *Journal of Law, Medicine and Ethics* 33/2 (2005), pp. 363–371 at p. 368.

60. American Academy of Neurology, 'Position of the American Academy of Neurology on Certain Aspects of the Care and Management of the Persistent Vegetative Patient', in R. Hamel and J. Walter (eds.), *Artificial Nutrition and Hydration and the Permanently Unconscious Patient: The Catholic Debate* (Georgetown: Georgetown University Press, 2007), p. 9.

61. As reported in the case of Terri Schiavo, Autopsy report of the Medical Examiner, J. Thogmartin (13 June 2005), p. 7 <http://www.sptimes.com/2005/06/15/schiavoreport.pdf> [accessed 8 September 2011]..

62. R. Cranford, 'Commentary Facts, Lies and Videotapes: The Permanent Vegetative State and the Sad Case of Terri Schiavo' in *Journal of Law, Medicine and Ethics* p. 368.

63. See J. Berkman, 'Medically Assisted Nutrition and Hydration in Medicine and Moral Theology', in J. Morris (ed.), *Medicine, Health Care, and Ethics: Catholic Voices* (Washington: Catholic University of America Press, 2007), p. 149.

64. See R. Cranford, 'Commentary Facts, Lies and Videotapes: The Permanent Vegetative State and the Sad Case of Terri Schiavo' in *Journal of Law, Medicine and Ethics* 363–371.

65. J. Berkman, 'Medically Assisted Nutrition and Hydration in Medicine and Moral Theology' in *Medicine, Health Care, and Ethics: Catholic Voices* ,pp. 156–157.

66. K. O'Rourke, P. Norris, 'Care of PVS Patients: Catholic Opinion in the US' in *Linacre Quarterly* 68/3 (2001), pp. 207–217.

67. B. Jennett, *The Vegetative State: Medical Facts, Ethical and Legal Dilemmas* p. ix.

68. B. Jennett, 'Thirty years of the vegetative state: clinical, ethical and legal problems' in *Progress in Brain Research* 150 (2005), 537–543.

69. F. Plum, B. Jennett, 'Persistent vegetative state after brain damage. A syndrome in search of a name' in *Lancet* at p. 736.

70. B. Jennett, *The Vegetative State: Medical Facts, Ethical and Legal Dilemmas* p. 16.

71. *Ibid.*, p. 18.

72. C. J. Borthwick, R. Crossley, 'Permanent vegetative state: usefulness and limits of a prognostic definition' in *NeuroRehabilitation* at p. 381.

73. C. Watts, G. Livingston, 'Cogito ergo sum. A commentary' in *Surgical Neurology Int* 2/5 (2011) <http://www.surgicalneurologyint.com/text.asp?2011/2/1/5/76142> [accesed 7 November 2011].

74. See European Task Force on Disorders of Consciousness, 'Unresponsive wakefulness syndrome: a new name for the vegetative state or apallic syndrome' in *BMC Medicine* 8/68 (2010).

75. D. A. Shewmon, G. L. Holmes, P. A. Byrne, 'Consciousness in Congenitally Decorticate Children: Developmental Vegetative State as Self–Fulfilling Prophecy' in *Dev Med Child Neurol* 41 (1999), pp. 364–374.

76. J. Bernat, *Ethical Issues in Neurology* (Philadelphia: Lippencort Williams and Wilkins, 2008), p. 293; B. Kotchoubey, 'Apallic syndrome is not apallic: is vegetative state vegetative?' in *Neuropsychological Rehabilitation* 15/3–4 (2005), 333–356 at p. 336; D. A. Shewmon, G. L. Holmes, and P. A. Byrne 'Consciousness in Congenitally Decorticate Children: Developmental Vegetative State as Self–Fulfilling Prophecy' in *Dev Med Child Neurol* 41 (1999), pp. 364–374.

77. B. Kotchoubey, 'Apallic syndrome is not apallic: is vegetative state vegetative?' in *Neuropsychological Rehabilitation* at p. 351.

78. B. Jennett, 'Letting Vegetative Patients Die' in *BMJ* 305 (1992), 1305–1306.

79. J. Bernat, *Ethical Issues in Neurology* p. 300.

80. B. Jennett, *The Vegetative State: Medical Facts, Ethical and Legal Dilemmas* p. ix.

81. B. Lo, *Resolving ethical dilemmas: a guide for clinicians* p. 163.

82. G. Kahane, J. Savulescu, 'Brain Damage and the Moral Significance of Consciousness' in *Journal of Medicine and Philosophy* 34/1 (2009), 6–26 at p. 10.

83. G. Kahane, J. Savulescu, 'Brain Damage and the Moral Significance of Consciousness' in *Journal of Medicine and Philosophy* p. 11.

84. *Ibid.,* p. 15.

85. *Ibid.,* p. 20.

86. *Ibid.,* p. 21.

87. *Ibid.,* p. 11.

88. G. Lancioni et al, 'A learning assessment procedure to re–evaluate three persons with a diagnosis of post–coma vegetative state and pervasive motor impairment' in *Brain Injury Feb.* 23/2 (2009), pp. 154–162.

89. See C. J. Borthwick and R. Crossley, 'Permanent vegetative state: usefulness and limits of a prognostic definition' in *NeuroRehabilitation* p. 388.

90. See B. Jennett, 'Letting Vegetative Patients Die' in *BMJ* 1305–1306; B. Jennett, *The Vegetative State: Medical facts, Ethical and Legal Dilemmas,* p. 16; G. Kahane and J. Savulescu, 'Brain Damage and the Moral Significance of Consciousness' in *Journal of Medicine and Philosophy* p. 20.

91. Lord Goff in *Airedale NHS Trust v Bland* [1993] 2WLR 359 p. 336.

92. Pope John Paul II, Speech *To the 18th International Congress of the transplantation Society* (29 August 2000).

93. Pope John Paul II, *Letter to the Pontifical Academy of Sciences* (1 February 2005), 3,4.

94. Pope John Paul II, Speech *To the participants in the International Congress on " life sustaining treatments and vegetative state: scientific advances and ethical dilemmas"* (20 March 2004).

95. See comments by R. Fine, 'From Quinlan to Schiavo: medical, ethical and legal issues in severe brain injury' in *Proc (Bayl Univ Med Cent)* 18/4 (2005), pp. 303–310.

96. Pope John Paul II, *To the participants in the International Congress on "life–sustaining treatments and vegetative state: scientific advances and ethical dilemmas"*, 3.

97. *Ibid.,* 6.

98. *Ibid.*

99. B. Jennett *The Vegetative State: Medical Facts, Ethical and Legal Dilemmas* p. 16.

100. Pope John Paul II, *To the participants in the International Congress on "life–sustaining treatments and vegetative state: scientific advances and ethical dilemmas"*, 6.

101. *Ibid.*

102. D. Callahan, 'On feeding the dying' in *Hastings Center Report*, 13/5 (1983), 22.

103. B. Jennett, C, Dyer, 'Persistent vegetative state and the right to die: the United States and Britain' in *BMJ* 302 (1991), 125–1258.

104. Lord Keith of Kinkel *Airedale Trust NHS* v *Bland* [1993] 2WLR 359 p. 361.

105. Lord Browne–Wilkinson *Airedale Trust NHS* v *Bland* [1993] 2WLR 359 p. 383.

106. B. Jennett, C. Dyer, 'Persistent vegetative state and the right to die: the United States and Britain' in *BMJ* p. 1258.

107. Autopsy report of the Medical Examiner, J. Thogmartin (13 June 2005), p. 1–2

108. Autopsy report of the Chief Medical Examiner, S. Nelson (8 June 2005), p. 9 <http://www.sptimes.com/2005/06/15/schiavoreport.pdf> [accessed 8 September 2011].

109. Autopsy report J. Thogmartin (13 June 2005), p. 9.

110. *NHS Trust A* v *M and NHS Trust B* v *H* [2001] Fam 348.

111. GMC, *Treatment and care towards the end of life: good practice in decision making*, (2010), 114. <http://www.gmc–uk.org> [accessed 7 February 2011].

112. GMC, *Treatment and care towards the end of life: good practice in decision making*, 115; see also *Burke* v *GMC* [2005] EWCA Civ 1003.

113. GMC, *Treatment and care towards the end of life: good practice in decision making*, 119–120.

114. *Ibid.*, 123.

115. *Ibid.*, 126.

116. The Multi–Society Task Force on Persistent Vegetative State, 'Medical Aspects of the Persistent Vegetative State (First of Two Parts)' in *New England Journal of Medicine* 330/21 (1994), 1499–1508.

117. J. Panksepp, T. Fuchs, V. Garcia, and A. Lesiak, 'Does any aspect of mind survive brain damage that typically leads to a persistent vegetative state? Ethical considerations' in *Philosophy, Ethics and Humanities in Medicine* 2/32 (2007) <http://www.peh–med.com/content/2/1/32.> [accessed 30 January 2012].

118. Pope John Paul II, *To the participants in the International Congress on "life–sustaining treatments and vegetative state: scientific advances and ethical dilemmas"*, 4.

119. Pope John Paul II, *Evangelium vitae*, 19.

120. *Ibid.*

121. *Ibid.*, 2.

122. *Ibid.*, 19 his italics.

123. *Ibid.*

124. T. Shannon, J. Walter, 'Assisted Nutrition and Hydration and the Catholic Tradition', in R. Hamel and J. Walter (eds.), *Artificial Nutrition and Hydration and the Permanently Unconscious Patient The Catholic Debate* (Washington: Georgetown University Press, 2007).

125. Pope Pius XII, 'Address to an International Congress of Anaethesiologists' in *L'Osservatore Romano* (25–26 November 1957).

126. B. Jennett, *The Vegetative State: Medical Facts, Ethical and Legal Dilemmas* p. 105.

127. Congregation for the Doctrine of the Faith, *Declaration on Euthanasia*, 1980, Part IV.

128. Pontifical Council Cor Unum, *Questions of Ethics regarding the Gravely Ill and Dying* (27 June 1981); Pontifical Academy of Sciences, *The Artificial Prolongation of Life and Exact Determination of the Moment of Death* (21 October 1985).

129. Pontifical Council for Pastoral Assistance to Health Care Workers, *Charter for Health Care Workers* (1995), 120.

130. Texas Bishops and the Texas Conference of Catholic Health Facilities, 'On Withdrawing Artificial Nutrition and Hydration' in *Artificial Nutrition and Hydration and the Permanently Unconscious Patient: The Catholic Debate* p. 112.

131. Pope John Paul II, Speech *To the Bishops of California, Nevada and Hawaii USA on their 'ad limina' visit* (2 October, 1998), 4.

132. Pope John Paul II, *To the participants in the International Congress on "life–sustaining treatments and vegetative state: scientific advances and ethical dilemmas"*, 4.

133. *Ibid.*

134. United States Conference of Catholic Bishops, *Ethical and Religious Directives for Catholic Health Care Services* (5th edition), 17 November 2009, directive 58 <http://www.usccbpublishing.org> [accessed 10 January 2012].

135. K. O'Rourke, J. Hardt, 'Nutrition and Hydration: The CDF response, In Perspective' in *Health Progress* 88/6 (2007), pp. 44–47.

136. P. Clark, 'Tube feeding and Persistent Vegetative Patients: Ordinary or Extraordinary means?' in *Christian Bioethics* 12/1 (2006), pp. 43–64 at p. 44.

137. *Ibid.* at pp. 55–56.

138. K. O'Rourke, 'Reflections on the Papal Allocution concerning care for persistent vegetative state patients' in *Christian Bioethics* 12/1 (2006), pp. 83–97 at p. 83.

139. *Ibid.*; Clark, 'Tube feeding and Persistent Vegetative Patients: Ordinary or Extraordinary means?' in *Christian Bioethics* p. 50.

140. T. Shannon, J. Walter, 'Assisted Nutrition and Hydration and the Catholic Tradition' in *Artificial Nutrition and Hydration and the Permanently Unconscious Patient The Catholic Debate* p. 230.

141. D. Amundsen, *Medicine, Society and Faith in the Ancient and Medieval Worlds* (London: John Hopkins University Press, 1996), p. 7.

142. *Ibid.*, pp. 6–7.

143. St Augustine, *Sermon* 344.

144. A. Fisher, 'Why Do Unresponsive Patients Still Matter?', in C. Tollefsen (ed.), *Artificial Nutrition and Hydration: the New Catholic Debate* (Netherlands: Springer, 2008), pp. 16–17.

145. St Pachomius, *Precepts*, 40, 42.

146. *Ibid.*, 53, 54.

147. St Pachomius, *Letter* 5.2.

148. Horsiesios, 'Regulations of Horsiesios', in *Pachomian Koinonia* Vol.2, 24, 42, 13.

149. St Jerome, 'Preface to the Rules of St Pachomius' in *Pachomian Koinonia* Vol. 2, 5.

150. St Basil, *Letter 94*.

151. St Basil, *Long Rules, Q.55*.

152. A. Crislip, *From Monastery to Hospital: Christian Monasticism and the Transformation of Healthcare in Late Antiquity* (USA: University of Michigan Press, 2005), pp. 16–17.

153. St Augustine, *Rule*, 3.1; 5.8.

154. *Ibid.*, 3.5.

155. T. Shannon, J. Walter, 'Assisted Nutrition and Hydration and the Catholic Tradition' in *Artificial Nutrition and Hydration and the Permanently Unconscious Patient The Catholic Debate* pp. 227–228.

156. P. Clark, 'Tube feeding and Persistent Vegetative Patients: Ordinary or Extraordinary means?' in *Christian Bioethics* p. 49.

157. *Ibid.*, p. 50.

158. *Ibid.*, pp. 49–51.

159. *Ibid.*, p. 51.

160. *Ibid.*, p. 51.

161. *Ibid.*, p. 56.

162. *Ibid.*, p. 58.

163. F. de Vitoria, *On Homicide*, 35.

164. *Ibid.*, 33, 35.

165. See P. Taboada, 'Ordinary and Extraordinary Means and the Preservation of Life: The Teaching of Moral Tradition', in E. Sgreccia, and J. Lafitte (eds.), *Proceedings of the XIV's General Assembly: Close by the Incurable Sick Person and the Dying, Scientific and Ethical Aspects* (Vatican City: Libreria Editrice Vaticana, 2009).

166. T. Shannon, J. Walters, 'Assisted Nutrition and Hydration and the Catholic Tradition' in *Artificial Nutrition and Hydration and the Permanently Unconscious Patient. The Catholic Debate* Ch.18.

167. St Thomas Aquinas, *Summa Theologiae*, II–II.33.2.

168. Congregation for the Doctrine of the Faith, *Responses to Certain Questions of the United States Conference of Catholic Bishops Concerning Artificial Nutrition and Hydration, Vatican commentary* (1 August 2007).

169. P. Taboada, 'Ordinary and Extraordinary Means and the Preservation of Life: The Teaching of Moral Tradition' in *Proceedings of the XIV's General Assembly: Close by the Incurable Sick Person and the Dying, Scientific and Ethical Aspects,* 2.1.5.

170. *Ibid.*, 2.1.4.

171. See K. Wildes, 'Ordinary and Extraordinary Means and the Quality of Life' in *Theological Studies* 57 (1996) 500–512; D. Sulmasy, 'Preserving Life? The Vatican and PVS' in *Commonweal* (2007) <http://www.commonwealmagazine.org/preserving-life-0> [accessed 13 September 2011].

172. See C. Constable, 'Withdrawal of Artificial Nutrition and Hydration for Patients in a Permanent Vegetative State: Changing Tack' in *Bioethics* 26/3 (2012), pp. 157–163.

173. Pope John Paul II, *To the participants in the International Congress on "life–sustaining treatments and vegetative state: scientific advances and ethical dilemmas"*, 4 where the Pope refers to the Pontifical Council for Pastoral Assistance to Health Care Workers, *Charter of Healthcare Workers,* 120. <http://www.ewtn.com/library/curia/pcpaheal.htm> [accessed 13 January 2009].

174. Pontifical Council for Pastoral Assistance to Health Care Workers, *Charter of Healthcare Workers,* 121.

175. P. Clark, 'Tube feeding and Persistent Vegetative Patients: Ordinary or Extraordinary means?' in *Christian Bioethics* p. 57; K. O'Rourke, 'Reflections on the Papal Allocution concerning care for persistent vegetative state patients' in *Christian Bioethics* p. 93.

176. P. Clark, 'Tube feeding and Persistent Vegetative Patients: Ordinary or Extraordinary means?' in *Christian Bioethics* p. 49; K. O'Rourke 'Reflections on the Papal Allocution concerning care for persistent vegetative state patients' in *Christian Bioethics* p. 93.

177. P. Clark, 'Tube feeding and Persistent Vegetative Patients: Ordinary or Extraordinary means?' in *Christian Bioethics* p. 57; K. O'Rourke, P. Norris, 'Care of PVS Patients: Catholic Opinion in the US' in *Linacre Quarterly* 68/3 (2001), 207–217.

178. The Multi–Society Task Force on Persistent Vegetative State, 'Medical Aspects of the Persistent Vegetative State (Second of Two Parts)' in *New England Journal of Medicine* 330/22 (1994), 1572–1579 at p. 1578. Fred Plum was a member of this task force.

179. K. O'Rourke, 'Reflections on the Papal Allocution concerning care for persistent vegetative state patients' in *Christian Bioethics* 83–97.

180. K. O'Rourke, J. Hardt, 'Nutrition and Hydration: The CDF Response In Perspective' in *Health Progress* 44–47.

181. K. O'Rourke, 'The A.M.A. Statement on Tube Feeding: An Ethical Analysis' in *America* VII/8 (1986), 321–323 at p. 322.

182. K. O'Rourke, 'Development of Church Teaching on Prolonging Life' in *Health Progress* 8 (1988), pp. 29–35.

183. K. O'Rourke, P. Norris, 'Care of PVS Patients: Catholic Opinion in the US' in *Linacre Quarterly* 201–217.

184. P. Clark, 'Tube feeding and Persistent Vegetative Patients: Ordinary or Extraordinary means?' in *Christian Bioethics* p. 58.

185. K. O'Rourke, 'Reflections on the Papal Allocution Concerning Care for Persistent Vegetative State Patients' in *Christian Bioethics* p. 93.

186. *Ibid.,* pp. 95 and 93.

187. Pope Pius XII, 'Address to an International Congress of Anesthesiologists' in *L'Osservatore Romano* (25–26 November 1957).

188. Pope John Paul II, *To the participants in the International Congress on "life-sustaining treatments and vegetative state: scientific advances and ethical dilemmas"*, 2–3.

189. K. O'Rourke, 'Reflections on the Papal Allocution Concerning Care for Persistent Vegetative State Patients' in *Christian Bioethics* p. 93.

190. Pope John Paul II, 'Mentally Ill Are Also Made in God's Image' in *L'Osservatore Romano* (11 December 1996).

191. St Augustine, *On the Trinity*, XIV,4.6; XIV, 8.11.

192. K. O'Rourke, 'Development of Church Teaching on Prolonging Life' in *Health Progress* 29–35.

193. J.W. Block, *Copious Hosting: a theology of access for people with disabilities* (New York: Continuum International, 2002), p. 39.

194. M. Otlowski, *Voluntary Euthanasia and the Common Law* (Oxford: Oxford University Press, 1997), p. 221.

195. *Ibid.*

196. *Ibid.*, pp. 190–191.

197. See M. Warnock, E. Macdonald, *Easeful Death: is there a case for assisted dying?* (Oxford: Oxford University Press, 2008), p. 104ff.

198. As reported in *The Times* (12 December 2004).

199. M. Warnock, E. Macdonald, *Easeful Death* p. 64.

200. M. Otlowski, *Voluntary Euthanasia and the Common Law*, p. 221.

201. *Ibid.*, p. 222.

202. B. Jennett and C. Dyer make such a move in 'Persistent vegetative state and the right to die: the United States and Britain' in *BMJ* 302 (1991), 1256.

203. M. Warnock, E. Macdonald, *Easeful Death* p. 134.

204. H. Lindemann, M. Verkerk, 'Ending the Life of a Newborn' in *Hastings Center Report* 38:1 (2008), pp. 42–51 at p. 48.

205. *Ibid.*, p. 44.

206. *Ibid.*, p. 47.

207. *Ibid.*, p. 43.

208. A. Giubilini, F. Minerva, (2012) 'After-birth abortion: why should the baby live' <http://www.jme.bmj.com/content/early/2012/03/01/medethics-2011-100411 full> [accessed 3 April 2012].

209. J. Savulescu, (2012) <http://www.blogs.bmj.com/medical-ethics/2012/02/28/liberals-are-disgusting-in-defence-of-the-publication-of-after-birth-abortion/ [accessed 3 April 2012].

210. Aristotle, *Nicomachean Ethics*, IX.9.9.1170b.

211. Plato, *Apology*, 38a.

212. See discussions in *The Metaphysics of Death* J. Fischer (ed.), (Stanford: Stanford University Press, 1993).

213. See for instance L. Dugdale, A. A. Ridenour, 'Making Sense of the Roman Catholic Directive to Extend Life Indefinitely' in *Hastings Center Report* 41:2 (2011), pp. 28–29 at p. 29.

214. Died c.154.

215. St Gregory of Nyssa, *On Infants' Early Deaths;* see also *Ws* 7:27.

216. Pope John Paul II, *Evangelium vitae,* 2.

217. *Ibid.,* 21–23.

218. *Ibid.*

219. K. O'Rourke, P. Norris, 'Care of PVS Patients: Catholic Opinion in the US' in *Linacre Quarterly* pp. 207–217.

220. Pope John Paul II, *To the participants in the International Congress on Life–sustaining Treatments and Vegetative State: Scientific Advances and Ethical Dilemmas,* 3.

10

KAROL WOJTYŁA, SAINT JOHN OF

THE CROSS AND THE APPARENTLY

NON-ACTING PERSON

For many people the person in persistent vegetative state is the archetypal 'non-acting' person. According to Father Kevin O'Rourke and his colleague Father Patrick Norris not only does the patient 'function only at the biological level' but also spiritual activity is no longer possible,[1] indeed it is precluded.[2] The evangelical theologian Robert Rakestraw believes that whilst there may be some kind of 'residual life, the person is dead'. He adds there is 'no communication with God'.[3] Indeed, for writers like Robert Rakestraw and the Anglican theologian Nigel Biggar 'a person is constituted *both* by his vocation *and* by his capacity for response to it' (his italics).[4] So, a living human being 'rendered permanently incapable of responding to a vocation, whether by severe brain damage or by intense pain that cannot be relieved so as to permit the recovery of responsible life, generously conceived' is no longer a person never mind an acting person. Therefore according to Father O'Rourke there is no moral obligation to prolong the patient's life;[5] for Robert Rakestraw the patient can already be declared dead 'theologically' and so artificial nutrition and hydration can be discontinued;[6] Nigel Biggar says intentional killing of any such patient could be permissible.[7]

This apparently non-acting person, the patient in persistent vegetative state, is vulnerable not only to philosophers and bioethicists who use science to affirm a view of the acting person that relies on the vagary of human choice but also to some theologians who seem to have given up the hope that God can act even with the most profoundly of disabled people. In defence of this apparently non-acting person Pope John Paul is adamant that all human beings remain persons and whatever their condition or situation they are acting persons. Moreover intentional killing of the patient in persistent vegetative state is the killing of a human person. And all persons are in relationship with God who is the 'sole Lord of this life' and who holds life and death in his hands as 'part of his loving concern'.[8]

Whilst Nigel Biggar and Pope John Paul differ on the status of people with the most profound disabilities, they both agree that the notion of vocation is essential. As Pope John Paul explains vocation 'indicates that *there is a proper course for every person's development to follow......his or her love is fixed on some particular goal*' (his italics).[9] Moreover Pope John Paul seems to share a similar concern with Nigel Biggar for he adds 'vocations are meaningful only within the framework of a personalistic vision of human existence, in which conscious choice determines the direction which a person's life and actions will take'.[10] Nevertheless Pope John Paul constantly speaks about the vocation of people with even the most profound disabilities and the part they play in God's plan of salvation and he encourages their participation as far as they are able in this task. This is because Pope John Paul's personalistic vision of human existence, unlike Nigel Biggar's, includes all human beings whatever their capacities.

No doubt Nigel Biggar would agree with Pope John Paul that the interior life of the person is not the only source of vocation: a person's interior life encounters first 'an objective call from God'.[11] However in his endorsement of the distinction between biographical personal life and biological human life Nigel Biggar appears to give priority to the response of a person to his or her vocation since, he says, 'the value of biographical life lies…in the individual's obedient response to God's vocation':[12] everything seems to depend on what the person does. In similar fashion Father O'Rourke and Robert Rakestraw believe that in the case of the patient in persistent vegetative state there is no communication with God. This is because, they argue, the patient no longer has the cognitive-affective capacities to engage in the relationship. But according to Pope John Paul, whilst human co-operation is necessary 'the operations of Grace take man beyond the confines of his personal life and bring him within the orbit of God's activity and His love'.[13] Grace supplies when human capacity fails.

According to Pope John Paul every human person has an inner life, that is a spiritual life that 'communicates... not only with the visible, but also with the invisible world, and most importantly, with God'.[14] This inner life has already been discovered in people, admittedly with functioning cerebral cortexes, who were once written off as incapable of communication through new therapies such as intensive interaction. People with profound disabilities and in particular people in vegetative state are still living an earthly human life albeit an apparently diminished one. Since they are still alive on earth they are not in full union with God. Although some may not appear to be able to communicate with the visible world it cannot be said definitively that they do not have an inner life, even if perhaps not one that most would recognise and most surely it cannot be said that they are beyond the reach of God. Perhaps a return to one of Karol Wojtyła's earliest work, his thesis on faith in the spirituality of St John of the Cross can give a sense of direction.

Karol Wojtyła and the Carmelites

Pope John Paul's attraction to St John of the Cross (1542–1591) and the spirituality of Mount Carmel is well recorded. He tells of receiving the scapular of Carmel, a small cloth representation of the habit which monks wear as a sign of their vocation and devotion, on the day of his First Holy Communion in his home town of Wadowice the home also of a Carmelite monastery.[15] Even before entering the seminary Karol Wojtyła was introduced to the works of the Spanish mystics, in particular St John of the Cross by Jan Tyranowski, a lay youth worker who guided young men during the Nazi occupation in Krakow after the Salesian fathers who had run the parish were deported by the Nazis to a concentration camp.[16] In his reflections on his priesthood Pope John Paul adds that at one time he thought of joining the Carmelites but Archbishop Cardinal Sapieha 'in his typical manner said tersely: "First you have to finish what you have begun". And that is what happened'.[17] However, the influence of Jan Tyranowski remained leading him to study Spanish and in 1948 he presented his doctoral thesis on *Faith in St John of the Cross* (translated into English from Latin in 1981). Certainly Pope John Paul cannot be defined or limited by his early adherence to Carmelite spirituality. However undoubtedly it is one of the influences that have shaped his thought.

St John of the Cross and Faith, with Hope and Charity

In his thesis Karol Wojtyła sees as his task to learn 'what faith is as a means of union with God; what that reality means psychologically, on the one hand, and on the other, as a participation in the divine; how it exists and operates in the soul; and how the symbiosis is effected between the participated divine reality and the human intellect'.[18] Although Karol Wojtyła focuses on faith in St John's writing he notes that this is only one aspect of St John's work. To begin with Karol Wojtyła locates the work of St John of the Cross clearly in the tradition of St Thomas Aquinas and St Augustine. He further notes that St John takes Scripture as a primary source and St John also uses mystical experience.[19] No doubt this has resonance with Karol Wojtyła's own approach if we recall both the scriptural emphasis and the significance of experience in Karol Wojtyła's own reflections. According to Karol Wojtyła St John is one with St Thomas in asserting that for the soul to be united with God nature must be purified by grace and radically elevated so the work of union depends on the supernatural power of a living faith, a faith energised by hope and charity.[20]

Karol Wojtyła takes a step-by-step approach to St John's writing in order to demonstrate that the three theological virtues of faith, hope and charity are instruments of union with God with regard to the human faculties in which they reside and that logically faith belongs to the supernatural order.[21] Karol Wojtyła points out that in his work *Ascent of Mount Carmel* St John identifies two types of union of the soul with God.[22] The first is a 'natural' union which is effected by the substantial presence of God in the soul: as St John puts it 'God sustains and is present substantially in every soul'.[23] This is a union 'by very reason of its [the created thing's] being'. The second is a 'supernatural' union, a 'union of likeness'. However no creature bears any essential likeness to God so no created thing can serve as a means of supernatural union, though Karol Wojtyła does admit that there is analogical likeness by the very fact that a created thing exists.[24] But, Karol Wojtyła adds, faith does possess an essential likeness to God, it belongs to the supernatural order because the virtue of faith is elevated above the highest creatures.[25]

Karol Wojtyła argues that for St John the virtue of faith resides in the intellect, the rational higher part of the soul although he recognises that this is not explicit in St John's work.[26] However, Karol Wojtyła notes that according to St John the intellect is absolutely incapable of attaining union with God by its own natural powers. St John says this is because the intellect can only know of natural things through the senses and so cannot grasp the divine essence.[27] Instead 'in order to reach him, a soul must proceed rather by not understanding than by desiring to understand, by blinding itself and putting itself in darkness, rather than opening its eyes to approach the divine ray more closely'.[28] What is significant here is that all human intellects are inadequate. Although the intellect, the rational higher part of the soul, cannot by its natural powers lead to the divine essence, faith enables the intellect to attain God.[29] Whereas at the end of this mortal life and in the beatific vision God is seen, in this life God is believed, that is, there is not the clarity of the beatific vision for the divinity is hidden in darkness. Moreover, in a way it is the disabling, the blindness, that leads to a deeper awareness of God. As St John says about the light, 'by this means alone, God manifests himself to the soul in divine light that surpasses all understanding'.[30] Notably, for St John primacy goes to God manifesting himself rather than the response of the recipient of this manifestation. As Pope John Paul is later to point out, disability such as blindness allows the person to become closer to Christ because through disability a person realises that he or she is not self-sufficient; rather he or she is dependant on God.

Karol Wojtyła explains that in contrast to the natural union the supernatural union is a different kind of communication of God's, one effected 'only through grace and charity' and he adds that for St John there are varying degrees of supernatural communication according to the immensity of grace and charity in each person. Undoubtedly for Karol Wojtyła and for St John the will of the person is significant since, as Karol Wojtyła puts it, the psychological aspect of this union is 'the conformity of the human will with the divine'.[31] As Karol Wojtyła sees it what makes a person unique and unrepeatable is that no one else can will or want for that person. This incommunicability of a person is 'intrinsic to that person's inner self, to the power of self-determination, free will'.[32] Moreover, alongside the will, knowledge and experience are vital since faith 'enables the intellect to know God intimately and subjectively' and 'even more to experience what God is'.[33]

However Karol Wojtyła also explains that the existence of these essential capacities does not depend on an ability to exercise them. Rather they belong to the rational nature that every human being has simply by virtue of being human.[34] Reaffirming Church tradition Pope John Paul says that the rational soul is the form of the body and 'the spiritual and immortal soul is the principle of unity of the human being, whereby it exists as a whole... as a person'.[35] Thus he can say that 'an unborn child cannot be denied personality in its most objective ontological sense',[36] and by analogy this presumably applies to the profoundly disabled. If it is the case that all live human beings have a rational nature even if they cannot exhibit any rational behaviour then they still have an intellect (in the sense of rational nature) with which God can work. Father O'Rourke's view that in persistent vegetative state 'the soul of the person still maintains the radical power to perform human acts of cognitive-affective function but the actual performance of these acts is impossible'[37] seems in agreement with the Pope's view even if Father O'Rourke then goes on to deny any possible spiritual activity. In contrast for Pope John Paul the 'predominant element' in the virtue of faith is light: divine light is essential and 'once the intellect is disposed supernaturally by a divine infusion, it is capable of receiving the light of divine truths'.[38] This is not to say that the human person is reduced to what is immaterial or to having a purely 'spiritual' freedom. Rather it is to acknowledge the primacy of God's action on each living human being who is a unity of body and soul. This may perhaps come clearer in a discussion of the errors to which St John of the Cross himself responded.

St John of the Cross and the Alumbrados

What seems highly significant for an exploration of the apparently 'non-acting' human being and spirituality or response to vocation is the distance Karol Wojtyła identifies between the thought of St John of the Cross and the errors of Quietism as represented by the *alumbrados*.[39] The *alumbrados* were active in Seville and Cadiz in 1575. As Karol Wojtyła explains they were 'pseudo-mystics' who claimed to be under the guidance of the Holy Spirit such that they were not subject to any human authority and so they rejected the activity and authority of the Church. They claimed to enjoy an immediate vision of God which meant that they became unable to sin whatever they did. By their exaggerated passivity of the soul in relation to God Karol Wojtyła links them to the error of quietism.[40] Quietism as developed through the later thinking of the Spanish priest Michael de Molinos (1640–1697) encourages total abandonment of the soul to God so that the person remains a lifeless body. With the mind wholly inactive the soul stays passive while God acts within it and by doing nothing the soul in effect annihilates itself.

At first sight it may seem that this is precisely the situation of the patient in persistent vegetative state: a lifeless body with an inactive mind. Any suggestion that the patient has a spiritual though passive aspect appears to risk falling into the error of quietism. However in quietism the person deliberately aims at inactivating his or her mind and at obliterating the activity of the soul. In the case of profoundly disabled people theirs is not a situation of choice and whilst some observers may claim they have an inactive mind they are still alive so the soul, traditionally the form of the body, is still active. True, in Karol Wojtyła's thesis and in St John's writings neither author is considering the situation of an apparently 'mindless' human being. Moreover as Pope, John Paul is keen to point out that rationality is not factored out of St John's treatment of faith. He explains that John of the Cross 'earnestly' extols the value of human reason and he quotes St

John's saying that 'one thought alone of man is worth more than the entire world; hence God alone is worthy of him'.[41] Indeed Pope John Paul adds that rationality should serve to guide the person towards his or her proper end, union with God and 'for that reason, faith does not justify scorning human reason'.[42] No doubt Pope John Paul is acutely aware of the modern opposition some make between faith and reason and so he is even more concerned to demonstrate how they work together. To illustrate this he explains that 'faith is not a disincarnate reality. Its proper subject is man a rational being, with his lights and limits. The theologian and the believer cannot renounce their rationality; instead they must open it to the horizons of mystery'.[43]

Arguably, rather than a mindless vegetative existence this is more precisely the situation of the person with profound disabilities. According to Pope John Paul the experiences of illness, disability and suffering concern not only the person's physicality but also 'man in his entirety and in his somatic-spiritual unity'.[44] He or she remains 'a rational being' even though severely limited in his or her exercise of reason and he or she is called to open up to 'the horizons of mystery' enabled by the grace of God. This enabling is explained by the point that God's communication with a human being and the human being's response to God turn upon the theological virtues of faith, hope and love that are, after all, gifts of God who prepares the soul to receive them.[45]

Naturally any kind of assumption about the spiritual life of someone with profound disability can only be speculative. However it seems that what cannot be done is to claim that a person's spirituality is lessened because that person's ability consciously to express him or herself is diminished. Nor can anyone discount God's action and the workings of grace. Moreover, if spirituality involves the whole person and not just the brain it cannot be said that there is no spirituality if there is no apparent activity in the mind. Indeed many people who work with people with disabilities note that those who are physically and mentally impaired are also deeply open and pure in heart, happy simply 'to be'.

Still despite the speculative nature of the exercise, it seems that interesting parallels can be drawn between the interior life of the person with profound disabilities such as the person in persistent vegetative state and the person who is entering the contemplative Carmelite way of the dark night of the soul. To be sure the cases are not identical: the follower of Carmel chooses his or her path, there is not choice for people with profound disabilities. Nevertheless the dark night of the soul seems to lead to an 'in-betweenness' that may be especially apposite given that the person in persistent vegetative state appears to be suffering because he or she is not united with God; the person exists in finitude but on the edge of infinitude.

The 'dark night' of the soul

The keys to Carmelite spirituality lie in silence, in solitude, in the desert and the thirst for God. These have their roots in the story of Elijah retold in the *First Book of Kings* Chapters 17–19. Fleeing from Ahab the king of Israel, who 'was worse than all his predecessors', Elijah enters the desert and despairs, wishing he were dead. However Yahweh's angel gives him food and drink and he is led by the Spirit until he reaches Horeb, God's mountain, the holy place where Moses had encountered Yahweh in the burning bush.[46] There Elijah experiences hurricane, earthquake and lightening and finally 'a light murmuring sound' manifests Yahweh's presence.[47]

Historical documents suggest that there were early hermits following in the footsteps of Elijah on Mount Carmel in search of the Yahweh of the Old Testament. With the coming of the Son of God Christian hermits gathered following the monastic traditions and now in Carmelite spirituality Carmel watches and waits for the one who is to come.

Elijah's story indicates the possibility of a personal experience with God in the here-and-now through fostering a return to solitude and silence and so Carmelite spirituality takes this as its inspiration. For such an experience a person needs a contemplative spirit and a profound sense of God, both of which are placed in the soul and maintained there by God's grace. The gift of contemplation is the 'secret wisdom of God; for it is secret even to the understanding that receives it'.[48] As a gift no special activity, technique or practical disposition is required. Indeed, Celine, the sister of St Therese of Lisieux is reported to have called the spirit of Carmel the spirit of childhood. Thus prayer is not so much an exercise as a being present to God and depending on him alone. If an extension of this spirituality is taken to be being present and open to God in childlike simplicity then this may reflect the kind of spirituality that many profoundly disabled people seem to enjoy.

According to Karol Wojtyła this being present to God and hope of union involves the 'absolute necessity of the dark night'.[49] The notion of the 'dark night' is complex for it relates to mysticism and so involves a reality and knowledge beyond normal human grasp of things but one that is discovered through love. Moreover for Pope John Paul the dark night is related to suffering since suffering gives 'a great spiritual capacity'.[50] Karol Wojtyła explains the passage to union through the dark night in three steps: firstly because God is not comparable to any creature, rather there is an infinite distance between the divine reality and all created things, the person feels themselves as finite on the brink of infinitude. For Pope John Paul the experience of sickness and suffering in particular point to human beings as 'fragile' and 'limited creatures'[51] and it can lead to a deeper understanding that human existence is 'gratuitous' and that 'health is an immense gift of God'.[52] Pope John Paul sees that this perspective of the natural limitations of human beings and their dependence on God is especially relevant given the contemporary tendency to see humanity as self-sufficient by its 'Promethean attitude' to life and death.[53]

Secondly God takes over and enlivens this solitude, this desert experience, according to the soul's generosity. The desert is seen as the dwelling place of the Spirit for the Word of God is heard in the desert and the Promised Land is reached through the desert experience of the Exodus. Moreover, the desert embraces silence and solitude and it indicates thirst, so as prayer begins to quench thirst it also creates a deepening desire for the infinite. The significance in Carmel of solitude and its potential for opening up to the infinite may perhaps explain the importance of solitude for Pope John Paul's Theology of the Body. The experience of solitude itself is ambiguous as on the one hand it is where a person stands before God. Here 'the soul takes pleasure in being alone, with loving attentiveness upon God, without any particular conversation but with inner peace and quiet and rest, and without any acts and exercises of the faculties of memory, intellect and will'.[54] On the other hand it indicates a reaching out for relationship with others. In the case of the profoundly disabled and the sick in general Pope John Paul notes that suffering and sickness tend to lead to isolation and exclusion and he calls on all not only to help the sick but also to reintegrate them in society.[55] It would seem that such reintegration where people with disabilities are *seen* and *heard* would do much to redress the culture of indifference, discrimination and abuse suffered by many. Pope John Paul also notes that there is often a particular sense of communion and solidarity between people who suffer.[56] This is particularly noticeable with people with certain conditions, for instance sufferers from Rett Syndrome. Rett Syndrome is a very severe neurological problem and its sufferers tend to operate on the cognitive level of infants under one year old. Nonetheless a perhaps surprising feature is that those with Rett Syndrome seem to have an instinctive empathy with each other and this results in an almost secretive sharing. That seeing of the other as another within the experience of the profound solitude of severely limited capacities is perhaps a sound lesson for more capable people. This seems particularly so given the modern tendency towards rejecting the meaningfulness of being, nihilism, and the denial of humanity, which Pope John Paul says leads to 'a solitude without hope'.[57] Indeed for Pope John Paul currently 'one of our greatest threats is the temptation to despair'[58] and this is one area where the generosity of people with profound disabilities may lead in action.

Certainly Pope John Paul is aware that the invitation to turn the experience of illness, suffering and pain into something positive is a 'difficult path'. However he does think this is possible with Christ.[59] So, thirdly, it is God's love that is active in this work of discovery. In the Carmelite tradition this work of God is expressed as a wound because the immensity of God's love appears painful to the human spirit. Notably, God does not inflict this pain but rather the person in his or her finitude is overwhelmed by the infinite. For Pope John Paul the dark night appeals because even though it does not provide an answer to the 'appalling problem' of human suffering it does look into its 'unfathomable mystery' and the 'marvellous transformation which God effects in the darkness'.[60] According to Pope John Paul the experience of suffering provides an 'opportunity to release love'[61] because suffering brings an acute awareness of finitude and of dependence and its answer lies only in the love of God that transforms suffering.

Although according to both Karol Wojtyła and St John God communicates himself most to the soul that has progressed farthest in love in that the soul's will is more in conformity with the will of God, they both also discern the primacy of God's love as a transforming power. This is apparent in Karol Wojtyła's explanation of how a human being is 'God by participation' when he uses St John's analogy of sunlight passing through a window: as St John describes it, the cleaner the window the more sunlight passes through it, communicating its own brightness. If the window is so clean it is translucent it will give the same light as the sun's ray and will seem to be a ray of light but it still retains its own nature, 'it merely participates in the ray of light'.[62] The darkness experienced by the soul is not because of the absence of God rather 'it is a question of the intellect's incapacity to make the divine essence intelligible'.[63]

However, in this earthly life, the life to which the person in persistent vegetative state still clings, human beings are always drawn to the things that are 'not God'. The difficulty is that people with a 'Promethean attitude' find this draw even more powerful and so Pope John Paul thinks that this path of the dark night is 'not for the proud who think that everything is the fruit of personal conquest'.[64] Rather, quoting St John and once again highlighting strength in disability he says that the soul 'must be like a blind man, leaning upon dark faith, taking it for its guide and light, and leaning upon none of the things that he understands, experiences, feels and imagines'.[65]

When it comes to considering the acting person Pope John Paul notes that 'interior maturity and spiritual greatness in suffering are certainly the *result* of a particular *conversion* and cooperation with the grace of the Crucified Redeemer' (his italics). Nevertheless the acting person is not simply the human being whether acting or apparently non-acting. As Pope John Paul explains it is Christ himself 'who acts at the heart of human sufferings through his Spirit of truth, through the consoling Spirit. It is he who transforms, in a certain sense, the very substance of the spiritual life, indicating for the person who suffers a place close to himself'.[66]

Certainly it is impossible speculation to suggest that certain profoundly disabled people may have reached an advanced stage in their relationship with God. However it is interesting to note that in Carmelite spirituality the stage of contemplation is marked by what many might consider non-acting as distinct from quietism. As St John explains the surest sign that the soul has entered contemplation 'is that the soul takes pleasure in being alone, with loving attentiveness upon God, without any particular conversation but with inward peace, quiet and rest and without any acts and exercises of the faculties of memory, intellect and will'.[67] Comparing the dark night of the soul to purgatory St John says that in it 'God secretly teaches the soul and instructs it in perfection of love', he 'prepares it for the union of love'.[68] Finally when the soul is ready 'all that is required now is to die, so that one may enjoy the face-to-face vision'.[69] Of course Pope John Paul is at pains to point out that life as a gift from God is neither to be hastened nor to be artificially extended: both demonstrate the same fault that of believing that life is purely the subject of human will.[70] Moreover he emphasises that the Church's defence of the sacredness of human life, even of those who are dying, is not to absolutise physical life but rather to confirm respect for the dignity of the person.[71]

Just as St John took a stand against the *alumbrados* for removing the need of the Church in their spiritual life Pope John Paul also recognises the significance of the role of the Church not only as a witness to the dignity of all human beings. He sees that the task of the Church is to ensure that the sick and dying are embraced 'in a bond of love and solidarity' so that they do not feel abandoned.[72] He appreciates that suffering overwhelms people and he reminds those who suffer that the Church's action in its pastoral care of the sick, notably its rites of anointing and viaticum, addresses fear and despair as it continues Jesus's ministry of care.[73] Through its rite of anointing the Church acts as the Good Samaritan and in its care of the dying it supports them in the faith and hope that 'Christ truly awaits them in the new life'.[74]

Summary

Clearly any discussion on the spirituality of people with the most profound disabilities can only be speculative. Moreover Karol Wojtyła's work on faith in the writing of St John of the Cross is concerned with how a person through the exercise of the will and submission of the intellect follows the stages of Carmelite spirituality on the path to participation and ultimate union with God. However, Karol Wojtyła and St John of the Cross make a distinction between what happens in the natural order of knowledge and in the supernatural order. In the natural order both agree that 'the will cannot love anything unless the intellect first knows it'. But in the supernatural order 'God can infuse love and increase it without any corresponding increase of knowledge in the intellect'. Karol Wojtyła continues,

> an increase in the experience of love does not necessarily imply an increase in cognitive awareness... we are not dealing with the natural order which is subject to the norms of psychology; we are dealing with the supernatural order, the order of gratuitous infusion, and the principles of psychology do not suffice to explain this type of experience.[75]

Moreover St John makes certain parallels with those who are disabled notably the blind in order to draw out the strength of those who realise they are dependent over those who believe they can achieve everything through their own efforts. As Pope John Paul points out, 'many simple and unselfish souls receive it [experience the awareness of God] from God by means of the Spirit'.[76] The apparently hopeless situation of the person is not the issue for everything is possible for God. Perhaps a poignant parallel can be drawn between the story of Elijah and the profoundly disabled person. Like Elijah's journey the situation of the profoundly disabled person may seem to be an entry into the desert where despair leads to thinking death is preferable.

However, given food and drink and led by the Spirit the person may yet experience God's presence. This is not to say that every human being is to be kept alive no matter what: vitalism does not respect the true nature and dignity of the human person whose ultimate destiny is friendship with God in eternal life. Rather it is to maintain that no living human being is beyond the reach of God.

It is often said that people with the profoundest disabilities have childlike qualities. This is not only on account of their reduced capacities, limited or apparently absent skills, or lack of communication. Rather it is frequently recognised that they have innocence and purity of heart. They do not suffer the disabling effects of the spiritual sins spoken of by St John of the Cross in *Dark Night of the Soul:* pride and a reliance on one's own capacities;[77] spiritual avarice as a discontentment with the spirituality God has given;[78] spiritual luxury whereby pleasure is taken in spiritual things yet the love of God is allowed to grow cold;[79] wrath that is a bitterness, impatience and irritation with others;[80] spiritual gluttony that encourages one to act on one's own opinion and to go to extremes;[81] spiritual envy and sloth that promotes displeasure at the spiritual good of others or that advocates abandoning the way of perfection in favour of satisfying one's own will.[82] Still St John also points out that people crippled by spiritual sins are like children in that they require education and purification in the path of perfection.[83] All human beings, whatever their condition and so even the profoundly disabled, need the activity of God's grace to grow in holiness.

That being said, Pope John Paul constantly urges a return to the reflection of the Fathers of the Second Vatican Council that the search for holiness is in part found in a sincere gift of self through which the person fully discovers his or her self. [84] And, taking the profoundly disabled to be most childlike, as Karol Wojtyła explains, 'it is significant that the child—although deprived for a long time of the personal fullness of activity— nevertheless enters at once into the community as a person, as someone capable not only of receiving but also of giving… [the child] makes a gift of its humanity' and from conception every human being whatever his or her condition or situation 'presents itself as a person and a gift'.[85]

Pope John Paul takes the words of *Gaudium et spes* 24, the call to be a gift for the other, as foundational when he writes his encyclical letter *Veritatis splendor*, the *Splendour of Truth*. In *Veritatis splendor* the Pope has the acting person in mind as he reflects on how human beings learn to walk 'in the light', that is walk in the truth with Christ. He explains that 'truth enlightens man's intelligence and shapes his freedom, leading him to know and love the Lord'[86] and true freedom is acquired 'in love, that is the gift of self'.[87] However he also says that imitating and living out the love of Christ is not possible by a person's own strength. Rather it is itself a gift received from God.[88] Referring to the prophet Micah he reminds his readers that *'the good is belonging to God, obeying him,* walking humbly with him in doing justice and in loving kindness' (his italics).[89] He points out that all Christians are called 'to walk on the same road' as Christ.[90] The profoundly disabled person, the apparently non-acting person, belongs to God and is sent by God as a gift. The profoundly disabled person may not appear to be able to 'walk' in the same way as the apparently acting person. Indeed, according to some, the profoundly disabled human being is not able to 'walk' at all. Nevertheless as Pope John Paul himself witnesses, the profoundly disabled person passes through the Holy Door 'in the company of the crucified Lord'.[91]

Notes

1. K. O'Rourke, P. Norris, 'Care of the PVS Patient: Catholic Opinion in the US' in *Linacre Quarterly* 68/3 (2001), pp. 207–217.

2. K. O'Rourke, 'Development of Church teaching on prolonging life' in *Health Progress* 8 (1988), pp. 29–35.

3. R. Rakestraw, 'The Persistent Vegetative State and the Withdrawal of Nutrition and Hydration', in D. Clark and R. Rakestraw (eds.), *Readings in Christian Ethics Vol.2 Issues and Applications* (Grand Rapids: Baker Publishing, 1992), pp. 127–128.

4. N. Biggar, *Aiming to Kill: the Ethics of Suicide and Euthanasia* (Cleveland: The Pilgrim Press, 2004), p. 39.

5. K. O'Rourke, 'Reflections on the Papal Allocution Concerning Care for Persistent Vegetative Patients' in *Christian Bioethics* 12/1 (2006), pp. 83–97 at p. 93.

6. R. Rakestraw, 'The Persistent Vegetative State and the Withdrawal of Nutrition and Hydration' in *Readings in Christian Ethics Vol.2 Issues and Applications* p. 128.

7. N. Biggar, *Aiming to Kill: the Ethics of Suicide and Euthanasia* p. 114.

8. Pope John Paul II, *Evangelium vitae*, 39.

9. K. Wojtyła, *Love and Responsibility* (London: Fount, (1979) 1982), p. 256.

10. *Ibid.*, p. 257.

11. *Ibid.*

12. N. Biggar, *Aiming to Kill: the Ethics of Suicide and Euthanasia* p. 47.

13. K. Wojtyła, *Love and Responsibility* p. 258.

14. *Ibid.*, pp. 22–23.

15. Pope John Paul II, *General Audience Castelgandolfo* (16 July 2003).

16. Pope John Paul II, *Crossing the Threshold of Hope* (London: Jonathan Cape, 1994), p. 142; Pope John Paul II, *Gift and Mystery* (London: CTS, 1996), p. 23.

17. Pope John Paul II, *Gift and Mystery* p. 25.

18. K. Wojtyła, *Faith in St John of the Cross* (Oregon: Wipf and Stock, (1948) 1981), p. 22.

19. *Ibid.*, pp. 19–22.

20. *Ibid.*, pp. 20–21.

21. *Ibid.*, pp. 54–55.

22. *Ibid.*, pp. 48–54; St John of the Cross, *Ascent of Mount Carmel* (USA: Wilders Publications, 2008), Bk II Ch.5 no.3.

23. K. Wojtyła, *Faith in St John of the Cross* pp. 48–50; St John of the Cross, *Ascent of Mount Carmel* Bk II ch 5 no 3.

24. K. Wojtyła, *Faith in St John of the Cross* pp. 39–40.

25. *Ibid.*, p. 42.

26. *Ibid.*, p. 53.

27. *Ibid.*, p. 60.

28. *Ibid.*, p. 61; St John of the Cross, *Ascent of Mount Carmel* Bk II ch 8 no 5.

29. K. Wojtyła, *Faith in St John of the Cross* p. 44.

30. *Ibid.*, p. 66; St John of the Cross, *Ascent of Mount Carmel* Bk II ch 9 no1.

31. K. Wojtyła, *Faith in St John of the Cross* p. 52.

32. K. Wojtyła, *Love and Responsibility* p. 24.

33. K. Wojtyła, *Faith in St John of the Cross* p. 69.

34. K. Wojtyła, *Love and Responsibility* p. 22.

35. Pope John Paul II, *Veritatis splendor*, 48.

36. K. Wojtyła, *Love and Responsibility* p. 26.

37. K. O'Rourke, P. Norris, 'Care of PVS Patients: Catholic Opinion in the US' in *Linacre Quarterly* 68/3 (2001), 207–217.

38. K. Wojtyła, *Faith in St John of the Cross* pp. 67, 72.

39. *Ibid.,* p. 16.

40. *Ibid.,* p. 16 footnote 3.

41. Pope John Paul II, *Apostolic Letter on the IV Centenary of the Death of St John of the Cross*, 12.

42. *Ibid.*

43. *Ibid.*

44. Pope John Paul II, *Dolentium Hominum*, 2.

45. Pope John Paul II, *Apostolic Letter on the IV Centenary of the Death of St John of the Cross,* 10.

46. *Ex* 3:1–6.

47. *1K* 19:9–13.

48. K. Wojtyła, *Faith in St John of the Cross* p. 62; St John of the Cross, *Ascent of Mount Carmel* Bk II ch 8 no 6.

49. K. Wojtyła, *Faith in St John of the Cross* pp. 112–113.

50. Pope John Paul II, Speech *To the Sick and Disabled* (19 August 1989), 2.

51. Pope John Paul II, *World Day of the Sick, 5,* 4.

52. Pope John Paul II, *To the Sick and Disabled,* 4.

53. Pope John Paul II, *Evangelium vitae,* 15.

54. K. Wojtyła, *Faith in St John of the Cross* p. 150.

55. Pope John Paul II, *World Day of the Sick, 8,* 9.

56. Pope John Paul II, *Salvifici Doloris,* 8.

57. Pope John Paul II, *Fides et Ratio,* 90.

58. *Ibid.,* 91.

59. Pope John Paul II, *World Day of the Sick, 8,* 7.

60. Pope John Paul II, *Apostolic Letter on the IV Centenary of the Death of St John of the Cross,* 14.

61. Pope John Paul II, *World Day of the Sick, 1,* 2.

62. K. Wojtyła, *Faith in St John of the Cross* pp. 48–50.

63. *Ibid.,* p. 209.

64. Pope John Paul II, *Fides et Ratio,* 18.

65. K. Wojtyła, *Faith in St John of the Cross* p. 115; St John of the Cross, *Ascent of Mount Carmel* Bk II ch 4 no 2.

66. Pope John Paul, *Salvifici Doloris,* 26.

67. K. Wojtyła, *Faith in St John of the Cross* p. 150; St John of the Cross, *Ascent of Mount Carmel* BkII ch13 nos2–5.

68. K. Wojtyła, *Faith in St John of the Cross* p. 189; St John of the Cross, *Dark Night of the Soul* BkII ch 5 no1; ch 7 and 10.

69. K. Wojtyła, *Faith in St John of the Cross* p. 193.

70. Pope John Paul II, Speech *To the staff and residents at Rennweg Hospice* (21 June 1998).

71. Pope John Paul II, Speech *To the General Assembly of the Pontifical Academy for Life* (27 February 1999).

72. Pope John Paul II, *To the General Assembly of the Pontifical Academy for Life* (27 February 1999).

73. Pope John Paul II, Speech *To the sick, elderly and the handicapped* (23 November 1986), 2, 4, 5.

74. Pope John Paul II, *To the staff and residents at Rennweg Hospice* (21 June 1998), 9, 5.

75. K. Wojtyła, *Faith in St John of the Cross* p. 224.

76. Pope John Paul II, *Apostolic Letter on the IV Centenary of the Death of St John of the Cross* 1990, 10.

77. St John of the Cross, *Dark Night of the Soul*, Ch. II.

78. *Ibid.*, Ch. III.

79. *Ibid.*, Ch. IV.

80. *Ibid.*, Ch. V.

81. *Ibid.*, Ch. VI.

82. *Ibid.*, Ch. VII.

83. *Ibid.*, Ch. I.

84. K. Wojtyła, *Sources of Renewal* (London: Fount, (1975) 1980), p. 224.

85. K. Wojtyła, 'Parenthood as a Community of Persons'(1975) in *Catholic Thought from Lublin Vol.IV Person and Community* (New York: Peter Lang, 1993), p. 333.

86. Pope John Paul II, *Veritatis splendor*, Blessing.

87. *Ibid.*, 87.

88. *Ibid.*, 22.

89. *Ibid.*; Micah 6:8.

90. Pope John Paul II, *Veritatis splendor*, 89.

91. Pope John Paul II, Angelus *Jubilee of the Disabled* (3 December 2000), 1–2.

BIBLIOGRAPHY

Karol Wojtyła and Pope John Paul II

Wojtyła, K. *Faith According to St John of the Cross* (1948), translated by J. Aumann. Oregon: Wipf and Stock, 1981.

Wojtyła, K. *Catholic Thought from Lublin Vol.IV. Person and Community. Selected Essays* (1950–1978), translated by T. Sandok. New York: Peter Lang, 1993.

Wojtyła, K. *The Acting Person* (1969), translated by A. Potocki. Dordrecht: Reidel, 1979.

Wojtyła, K. *Sources of Renewal* (1975), translated by P. S. Falla. London: Fount, 1980.

Wojtyła, K. *Love and Responsibility* (1979), translated by H.T. Willets. London: Fount, 1982.

Pope John Paul II. Speech *To members of the 3rd General Conference of the Latin American Episcopate, Puebla.* 28 January 1979.

Pope John Paul II. Encyclical Letter *Redemptor Hominis.* 4 March 1979.

Pope John Paul II. Encyclical Letter *Dives in Misericordia.* 30 November 1980.

Pope John Paul II. Speech *To Teachers and University Students in Cologne Cathedral: Science and Faith in the Search for Truth.* 15 November 1980.

Pope John Paul II. Documento de la Sancta Sede para el 'año internacional de los minusválidos'. In: *L'Osservatore Romano* (Spanish edition) 4 March 1981.

Pope John Paul II. Speech *To the participants in the International Games for disabled persons.* 3 April 1981.

Pope John Paul II. Encyclical Letter *Laborem Exercens.* 14 September 1981.

Pope John Paul II. Apostolic Exhortation *Familiaris Consortio.* 22 November 1981.

Pope John Paul II. *Address at Southwark Cathedral Anointing the Sick.* 28 May 1982

Pope John Paul II. Apostolic Letter *Salvifici Doloris.* 11 February 1984.

Pope John Paul II. Motu Proprio *Dolentium Hominum.* 11 February 1985.

Pope John Paul II. Encyclical Letter *Dominum et Vivificantem.* 18 May 1986.

Pope John Paul II. Letter *To the Bishops of Brazil.* 9 April 1986.

Pope John Paul II. Speech *To the sick, elderly and the handicapped.* 23 November 1986.

Pope John Paul II. Encyclical Letter *Redemptoris Mater.* 25 March 1987.

Pope John Paul II. Encyclical Letter *Sollicitudo Rei Socialis.* 30 December 1987.

Pope John Paul II. Apostolic Letter *Mulieris Dignitatem.* 15 August 1988.

Pope John Paul II. Apostolic Exhortation *Christifideles Laici.* 30 December 1988.

Pope John Paul II. Speech *To the Sick and Disabled.* 19 August 1989.

Pope John Paul II. Apostolic Letter *On the IV Centenary of the Death of St John of the Cross.* 14 December 1990.

Pope John Paul II. Speech *To the International Congress on the care of the dying.* 17

March 1992.Pope John Paul II. Letter *Instituting the World Day of the Sick.* 13 May 1992.

Pope John Paul II. Annual Letters *For the World Day of the Sick I–XIII.* 1992–2004.

Pope John Paul II. Encyclical Letter *Veritatis Splendor.* 6 August 1993.

Pope John Paul II. Letter *To Families.* 2 February 1994.

Pope John Paul II. Motu proprio establishing the Pontifical Academy for Life *Vitae mysterium.* 11 February 1994.

Pope John Paul II. *Crossing the Threshold of Hope.* London: Jonathan Cape, 1994.

Pope John Paul II. Encyclical Letter *Evangelium vitae*. 25 March 1995.

Pope John Paul II. Pontifical Message *To the Pontifical Academy of Sciences: On Evolution*. 22 October 1996.

Pope John Paul II. 'Mentally Ill Are Also Made in God's Image'. In: *L'Osservatore Romano* (English edition) 11 December 1996.

Pope John Paul II. 'Incarnation Inspires Christian Genius: Address to the joint session of all the Pontifical Academies'. In: *L'Osservatore Romano* (English edition) 4 December 1996.

Pope John Paul II. *Gift and Mystery*. London: CTS, 1996.

Pope John Paul II. *The Theology of the Body: Human Love in the Divine Plan*. Boston: Pauline Books, 1997.

Pope John Paul II. Speech *To the Staff and Residents at Rennweg Hospice, Vienna*. 21 June 1998.

Pope John Paul II. Speech *To the Bishops of California, Nevada and Hawaii USA on their 'ad limina' visit*. 2 October 1998.

Pope John Paul II. Encyclical Letter *Fides et Ratio*. 14 September 1998.

Pope John Paul II. Speech *To the General Assembly of the Pontifical Academy for Life*. 27 February 1999.

Pope John Paul II. 'To the Congress on Integration of Disabled Children'. In:

L'Osservatore Romano (English edition) 5 January 2000.

Pope John Paul II. Speech *To the 18th International Congress of the Transplantation Society*. 29 August 2000.

Pope John Paul II. Angelus *Jubilee of the Disabled*. 3 December 2000.

Pope John Paul II. Homily *Jubilee of the Disabled*. 3 December 2000.

Pope John Paul II. Message *For the Celebration of the World Day of Peace*. 1 January 2001.

Pope John Paul II. Apostolic Letter *Novo Millennio Ineunte*. 6 January 2001.

Pope John Paul II. General Audience *Castelgandolfo*. 16 July 2003.

Pope John Paul II. Speech *On the occasion of the International Symposium on the dignity and rights of the mentally disabled person*. 5 January 2004.

Pope John Paul II. Speech *To the participants in the International Congress on 'Life-sustaining Treatments and Vegetative State: Scientific Advances and Ethical Dilemmas'.* 20 March 2004.

Pope John Paul II. Speech *Letter to the Pontifical Academy of Sciences.* 1 February 2005.

Pope John Paul II. *Memory and Identity.* London: Weidenfeld & Nicolson, 2005.

Person and Community is a collection of essays, articles, papers and lectures written by Karol Wojtyła from the early 1950s to his election to the papacy in 1978.

Other Papal Texts and Church Documents

Pope Leo XIII. Encyclical Letter *Quod Apostolici Muneris.* 28 December 1878.

Pope Leo XIII. Encyclical Letter *Rerum Novarum.* 15 May 1891.

Pope Pius XII. 'Address to an International Congress of Anaethesiologists'. In: *L'Osservatore Romano* (English edition) 25–26 November 1957.

Pope John XXIII. Pontifical Message *Christmas Message.* 23 December 1959.

Pope John XXIII. Encyclical Letter *Mater et Magistra.* 15 May 1961.

Pope Paul VI. Apostolic Letter *Octogesima Adveniens.* 14 May 1971.

Pope Benedict XVI.Homily *On the Beatification of Pope John Paul II.* 1 May 2011.

Second Vatican Council. Dogmatic Constitution on the Church *Lumen Gentium.* 21 November 1964.

Second Vatican Council. Decree on the Apostolate of Lay People *Apostolicam actuositatem.* 18 November 1965.

Second Vatican Council. Pastoral Constitution on the Church in the Modern World *Gaudium et spes.* 7 December 1965.

Committee for the Jubilee Day of the Community with People with Disabilities: Preparation for the Jubilee Day. 3 December 2000.

Conclusions of a Vatican Conference on the Family and Integration of the Disabled (1999) <www.vatican.va/.../family/.../rc_pc_family_doc_20000304_integration-disabled_en.html> (accessed 2 October 2010).

Sacred Congregation for the Doctrine of the Faith, *Declaration on Euthanasia,* (30 May 1980).

Congregation for the Doctrine of the Faith, *Responses to Certain Questions of the United States Conference of Catholic Bishops Concerning Artificial Nutrition and Hydration, Vatican commentary,* (1 August 2007).

Pontifical Council for Justice and Peace. *Compendium of the Social Doctrine of the Church.* Washington: Libreria Editrice Vaticana, 2004.

Pontifical Council for Pastoral Assistance to Health Care Workers *The Charter for Health Care Workers.* 1 January 1995. <http://www.ewtn.com/library/curia/pcpaheal.htm> [accessed 13 January 2009].

General Bibliography

Airedale NHS Trust v *Bland* [1993] 2 WLR 359.

American Academy of Neurology. 'Position of the American Academy of Neurology on Certain Aspects of the Care and Management of the Persistent Vegetative patient'. In: R, Hamel, J. Walter (eds.), *Artificial Nutrition and Hydration and the Permanently Unconscious Patient: The Catholic Debate.* Georgetown: Georgetown University Press, 2007.

Amundsen, D. *Medicine, Society, and Faith in the Ancient and Medieval Worlds.* London: Johns Hopkins University Press, 1996.

Annetts, Deborah. <http://www.dignityindying.org.uk/news/general/n4-voluntary-euthanasia-society-changes-name> (January 2006) [accessed 14 November 2011].

Apollinarius (c.315–392). 'Apodeixis', In: Gregory of Nyssa *Antirreticus: Treatise Against Apollinarius* <http://www.sage.edu/faculty/salmond/nyssa/appolin.html.> [accessed 17 January 2009].

Aquinas, Thomas (St) (c.1225–1274). *Summa Theologiae.* London: Spottiswoode, 1970.

Aristotle (c.384 BCE–322 BCE). *Nicomachean Ethics Book V.* <http://classics.mit.edu/Aristotle/nicomachaen.5.v.html> [accessed 10 November 2010].

Augustine (St) (354–430). *Confessions* translated by R.S. Pine-Coffin. London: Penguin, 1961.

Augustine (St) (354–430). *City of God* translated by H. Bettenson. London: Penguin, 2003.

Augustine (St) (354–430). *The Rule of Saint Augustine* translated by R. Canning. London: Darton, Longman & Todd, 1996.

Augustine (St) (354–430). *Sermons 1–19* translated by E. Hill. New York: New City Press, 1990.

Augustine (St) (354–430). 'On the good of widowhood'. In: P. Schaff (ed.), *Nicene and Post Nicene Fathers* Vol.3. New York: Cosimo, 2007.

Augustine (St) (354–430). 'On the Trinity'. In: P. Schaff (ed.), *Nicene and Post Nicene Fathers* Vol.3. New York: Cosimo, 2007.

Basil the Great (St) (330–379). 'Ascetical Works: Long Rules'translated by M. Wagner. In: *The Fathers of the Church* Vol.9. Washington: Catholic University of America Press, 1962.

Basil the Great (St) (330–379). 'Letter 94'. In: G. Barrois (ed.), *The Fathers Speak: St Basil the Great, St Gregory Nazianzus, St Gregory Nyssa.* Crestwood, New York: St Vladimir's Seminary Press, 1986.

Beauchamp, T., Childress, J. *Principles of Biomedical Ethics.* Oxford: Oxford University Press, 2009.

Bernat, J. *Ethical Issues in Neurology* 3rd edition. Philadelphia: Lippincott Williams and Wilkins, 2008.

Betcher, S. *Spirit and the Politics of Disablement.* Minneapolis: Fortress Press, 2007.

Betcher, S. 'Becoming Flesh of My Flesh: Feminist and Disability Theologies on the Edge of Posthumanist Discourse'. In: *Journal of Feminist Studies in Religion* 26/2 (2010), 107–139.

Bickenbach, J. 'Disability, Non-talent and Distributive Justice'. In: K. Kristiansen, S. Vehmas, and T. Shakespeare (eds.) *Arguing About Disability: Philosophical Perspectives.* New York: Routledge, 2009.

Biggar, N. *Aiming to Kill: The Ethics of Suicide and Euthanasia.* Cleveland: The Pilgrim Press, 2004.

Blandford, J. 'An Examination of the Revisionist Challenge to the Catholic Tradition on Providing Artificial Nutrition and Hydration to Patients in a Persistent Vegetative State'. In: *Christian Bioethics* 17/2 (2011), 153–164.

Block, J.W. *Copious Hosting: a theology of access for people with disabilities.* New York: Continuum International, 2002.

Borthwick, C.J., Crossley, R. 'Permanent vegetative state: usefulness and limits of a prognostic definition'. In: *NeuroRehabilitation* 19 (2004), 381–389.

Braddock, D., Parish, S. 'An Institutional History of Disability'. In: G. Albrecht, K. Seelman, and M. Bury (eds.) *Handbook of Disability Studies.* London: Sage Publications, 2001.

Branson, J., Miller, D. *Damned for their Difference.* Washington: Gallaudet University Press, 2002.

Brierley, J.B., Adams, J.A.H., Graham, D.I., Simpson, J.A. 'Neocortical death after cardiac arrest'. In *Lancet* (1971), 560–565.

Brody, B. 'On the humanity of the fetus'. In: M. Goodman (ed.), *What is a person?.* Clifton New Jersey: Humana Press, 1988.

Brown, I., Brown, R. 'Family Quality of Life as an Area of Study'. In: A. Turnbull, I. Brown, and H.R. Turnbull III (eds.) *Families and Persons with Mental Retardation and Quality of Life: International Perspectives.* Washington: American Association on Mental Retardation, 2004.

Burke v *GMC* [2005] EWCA Civ 1003.

Buttiglione, R. *Karol Wojtyła: The Thought of the Man who became Pope John Paul II,* translated by P. Guietti, F. Murphy. Grand Rapids: Eerdmans, 1997.

Caldwell, P. *Finding You Finding Me.* London: Jessica Kingsley Publishers, 2006.

Callahan, D. 'On Feeding the Dying'. In: *Hastings Center Report* 13/5 (1983), 22.

Cavalieri, P., Singer, P. 'The Great Ape Project'. In: H. Kuhse (ed.), *Peter Singer: Unsanctifying Human Life.* Oxford: Blackwell, 2002.

Chadwick, H. *The Early Church.* Middlesex: Penguin Books, 1974.

Chrislip, A. *From Monastery to Hospital. Christian Monasticism and the Transformation of Healthcare in Late Antiquity.* USA: University of Michigan Press, 2005.

Clark, P. 'Tube feeding and Persistent Vegetative State Patients: Ordinary or Extraordinary Means?'. In: *Christian Bioethics* 12 (2006), 43–64.

Clement of Alexandria (St) (c.150–215). 'Insrtuctor'. In: A. Roberts, J. Donaldson (eds.) *The Ante-Nicene Fathers* Vol.II. Grand Rapids: Eerdmans, 1983.

Clement of Alexandria (St) (c.150–215). 'Stromata'. In: A. Roberts, J. Donaldson (eds.) *The Ante-Nicene Fathers* Vol.II. Grand Rapids: Eerdmans, 1983.

Clement of Alexandria (St) (c.150–215). 'Exhortation to the Heathen'. In: A. Roberts, J. Donaldson (eds.) *The Ante-Nicene Fathers* Vol.II. Grand Rapids: Eerdmans, 1983.

Constable, C. 'Withdrawal of Artificial Nutrition and Hydration for Patients in a Permanent Vegetative State: Changing Tack'. In: *Bioethics* 26/3 (2012), 157–163.

Cranford, R. 'The case of Mr Stevens'. In: *Issues in Law and Medicine* 7/2 (1991), 199–211.

Cranford, R. 'Commentary Facts, Lies and Videotapes: The Permanent Vegetative State and the Sad Case of Terri Schiavo'. In: *Journal of Law, Medicine and Ethics* 33/2 (2005), 363–371.

Cranford, R., Smith, D. 'Consciousness: the most critical moral (constitutional) standard for human personhood'. In: *American Journal of Law and Medicine* 13 (1987), 233–248.

Creamer, D. 'Theological Accessibility: The Contribution of Disability'. In: *Disability Studies Quarterly* 26/4 (2006) <http://dsq-sds.org/article/view/812/987>

[accessed 8 March 2011].

Creamer, D. 'Embracing Limits, Queering Embodiment: Creating/Creative Possibilities for Disability Theology'. In: *Journal of Feminist Studies in Religion* 26/2 (2010), 123–127.

Crosby, J. *The Selfhood of the Human Person.* Washington: Catholic University of America Press, 1996.

Curran, C. *Catholic Social Teaching 1891– present: a historical, theological and ethical analysis.* Washington: Georgetown University Press, 2002.

Curry, S. 'Living patients in a permanent vegetative state as legitimate research subjects'. In: *Journal of Medical Ethics* 32/10 (2006), 606–607.

DeGrazia, D. *Taking Animals Seriously.* Cambridge: Cambridge University Press, 1996.

DeGrazia, D. 'Must we have full moral status throughout our existence?'. In: *Kennedy Institute of Ethics Journal* 17/4 (2007), 297–310.

Dennett, D. 'Conditions of Personhood'. In: A.O. Rorty (ed.), *The Identities of Persons.* London: University of California Press, 1976.

Descartes, R. (1596–1650). *Philosophical Essays and Correspondence. The World or Treatise on Man; Passions of the Soul; Discourse on Method; Meditations; Objections and Replies.* R. Ariew (ed.) Indiana: Hackett, 2000.

Descartes, R. 'To More'. In: *The Philosophical Writings of Descartes* Vol.III translated by J. Cottingham, R. Stoothoff, D. Murdoch, and A. Kenny. Cambridge: Cambridge University Press, 1997.

Dignity in Dying. <http://www.dignityindying.org.uk/research/slippery-slope.html> [accessed 14 November 2011].

Donagan, A. 'Thomas Aquinas on human action'. In: N. Kretzmann, A. Kenny, and J. Pinborg (eds.) *The Cambridge History of Later Medieval Philosophy* Cambridge: Cambridge University Press, 1982.

Draper, H. 'Research and patients in permanent vegetative state'. In: *Journal of Medical Ethics* 32/10 (2006), 607.

Dugdale, L., Ridenour, A.A. 'Making Sense of the Roman Catholic Directive to Extend Life Indefinitely'. In: *Hastings Center Report* 41/2 (2011), 28–29.

Eiesland, N. *The Disabled God; Toward a Liberatory Theology of Disability.* Nashville: Abingdon Press, 1994.

Engelhardt, H.T. *The Foundation of Bioethics.* Oxford: Oxford University Press, 1986.

Engelhardt, H.T. 'Infanticide in a post-Christian age'. In: R. Mc-Millan, H.T. Engelhardt, and S. Spicker (eds.) *Euthanasia and the Newborn*. Boston: D. Reidel, 1987.

European Task Force on Disorders of Consciousness. 'Unresponsive wakefulness syndrome: a new name for the vegetative state or apallic syndrome'. In: *BMC Medicine* 8/68 (2010) <http://www.biomedcentral.com/1741–7015/8/68> [accessed 7 March 2011].

Fine, R. 'From Quinlan to Schiavo: medical, ethical and legal issues in severe brain injury'. In: *Proc (Bayl Univ Med Cent)* 18/4 (2005), 303–310.

Firth, G., Elford, H., Leeming, C., and Crabbe, M. 'Intensive Interaction as a Novel Approach in Social Care: Care Staff's Views on the Practice Change Process'. In: *Journal of Applied Research in Intellectual Disabilities* 21 (2008), 58–69.

Fischer, J. (ed.) *The Metaphysics of Death*. Stanford: Stanford University Press, 1993.

Fisher, A. 'Why do Unresponsive Patients Still Matter?'. In: C. Tollefsen (ed.), *Artificial Nutrition and Hydration: the new Catholic Debate*. Netherlands: Springer, 2008.

Fletcher, J. *Morals and Medicine*. Boston: Beacon Press, 1972.

Fletcher, J. *Humanhood: Essays in biomedical ethics*. Buffalo New York: Prometheus Books, 1979.

Fletcher, J. *Situation Ethics: the new morality* (1966). London: Westminster John Knox Press, 1997.

Fletcher, J. 'Four Indicators of Humanhood – The Enquiry Matures' (1975). In: S. Lammers, A. Verhey (eds.) *On Moral Medicine: Theological Perspectives in Medical Ethics*. Grand Rapids: Eerdmans, 1998.

French National Consultative Ethics Committee. *Opinion on experimentation on patients in a chronic vegetative state, report*. 24 February 1986. <http://www.ccne-ethique-fr/docs/en/avis007.pdf > [accessed 2 March 2012].

Garin, O., Ayuso-Mateos, J.L., Almansa, J., Nieto, M., Chatterji, S., Vilagut, G., Alonso, J., Cieza, A., Svetskova, O., Burger, H., Racca, V., Francescutti, C., Vieta, E., Kostanjsek, N., Raggi, A., Leonardi, M., Ferrer, M., and the MHADIE Consortium. 'Validation of the "World Health organization Disability Assessment Schedule, WHODAS-2" in patients with chronic diseases'. In: *Health and Quality of Life Outcomes* 8/51 (2010) <http://www.hqlo.com/contents/8/1/51> [accessed 7 September 2011].

General Medical Council. *Treatment and care towards the end of life: good practice in decision-making.* 2010. <http://www.gmc-uk.org> [accessed 7 February 2011].

Gerstenberger, E. *Leviticus: A Commentary,* translated by D. Stott. London: Westminster John Knox Press, 1993.

Gervais, K. *Redefining death.* New Haven: Yale University Press, 1986.

Giubilini, A., Minerva, F. 'After-birth abortion: why should the baby live'. 2012. <http://www.jme.bmj.com/content/early/2012/03/01/medethics-2011-100411.full> [accessed 3 April 2012].

Glover, J. *Causing Death and Saving Lives.* London: Penguin, 1990.

Grant, C. 'Reinterpreting the Healing Narratives'. In: N. Eiesland, and D. Saliers (eds.) *Human Disability and the Service of God. Reassessing Religious Practice.* Nashville: Abingdon Press, 1998.

Gray, K., Knickman, T.A., Wegner, D. 'More dead than dead: Perceptions of persons in the persistent vegetative state'. In: *Cognition* 121/2 (2011), 275–280.

Green, M., Wikler, D. 'Brain death and personal identity'. In: *Philosophy and Public Affairs* 9/2 (1980), 105–133.

Gregory of Nazianzus (St) (329–390). 'To Cledonius Against Apollinaris Epistle 101 and 102'. In: E. Hardy (ed.), translated by C.G. Browne and J.E. Swallow *Christology of the Later Fathers* Vol III. London: SCM Press, 1954.

Gregory of Nyssa (St) (c. 331–395). 'On the Making of Man'. In: P. Schaff and H. Wace (eds.) *Nicene and Post Nicene Fathers* Vol. V. Grand Rapids: Eerdmans, 1972.

Gregory of Nyssa (St) (c.331–395). 'On Infants' Early Deaths'. In: P. Schaff and H. Wace (eds.) *Nicene and Post Nicene Fathers* Vol.V. Grand Rapids: Eerdmans, 1972.

Gunton, C. *The Promise of Trinitarian Theology.* London: T&T Clark, 1997.

Gutierrez, G. 'Renewing the Option for the Poor'. In: D. Batstone, E. Mendieta, L.A. Lorentzen, and D. Hopkins (eds.) *Liberation Theologies, Postmodernity and the Americas.* London: Routledge, 1997.

Gutierrez, G. *A Theology of Liberation: History, Politics and Salvation,* translated by M. O'Connell. New York: Orbis, 1988.

Harris, J. *The Value of Life: An Introduction to Medical Ethics.* New York: Routledge, 1985.

Harris, J. 'On the moral status of the embryo'. In: A. Dyson, and J. Harris (eds.) *Experiments on Embryos.* London: Routledge, 1991).

Harris, J. 'Euthanasia and the Value of Life'. In: J. Keown (ed.), *Euthanasia Examined.* Cambridge: Cambridge University Press, 1995.

Harris, J. *Enhancing Evolution: The Ethical Case for making Better People.* Princeton: Princeton University Press, 2007.

Harvard Medical School Report ('Harvard Report'). In: *Journal of the American Medical Association* 205/6 (1968), 337–340.

Hawkes, R. *Scope comment on assisted suicide debate in Parliament.* < http://www.scope.org.uk/news/assisted-suicide-debate-parliament > [accessed 28 March 2012]

Hebblethwaite, P. 'Liberation Theology and the Roman Catholic Church'. In: C. Rowland (ed.), *The Cambridge Companion to Liberation Theology.* Cambridge: Cambridge University Press, 2007.

Hobbes, T. (1588–1679). *The English Works* Vol I. Vol.11, Vol.III, Vol.VI. W. Molesworth, London, 1839.

Hoffenberg, R., Lock, M., Tilney, N., Casabona, C., Daar, A.S., Guttmann, R.D., Kennedy, I., Nundy, S., Radcliffe-Richards, J., Sells, R.A. (International Forum for Transplant Ethics). 'Should organs from patients in permanent vegetative state be used for transplantation?'. In: *Lancet* 350/9087 (1997), 1320–1321.

Horne, S. "'Those Who Are Blind See'": Some New Testament Uses of Impairment, Inability and Paradox'. In: N. Eiesland and D. Saliers (eds.) *Human Disability and the Service of God. Reassessing Religious Practice.* Nashville: Abingdon Press, 1998.

House of Lords Joint Committee on Human Rights Seventh Report of Session 2007–08. *A Life Like Any Other? Human Rights of Adults with Learning Disabilities.* <http://www.bild.org.uk/humanrights/docs/A life like any other vol 2 pdf> [accessed 2 August 2011].

House of Commons Science and Technology Committee Fifth Report of Session 2004–05 Vol.II. *Human reproductive technologies and the Law.* <http://www.publications.parliament.uk/pa/cm200405/cmselect/cmsctech/7/7ii.pdf> [accessed 3 April 2010].

International Classification of Functioning, Disability and Health (ICF). *Towards a Common Language for Functioning, Disability and Health 2002.* <http://www.who.int/classifications/icf/training/icfbeginnersguide.pdf.> [accessed 3 September 2011].

Jennett, B. 'The donor doctor's dilemma: observations on the recognition and management of brain death'. In: *Journal of Medical Ethics* 1 (1975), 63–66.

Jennett, B. 'Letting Vegetative Patients Die'. In: *BMJ* 305 (1992), 1305–1306.

Jennett, B. *The Vegetative State: Medical facts, Ethical and Legal Dilemmas.* Cambridge: Cambridge University Press, 2002.

Jennett, B. 'Thirty years of the vegetative state: clinical, ethical and legal problems'. In: *Progress in Brain Research* 150 (2005), 537–543.

Jennett, B. 'Development of Glasgow Coma and Outcome Scales'. In: *Nepal Journal of Neuroscience* 2 (2005), 24–28.

Jennett, B., Dyer, C. 'Persistent vegetative state and the right to die: the United States and Britain'. In: *BMJ* 302 (1991), 1256–1258.

John Chrysostom (St) (c.347–407). 'Homily 2'. In: *The Fathers of the Church: John Chrysostom Homilies on Genesis 1–17,* translated by R. Hill. USA: Catholic University of America Press, 1986.

John of the Cross (St) (1542–1591). *Ascent of Mount Carmel,* translated by E. Allison Peers. USA: Wilders Publications, 2008.

John of the Cross (St) (1542–1591). *Dark Night of the Soul,* translated by E. Allison Peers. USA: Wilders Publications, 2008.

Jones, D. 'The end of bioethics'. In: *The Pastoral Review* 6/1 (2010), 51–55.

Jonsen, A. *The Birth of Bioethics.* Oxford: Oxford University Press, 2003.

Jordan, M. 'Theology and Philosophy'. In: N. Kretzmann and E. Stump (eds.) *The Cambridge Companion to Aquinas.* Cambridge: Cambridge University Press, 1993.

Kahane, G., Savulescu, J. 'Brain damage and the moral significance of consciousness'. In: *Journal of Medicine and Philosophy* 34 (2009), 6–26.

Kass, L. 'Defending Human Dignity'. In: *Essays Commissioned by the President's Council on Bioethics: Human Dignity and Bioethics.* USA: US Government Printing Office, 2008.

Kotchoubey, B. 'Apallic syndrome is not apallic: is vegetative state vegetative?'. In: *Neuropsychological Rehabilitation* 15/3–4 (2005), 333–356.

Kuhse, H., Singer, P. *Bioethics: an Anthology.* Oxford: Blackwell, 2006.

Lancioni, G., Singh, N., O'Reilly, M., Sigafoos, J., de Tommaso, M., Megna, G., Bosco, A., Buonocunto, F., Sacco, V., Chiapparino,C. 'A learning assessment procedure to re-evaluate three persons with a diagnosis of post-coma vegetative state and pervasive motor impairment'. In: *Brain Injury* 23/2 (2009), 154–162.

Lewis, H. *Deaf Liberation Theology.* Aldershot: Ashgate, 2007.

Lindemann, H., Verkerk, M. 'Ending the Life of a Newborn'. In: *Hastings Center Report* 38/1 (2008), 42–51.

Lizza, J. 'Persons: natural, functional or ethical kind?'. In: *American Journal of Economics and Sociology* 66/1 (2007), 195–216.

Lo, B. *Resolving ethical dilemmas: a guide for clinicians.* Philadelphia: Lippencort Williams and Wilkins, 2009.

Locke, J. (1632–1704). *An Essay Concerning Human Understanding,* K. Winkler (ed.). Cambridge: Hackett Publishing, 1996.

Lockwood, M. 'The moral status of the human embryo: implications for IVF'. In: *Reproductive BioMedicine Online* 10/1 (2005), 17–20. <http://www.rbmonline.com/Article/1613> [accessed 1 February 2010].

Maier, B., Shibles, W.A. *The Philosophy and Practice of Medicine and Bioethics: A Naturalistic-Humanistic Approach.* London: Springer, 2011.

'Martyrdom of Polycarp' (155 or 156). In: B. Ehrman (ed.) *After the New Testament: A Reader in Early Christianity.* Oxford: Oxford University Press, 1999.

McMahan, J. *The Ethics of Killing: Problems at the margins of life.* Oxford: Oxford University Press, 2002.

Meilaender, G. 'Terra es animata: On having a Life'. In: S. Lammers and A. Verhey (eds.) *On Moral Medicine.* Grand Rapids: Eerdmans, 1998.

MENCAP. Treat me right!. 2004 <http://www.mencap.org.uk/document.asp?id=316w.m> [accessed 14 July 2010].

MENCAP. *Death by Indifference.* 2007 <http://www.mencap.org.uk/document.asp?id=284> [accessed 14 July 2010].

Messer, N. 'Human Genome Project, Health and the Tyranny of Normality'. In: C. Deane-Drummond (ed.), *Brave New World?.* London: Continuum, 2003.

'Multi-Society Task Force on PVS: medical aspects of the persistent vegetative state' (First of Two Parts) (no authors listed). In: *New England Journal of Medicine* 330/21 (1994), 1499–1508.

'Multi-Society Task Force on PVS: medical aspects of the persistent vegetative state' (Second of Two Parts) (no authors listed). In: *New England Journal of Medicine* 330/22 (1994), 1572–1579.

National Confidential Enquiry into Patient Outcome and Death, November. *An Age Old Problem: a review of the care received by elderly patients undergoing surgery.* 2010 <http://www.ncepod.org.uk/2010report3/downloads/EESE_summary.pdf> [accessed 3 March 2011].

Nelson, S. *Autopsy Report of the Chief Medical Examiner* (8 June 2005) <http://www.sptimes.com/2005/06/15/schiavoreport.pdf> [accessed 8 September 2011].

NHS Trust A v *M; NHS Trust B* v *H.* [2001] Fam 348.

O'Rourke, K. 'The A.M.A. Statement on tube feeding: an ethical analysis'. In: *America* VII/8 (1986), 321–323.

O'Rourke, K. 'Development of Church teaching on prolonging life'. In: *Health Progress* 8 (1988), 29–35.

O'Rourke, K., Norris, P. 'Care of PVS Patients and Catholic Opinion in the United States'. In: *The Linacre Quarterly* 68/3 (2001), 201–217.

O'Rourke, K. 'Reflections on the Papal Allocution concerning care for persistent vegetative state patients'. In: *Christian Bioethics* 12/1 (2006), 83–97.

O'Rourke, K., Hardt, J. 'Nutrition and Hydration: The CDF Response, In Perspective'. In: *Health Progress* 88/6 (2007), 44–47.

Oliver, M. *Understanding Disability from Theory to Practice.* New York: Palgrave, 1996.

Otlowski, M. *Voluntary Euthanasia and the Common Law.* Oxford: Oxford University Press, 1997.

Oxford English Dictionary. Oxford: Clarendon Press, 1989.

Pachomius (St), (c.290–346). *Pachomian Chronicles and Rules* Vol. 2, translated by A. Vielleux. Michigan: Cistercian Publications, 1981.

Pachomius (St), (c.290–346). *Instructions, Letters and Other Writings of Saint Pachomius and his Disciples* Vol.3, translated by A. Vielleux. Michigan: Cistercian Publications, 1982.

Panksepp, J., Fuchs, T., Garcia, V., Lesiak, A. 'Does any aspect of mind survive brain damage that typically leads to a persistent vegetative state? Ethical condiserations'. In: *Philosophy, Ethics and Humanities in Medicine* 2/32 (2007) <http://www.peh-med.com/content/2/1/32.> [accessed 30 January 2012].

Patients Association, *Listen to patients, speak up for change.* 2010 <http://www.patients-association.com/dbimgs/Listen%20to%20patients,%20Speak%20up%20for%20change%281%29.pdf> [accessed 6 April 2011].

Patterson, B. 'Redeemed Bodies: Fullness of Life'. In: N. Eiesland, and D. Saliers (eds.) *Human Disability and the Service of God. Reassessing Religious Practice.* Nashville: Abingdon Press, 1998.

Plum, F., Jennett, B. 'Persistent vegetative state after brain damage. A syndrome in search of a name'. In: *Lancet* 1 (1972), 734–737.

Rachels, J. *The End of Life: Euthanasia and Morality*. Oxford: Oxford University Press, 1986.

Rachels, J. *Created from Animals: The Moral Implications of Darwinism*. Oxford: Oxford University Press, 1990.

Rakestraw, R. 'The Persistent Vegetative State and the Withdrawal of Nutrition and Hydration'. In: D. Clark, and R. Rakestraw (eds.) *Readings in Christian Ethics Vol.2 Issues and Applications*. Grand Rapids: Baker Publishing, 1996.

Ramsey, P. *The Patient as Person* (1970). Yale: Yale University Press, 2002.

Ravelingien, A., Mortier, F., Mortier, E., Kerremans, I., Braeckman, J. 'Proceeding with clinical trials of animal to human organ transplantation: a way out of the dilemma'. In: *Journal of Medical Ethics* 30/1 (2004), 92–98.

Redmont, J. 'Letter to women bares John Paul's isolation'. In: *National Catholic Reporter*, 31/35 (1995), 11.

Reinders, H. *Receiving the Gift of Friendship*. Grand Rapids: Eerdmans, 2008.

Richmond, C. 'Obituary Fred Plum'. In: *Lancet* 376/9739 (2010), 412.

Ruddick, W. 'Biographical Lives Revisited and Extended'. In: *Journal of Ethics* 9/3–4 (2005), 501–515.

Rush, C. 'The history of the Glasgow Coma Scale: an interview with Professor Bryan Jennett'. In: *International Journal of Trauma Nursing* 3/4 (1997), 114–118.

Savulescu, J. '"Liberals are disgusting": in Defence of the Publication of "After-Birth Abortion"'. 2012. <http://blogs.bmj.com/medical-ethics/2012/02/28/liberals-are-disgusting-in-defence-of-the-publication-of-after-birth-abortion/> [accessed 3 April 2012].

Saxton, M. 'Disability Rights and Selective Abortion'. In: L. Davis (ed.), *The Disability Studies Reader*. New York: Routledge, 2006.

Segers, M. 'Feminism, liberalism and Catholicism'. In: R.B. Douglass, and D. Hollenbach (eds.) *Catholicism and Liberalism*. Cambridge: Cambridge University Press, 1994.

Shakespeare, T., Watson, N. 'The Social Model of Disability: an Outdated Model?'. In: *Research in Social Science and Disability* 2 (2002), 9–28.

Shannon, T. 'Grounding human dignity'. In: *Dialog A Journal of Theology* 43/2 (2004), 113–117.

Shannon, T., Walter, J. 'Assisted Nutrition and Hydration and the Catholic Tradition'. In: R. Hamel and J. Walters (eds.), *Artificial Nutrition and Hydration and the Permanently Unconscious Patient. The Catholic Debate.* Washington: Georgetown University Press, 2007.

Shea, N., Bayne, T. 'The Vegetative State and the Science of Consciousness'. In: *British Journal for the Philosophy of Science* 61 (2010), 459–484.

Sheets, J. 'The Spirituality of Pope John Paul II'. In: J. McDermott (ed.) *The Thought of Pope John Paul II.* Rome: Editrice Pontificia Universita Gregoriana, 1993.

Shewmon, D.A., Holmes, G.L., Byrne, P.A. 'Consciousness in Congenitally Decorticate Children: Developmental Vegetative State as Self-Fulfilling Prophecy'. In: *Dev Med Child Neurol* 41 (1999), 364–374.

Silvas, A. *The Asketikon of St Basil the Great.* Oxford: Oxford University Press, 2005.

Singer, P. *Rethinking Life and Death.* Oxford: Oxford University Press, 1995.

Singer, P. *Practical Ethics.* Cambridge: Cambridge University Press, 1997.

Singer, P. *Writings on an ethical life.* London: Fourth Estate, 2001.

Smith, T. 'Taming High Technology'. In: *BMJ* 289/6442 (1984), 393–394.

Stein, M. *Distributive Justice and Disability: Utilitarianism against Egalitarianism.* Yale: Yale University Press, 2006.

Stiker, H-J. *A History of Disability,* translated by W. Sayers. USA: University of Michigan Press, 1999.

Stikkers, K. 'Persons and Power: Max Scheler and Michel Foucault on the Spiritualization of Power'. In: *The Pluralist* 4/1 (2009), 51–59.

Sulmasy, D. 'Preserving Life? The Vatican and PVS'. In: *Common-weal* (2007) <http://www.commonwealmagazine.org/preserving-life-0> [accessed 13 September 2011].

Sulmasy, D. 'Dignity in Bioethics: History, Theory and Selected Applications'. In: *Essays Commissioned by the President's Council on Bioethics: Human Dignity and Bioethics*. USA: US Government Printing Office, 2008.

Taboada, P. 'Ordinary and Extraordinary means and the Preservation of Life: The Teaching of Moral Tradition'. In: E. Sgreccia, and J. Lafitte (eds.), *Proceedings of the XIV's General Assembly: Close by the Incurable Sick Person and the Dying, Scientific and Ethical Aspects*. (Vatican City: Libreria Editrice Vaticana, 2009).

Teasdale, G.M. 'The Glasgow Coma and Outcome Scales: Practical Questions and Answers'. In: M. Sindou (ed.), *Practical Handbook of Neurosurgery* Vol 3. Wien: Springer, 2009.

Tertullian (c.160–225). 'On the Resurrection of the Flesh'. In: A. Roberts and J. Donaldson (eds.) *Ante-Nicene Fathers*, Vol.III. Massachusetts: Hendrickson, 1995.

Thogmartin, J. *Autopsy Report of the Chief Medical Examiner* (13 June 2005). <http://www.sptimes.com/2005/06/15/schiavoreport.pdf> [accessed 8 September 2011].

Toulmin, S. 'How medicine saved the life of ethics'. In: *Perspectives in Biological Medicine* 25/4 (1982), 736–750.

United States Conference of Catholic Bishops. *Ethical and Religious Directives for Catholic Health Care Services*. 17 November 2009 <http://www.usccbpublishing.org> [accessed 10 January 2012].

US President's Commission Report. *Defining Death: Medical, Legal and Ethical Issues in the Definition of Death*. 1981. <http://bio-ethics.georgetown.edu/pcbe/reports/past_commissions/defin-ing_death.pdf>[accessed 31 January 2010].

Vanier, J. *Becoming Human*. London: Darton, Longman and Todd, 1998.

Veatch, R. 'The Ethics of Death and Dying: Changing Attitudes towards Death and Medicine'. In: A. Jonsen, R. Veatch, and L. Walters (eds.), *Source Book in Bioethics: A Documentary History*. Washington: Georgetown University Press, 1998.

Veatch, R. *Transplantation Ethics*. Washington: Georgetown University Press, 2000.

Veatch, R. 'The dead donor rule: true by definition'. In: *The American Journal of Bioethics* 3/1 (2003), 10–11.

Verhey, A. *Reading the Bible in the Strange World of Medicine*. Grand Rapids: Eerdmans, 2004.

Vitoria, Francisco de. *On Homicide and Commentary on Summa Theologiae IIa–IIae*, translated by J. Doyle. Milwaukee: Marquette University Press, 1997.

Warnock, M., Macdonald, E. *Easeful Death: Is There a Case for Assisted Dying?*. Oxford: Oxford University Press, 2008.

Wasserman, D. 'Disability, capability and thresholds for distributive justice'. In: A. Kaufman (ed.), *Capabilities Equality: Basic Issues and Problems*. New York: Routledge, 2006.

Watts, C., Livingston, G. 'Cogito ergo sum: A commentary'. In: *Surgical Neurology Int* 2/5 (2011). <http://www.surgicalneurologyint.com/text.asp?2011/2/1/5/76142> [accessed 7 November 2011].

Wikler, D. 'Not dead, not dying? Ethical categories and persistent vegetative state'. In: *Hastings Center Report* 18/1 (1988), 41–47.

Wildes, K. 'Ordinary and Extraordinary Means and the Quality of Life'. In: *Theological Studies* 57 (1996) 500–512.

Williams, G. 'Theorizing Disability'. In: G. Albrecht, K. Seelman, and M. Bury (eds.), *Handbook of Disability Studies*. London: Sage Publications, 2001.

Woll, B., Ladd, P. 'Deaf Communities'. In: M. Marschark, and P.E. Spencer (eds.), *Deaf Studies, Language and Education*. Oxford: Oxford University Press, 2003.

World Health Organisation, Document A29/INFDOCI/1. Geneva, Switzerland, 1976.

Young, A. *Theology and Down Syndrome*. Waco: Baylor University Press, 2007.

INDEX

SCRIPTURE INDEX